INDIA

UNDER

BRITISH RULE

INDIA

UNDER

BRITISH RULE

FROM THE

FOUNDATION OF THE EAST INDIA COMPANY

By

J. Talboys Wheeler

GYAN

India under British Rule
from the
Foundation of the East India Company

J. Talboys Wheeler

ISBN : 978-81-212-2217-4

First Published 1886, reprint 2013 in India by
Gyan Publishing House
23, Main Ansari Road, Daryaganj,
New Delhi - 110002
Phones : 23282060, 23261060

Fax : (011) 23285914
E-mail: books@gyanbooks.com
website: gyanbooks.com

Printed at : Sagar Color Scan, New Delhi.

BY THE SAME AUTHOR.

MADRAS IN THE OLDEN TIME, 1639—1748. 3 vols. sm. 8vo. Madras, 1861—62.

EARLY TRAVELS IN INDIA. First Series, comprising Purchas's "Pilgrimage" and the "Travels of Van Linschoten." 8vo. Calcutta, 1864.

EARLY TRAVELS IN INDIA. Second Series, comprising Sir Thomas Roe's "Embassy to the Great Mogul" and Fryer's "Travels in India." 8vo. London, 1873.

HISTORY OF INDIA FROM THE EARLIEST AGES. 5 vols. 8vo.
Vol. I. The Mahá Bhárata and the Vedic Period. Thick 8vo. Map. 1867.
II. The Rámáyana and the Brahmanic Period. Thick 8vo. Map. 1869.
III. Hindu, Buddhist, and Brahmanic Revival. 8vo. Map. 1874.
IV. and V. Mohammedan Rule. 2 vols. 8vo. 1876—82.

SHORT HISTORY OF INDIA, and of the Frontier States of Afghanistan, Nipal, and Burma. Thick crown 8vo, with Maps and Tables. Macmillan and Co. 12*s*. 1880.

HISTORY OF THE IMPERIAL ASSEMBLAGE AT DELHI, held on the 1st of January, 1877, to celebrate the assumption by Her Majesty Queen Victoria of the Title of Empress of India; with Historical Sketches of India and her Princes. Royal 4to, with 13 Portraits, Map, and 17 Illustrations, chiefly by Photographs. 1877.

EARLY RECORDS OF BRITISH INDIA; a History of the English Settlements in India. 8vo. Calcutta, 1878.

JOURNAL OF A VOYAGE UP THE IRRAWADDY TO MANDALAY AND BHAMO. 8vo. Rangoon, 1871.

TALES FROM INDIAN HISTORY. 12mo. 1881.

GEOGRAPHY OF HERODOTUS, Developed, Explained, and Illustrated from Modern Researches and Discoveries. Thick 8vo, with Maps and Plans. 1854.

LIFE AND TRAVELS OF HERODOTUS. 2 vols. post 8vo. 1855.

ANALYSIS AND SUMMARY OF HERODOTUS. Post 8vo. Bohn's Philological Library. 1852.

ANALYSIS AND SUMMARY OF THUCYDIDES. Post 8vo. Bohn's Philological Library. 1852.

TO

SIR CHARLES TREVELYAN, BART.,

WHO OPENED

THE OLD MADRAS RECORDS TO THE AUTHOR

IN 1860,

This Book is Dedicated.

PREFACE.

A HUNDRED years ago, when the lively Miss Frances Burney was weeping over the wrongs of Warren Hastings, and the learned and portly Gibbon was still lamenting that he had not entered on an Indian career, there were people in the British Isles who knew something of Indian history. They had picked up information respecting Indian affairs from the speeches of the grave Edmund Burke, the eloquent Charles James Fox, and the impassioned Richard Brinsley Sheridan. The facts may have come second hand, and been more or less distorted by the jealous and bitter fancies of Sir Philip Francis, the reputed author of the *Letters of Junius;* but facts or fables, they served to enlighten the British public on the Indian questions of the day.

During the present century, the march of intellect has turned away from India, except as regards an outlet for cotton goods, a field for speculation in railways and teas, or a provision for younger sons in the "Indian civil." Within the last few years, however, there has been a change for the better. The British public has been alarmed at the fall in silver. It has been cheered by the proposal to place British-born subjects under the magisterial jurisdiction of Hindus and Mohammedans. It has been aroused by the prospect of a war with Russia in Central Asia; but it has been comforted by the restoration of the fortress of Gwalior to Maharaja Sindia. Moreover, Burma is no longer confounded with Bermuda, and no one groans over the annexation of the country, or the destruction of brigandage by the new rulers. Still there is room for more knowledge. The author, however, has before him a letter from an old friend in high position in India, who tells him plainly that the British government does not want history. Accordingly, the present work is not called a *History of India*, but *India under British Rule*.

More than one British ruler in India has, however, sinned against history, and might well like to shut it up with confidential minutes and secret negotiations. Within the present century, India has been desolated by wars as cruel as those of the Heptarchy, and as unmeaning as those of the White and Red Roses. Within the present generation, it has been distracted and tortured by a military revolt, created by a scare about greased cartridges, but leading to crimes more horrible than those of the French Revolution. Yet Anglo-Indian statesmen have been known to ignore the past, and to propound schemes for India that would be too advanced for any European nation excepting Great Britain. They have blinded themselves against history, like ostriches burying their faces in the sand. They have dealt with India, as the German philosopher dealt with the "camel," not by the facts before them, but out of the sublime depths of their moral consciousness, stirred up by a political caucus, or a philanthropic gathering in Exeter Hall.

Controversy and fault-finding are to be deprecated. But reform is only possible after a due consideration of what has been accomplished up to date by British rule in India, and of the flaws and faults in the existing constitution.

It will be seen from the first chapter, that the British traders of the seventeenth century, who established factories, built fortresses, and created manufacturing towns, also attempted to introduce representative and municipal government into the East India Company's once famous city of Madras. The second chapter reveals the fact that the acquisition of Bengal in the eighteenth century was not the work of ambition, but an act of self-preservation. The third chapter shows that the peace of India could not have been maintained in any possible way except by the establishment of British supremacy as the paramount power. The fourth chapter proves that the first Afghan war, needless as it turned out to be at the time, was the outcome of Russian ambition which dates back to the times of Peter the Great and Nadir Shah.

The story of the sepoy mutinies of 1857 occupies a considerable space in the present volume. It is not a mere narrative of military revolt, but a revelation of Asiatic nature; a lesson which every Anglo-Indian statesman must study, if he would avoid defeat or failure. The masses in the British Isles may read Biblical accounts of rebellion and massacre, or the story in Josephus of the atrocities of Herod the Great; but very few seem to realise the fact that they are reading Asiatic history, which has no reflex in Europe, nor in any country under European rule except British India. The horrible intrigues and murders in the household of Herod; his frantic passion for the fair Mariamne; the malicious lies of Salome; the assassination of Mariamne by her jealous and infuriated husband; the alternations in the mind of Herod as regards Cleopatra, whether to accept her love or murder her;—find no parallels in European history, excepting perhaps in Turkey, or in the Russian court of the last century.

The last chapter in the present volume is devoted to the constitutional changes in the government of India, and in the local governments, since the mutinies. The author has not indulged in the hope of raising Asiatics to the level of Europeans by the premature introduction of representative government. He considers that such a scheme would for the present be as much out of place in Asia as a republic of boys for the control of schoolmasters. British India is treated as a political school for Asiatics, in which Europeans are the teachers; and so long as that theory of government is upheld, constitutional reforms in India are practical and possible.

In conclusion, the author has to express his obligations to Professor Terrien de Lacouperie of the London University College, and to his own son, Owen E. Wheeler of the Leicestershire Regiment, for revising the proofs of the present work, and for many valuable suggestions.

FULHAM,
12*th May*, 1886.

CONTENTS.

PART I.

EAST INDIA COMPANY.

CHAPTER I.

FIRST PERIOD: FACTORIES, FORTRESSES, TOWNS.

1600–1756.

§1. India in 1600. §2. British at Surat and Masulipatam: Commercial and Social Life, 1612—1638. §3. Rise and Growth of Madras, 1639—1680: Portuguese and Dutch Neighbours. §4. British Rule and Representative Government, 1686. §5. Mixed Corporation of Europeans and Natives, 1688. §6. Slavery and the Slave Trade in India. §7. Madras, Surat, Bombay, and Hughly. §8. Collision with the Great Mogul, 1686—1700. §9. Domestic Administration, 1700—1746. §10. Wars against France in Southern India, 1746—1756. §11. The Black Hole at Calcutta, June 1756 . . . . *Pages* 1—39

CHAPTER II.

SECOND PERIOD: BENGAL PROVINCES.

1756-1798.

§1. From Calcutta to Plassy, 1757-58. §2. Nawab Rule under British Protection. §3. British Arrogance: Massacre at Patna. §4. Lord Clive's Double Government, 1765-67. §5. Warren Hastings, 1772-85: Life and Career. §6. British Rule: Treatment of Bengal Zemindars. §7. British Collectors and Magistrates: Circuit Courts and Sudder. §8. Innovations of Parliament. §9. Collisions in Calcutta Council: Trial and Execution of Nundcomar. §10. Clashing of Supreme Court and Sudder. §11. Mahratta war: Goddard and Popham. §12. Triple Alliance against the British: the Mahrattas, the Nizam, and Hyder Ali. §13. Parliamentary Interference: the Two India Bills. §14. Charges against Warren Hastings. §15. Lord Cornwallis, 1786-93: Perpetual Settlement and Judicial Reforms. §16. Sir John Shore, 1793-98: Non-Intervention . . . . *Pages* 40—82

CHAPTER III.

THIRD PERIOD: IMPERIAL GOVERNMENT.

1798-1836.

§ 1. Lord Mornington (Marquis of Wellesley), 1798-1805: last war against Tippu, 1799. § 2. Carnatic confiscated and annexed to Madras Presidency. § 3. Wellesley's scheme of a paramount power. § 4. Second Mahratta war: successes of Arthur Wellesley and Lake. § 5. Disastrous war with Holkar. § 6. Return to non-intervention. § 7. Sepoy mutiny in Madras army. § 8. Lord Minto, 1807-13: wars and alliances against France. § 9. Evils of non-intervention in Rajputana: troubles in Nipal. § 10. Lord Moira (Marquis of Hastings), 1813-23: war with Nipal, 1814-15. § 11. Revival of the paramount power: Pindhari and Mahratta wars, 1817-18. § 12. Lord Amherst, 1823-28: wars with Burma and Bhurtpore. § 13. Lord William Bentinck, 1828-35; abolition of Suttee. § 14. Suppression of Thugs. § 15. Administrative reforms. § 16. North-West Provinces: Joint Village Proprietors. § 17. Madras and Bombay Presidencies: Ryotwari Settlements. § 18. Changes under the Charter of 1833. § 19. Sir Charles Metcalfe, 1835-36. *Pages* 83—140

CHAPTER IV.

FOURTH PERIOD: RISE TO ASIATIC POWER.

1836-56.

§ 1. Russian advance checked by Nadir Shah, 1722-38. § 2. First Cabul war under Lord Auckland, 1838-42. § 3. Lord Ellenborough, 1842-44: return from Cabul and conquest of Sind. § 4. War in Gwalior: reduction of Sindia's army. § 5. Lord Hardinge, 1845-48: Sikh rule in the Punjab. § 6. First Sikh war: Moodki, Ferozshahar, Aliwal, and Sobraon. § 7. Lord Dalhousie, 1848-56: Second Sikh war: Chillianwalla and Goojerat: annexation of the Punjab. § 8. British rule: patriarchal government. § 9. Second Burmese war, 1852: annexation of Pegu. § 10. Lord Dalhousie as an administrator: no roads in India. § 11. Trunk road, trunk railway, telegraphs, Ganges canal. § 12. Annexations of Nagpore, Satara, Jhansi, and Oudh. § 13. India Bill of 1853: new competitive Civil Service. § 14. New Legislative Council: Lord Macaulay and the Penal Code. § 15. Departure of Lord Dalhousie, 1856. § 16. Lord Canning, 1856-62: expedition to the Persian Gulf. § 17. Mogul family at Delhi. § 18. Condition of Oudh . . . *Pages* 141—184

CHAPTER V.

SEPOY REVOLT: BENGAL, DELHI, PUNJAB.

1857.

§ 1. European soldiers and Asiatic sepoys. § 2. Three British armies in India: Bengal, Bombay, and Madras. § 3. Sepoy army of Bengal: Brahmans and Rajputs. § 4. Enfield cartridges: general horror of pork: Hindu worship of the cow. § 5. Agitation of the sepoys at Barrackpore. § 6. First mutiny against the cartridges: Berhampore. § 7. Second mutiny: Barrackpore. § 8. Oudh: mutiny at Lucknow: suppressed. § 9. Mutiny and massacre at Meerut. § 10. Mohammedan revolt and massacre at Delhi: general excitement. § 11. British advance from the Punjab to Delhi. § 12. Siege of Delhi by Europeans, Sikhs, and Ghorkas. § 13. Punjab and John Lawrence: antagonism between Sikhs and Mohammedans. § 14. Sepoy plots at Lahore and Mian Mir: quashed. § 15. Peshawar and frontier mountain tribes. § 16. Execution of sepoy mutineers at Peshawar. § 17. Brigadier John Nicholson: worshipped by a Sikh brotherhood. § 18. Proposed withdrawal from Peshawar. § 19. Mutiny at Sealkote: wholesale executions. § 20. Siege and storm of Delhi, September 1857: peace in the North-West. *Pages* 185—231

CHAPTER VI.

SEPOY REVOLT: NORTH WEST, CAWNPORE, LUCKNOW.

1857–58.

§ 1. Bengal and Lord Canning: General Neill's advance from Calcutta. § 2. Sacred city of Benares: Hindu population overawed. § 3. Fortress at Allahabad: treachery and massacre. § 4. Cawnpore: extreme peril. § 5. Story of Nana Sahib. § 6. European refuge in the barracks. § 7. Nana Sahib at Cawnpore: aspirations after Hindu sovereignty: delusion of General Wheeler. § 8. Mutiny and treachery: barracks beleaguered by Nana Sahib. § 9. First massacre at Cawnpore: massacre at Jhansi. § 10. Advance of General Havelock. § 11. Second massacre of women and children: the well. § 12. Lucknow and Sir Henry Lawrence: May and June. § 13. Siege of British Residency at Lucknow: July to September: death of Sir Henry Lawrence. § 14 Havelock's advance and retreat. § 15. Advance of Havelock and Outram. § 16. Relief of Lucknow. § 17. Sir Colin Campbell's advance: deliverance of the garrison. § 18. Mutiny of the Gwalior contingent: defeated. § 19. End of the mutiny and rebellion: causes . . . . *Pages* 232—274

PART II.

BRITISH CROWN.

CHAPTER THE LAST.

CONSTITUTIONAL GOVERNMENT.

1858-1886.

§1. Awakening of the British nation. §2. Government Education in India: Toleration. §3. British Rule after the Mutiny: Legislative Council of 1854 and Executive Council: Wrongs of Non-Official Europeans. §4. Mr. James Wilson and his Income-Tax. §5. New Legislative Council of 1861-62. §6. New High Court: proposed District Courts. §7. Lord Canning leaves India. §8. Lord Elgin, 1862-63. §9. Sir John Lawrence, 1864-69: Governments of Madras and Bombay: Migrations to Simla: Foreign Affairs. §10. Lord Lawrence leaves India. §11. Lord Mayo, 1869-72. §12. Lord Northbrook, 1872-76: Royal visits to India. §13. Lord Lytton, 1876-80: Empress Proclaimed. §14. Second Afghan War. §15. Political and Judicial Schools. §16. Constitution of British India: proposed Reforms . . . . *Pages* 275—302

INDEX . . . . *Pages* 303—312

INDIA UNDER BRITISH RULE.

PART I.

EAST INDIA COMPANY.

CHAPTER I.

FIRST PERIOD: FACTORIES, FORTRESSES, TOWNS.

1600—1756.

§ 1. India in 1600. § 2. British at Surat and Masulipatam: Commercial and Social Life, 1612—1638. § 3. Rise and Growth of Madras, 1639—1680: Portuguese and Dutch Neighbours. § 4. British Rule and Representative Government, 1686. § 5. Mixed Corporation of Europeans and Natives, 1688. § 6. Slavery and the Slave Trade in India. § 7. Madras, Surat, Bombay, and Hughly. § 8. Collision with the Great Mogul, 1686—1700. § 9. Domestic Administration, 1700—1746. § 10. Wars against France in Southern India, 1746—1756. § 11. The Black Hole at Calcutta, June, 1756.

CHAP. I.

Rise of British rule.

THE rise of British rule in India is a problem in history. A single association of British traders established factories which grew into fortresses, and governed native towns which became the capitals of a British empire. The march of events is without a parallel in the annals of the world. In 1600 the East India Company obtained from Queen Elizabeth a charter of exclusive rights to trade in the Eastern seas. In 1612 it established its first factory at Surat. In 1639 it began to build a fortified factory at Madras,

CHAP. I. whilst a Hindu population of weavers and other manufacturers grew up by its side. Before the beginning of the eighteenth century, before Queen Anne ascended the throne of Great Britain, the British settlements at Madras, Bombay, and Calcutta had each a fortress and a town. How Hindu and Mohammedan populations were ruled by British traders will be told in the present chapter. How the British traders acquired provinces and established an empire belongs to the after chapters.

NORTHERN INDIA: the Great Mogul.

§ 1. In 1600 the whole of Northern India was under the dominion of a Mohammedan sovereign, known as the Great Mogul. His revenues and armies were the marvel of Europe. His empire extended from the mountains of Cashmere to the Bay of Bengal, from the slopes of the Himalayas to the table-land of the Deccan. It covered large Hindu populations and many Hindu principalities, for throughout this vast area the Great Mogul was sovereign lord of all, the emperor, the Padishah.

SOUTHERN INDIA: Mohammedan Sultans and Hindu Rajas.

South of the Mogul empire was the Deccan or "south." The country was a *terra incognita* to Europeans. The interior had been conquered by Mohammedan invaders from the north, and distributed into kingdoms under Sultans, who formed a barrier against the Moguls. East and west were hills and jungles stretching to the sea, mostly held by Hindu Rajas who were hostile alike to the Sultans and the Great Mogul. Mohammedan rule, however, had never as yet extended further south than the river Kistna. The whole region from the Kistna to Cape Comorin—sometimes known as the "Peninsula"—was under the dominion of Hindu Rajas.

Portuguese fortresses.

The western coast of the Deccan and Peninsula was dotted with Portuguese fortresses, mounted with cannon and garrisoned by Portuguese soldiers. The Portuguese had made their way to India round the Cape of Good Hope about the end of the fifteenth century, and for a hundred years had been building factories in the territories of Hindu Rajas, and converting them into fortresses. Nothing of the kind would have been allowed by the Great Mogul, or by the Sultans of the Deccan, but the Portuguese had persuaded the Hindu Rajas that they would help and protect them, and the Rajas never saw the danger until the fortresses were bristling with cannon and opposition was useless. The Portuguese capital was seated on the island of Goa, about half-way between Surat and Comorin, and was a centre of the Catholic religion as well as of Portuguese trade.[1]

British traders at Surat.

§ 2. British merchants in the service of the East India Company would gladly have traded on the same sea-board, which was known as the coast of Malabar, but they were shut out by the Portuguese fortresses. Accordingly they sailed further northward, and tried to get a footing in the Mogul port of Surat. This port was a centre of the Mohammedan religion and an emporium of Mogul trade. It was the starting-point for all pilgrims going to Mecca, and the point to which they returned when their pilgrimage was over. It was the rendezvous of Mogul merchants who despatched ships to the Persian Gulf and Red

[1] The island of Goa, and the fortress of Diu in Guzerat, were nominally within Mohammedan dominion, but they were really independent and were held by force of arms.

CHAP. I.

Sea, and sent goods overland to the great capitals of the Mogul empire—Agra, Delhi, and Lahore.

British defeat the Portuguese.

At Surat, however, the British were thwarted by the Portuguese. The Nawab of Surat was told that the British were pirates. The merchants of Surat were threatened with the capture of their ships if they had any dealings with the British. Fighting was the only way of meeting the difficulty. Accordingly the British attacked a Portuguese fleet outside the bar of Surat. The news of battle and the roar of cannon brought the Nawab, the merchants, and half the population of Surat to the sea-shore. The British sunk or burnt several Portuguese ships until the residue of the fleet steered back to Goa. The Moguls were fascinated by the victory. They saw that the British had not only superior strength on their side, but Allah and kismet. The Nawab of Surat feasted the conquerors in his tents on the sands, and the Surat merchants eagerly bought British cargoes and supplied Indian commodities to the brave men who had beaten the Portuguese.

British factory at Surat, 1612.

In 1612 the British set up a factory at Surat in a large Indian house, with warehouses and offices below and chambers and refection-rooms above. It was a London establishment transferred to a Mohammedan seaport. The British merchants, factors, and writers lodged and boarded together like members of one family. Native brokers or banyans were employed to buy cotton goods, silks, indigo, and other Indian commodities ; whilst public auctions were held in the factory for the sale of British broadcloths, glass and cutlery, especially sword-blades, and also for the sale of lead, copper, quicksilver, and other European commodities. The spirit of enterprise was as busy amongst the British as in after years. One factor urged the Company to send ships up the river Indus and open up a trade with Central Asia; whilst another tried to persuade the Great Mogul to lay down leaden pipes from the river Jumna to the city of Ajmere, a distance of more than two hundred miles, in order to convey drinking-water to the imperial palace in the heart of Rajputana.

Factory life.

In those early days no British ladies were allowed to reside in India. If a servant of the Company happened to be married he was obliged to leave his wife in England. The "English House," as it was called, was thus a bachelor establishment, without ladies, but not without Surat punch or Persian wine. An English chaplain read prayers every morning and evening, and preached two sermons on Sundays. An English surgeon attended the sick factors, and the Mogul authorities and other grandees often applied for his services, and thus enabled him to promote the Company's interests on more than one important occasion. The chief of the factory was known as the President, but all business was transacted by the President with the help of four or five senior merchants, who met twice a week in council. This management of affairs by a President in Council has survived the lapse of nearly three centuries. To this day the government of presidencies and the viceroyalty of India are in each case carried on by a President in Council.

Foreign guests.

Within a few years the "English House" at Surat was well known to all European sea-captains and voyagers. Not only British travellers, but Italians, Germans, and Frenchmen, were heartily welcomed by the honest factors at Surat. All were impressed with

CHAP. I. the order and regularity of the establishment, in which decorum and discipline were as strictly maintained as in Leadenhall Street or the Cheape. But when working hours were over the grave men of business proved to be convivial Britons of the old-fashioned type, and on Friday evenings especially, all the married men met together to drink the health of their absent wives to the detriment of their own. Foreign guests who could not speak the English tongue were in no want of amusement. In 1638 a young gentleman from Holstein, named Mandelslo, spent some months in the "English House," and passed the time very pleasantly, visiting the ships at anchor outside the bar of the river Tapty, and hearing the latest news of Europe from sea-captains versed in many languages, or wandering down the row of banyans' shops, which often contained as much wealth, hidden under dirt and squalor, as the houses of London merchants and goldsmiths. On Sundays, after sermon, the factors carried off their guest to their gardens outside Surat, where they all shot at butts, and were regaled with fruit and conserves.

British and Moguls. The European gentlemen at Surat were always polite to Mohammedan grandees, and were generally politely treated in return, excepting perhaps at the custom-house. British sailors and ill-mannered Englishmen would, however, occasionally show a contempt for Asiatics, which the President could not always restrain. British interlopers on the high seas set the Company's charter at defiance, and carried on a lawless trade, plundering the Mohammedan pilgrim ships and ill-treating the passengers. The Mogul authorities insisted that the Company's servants were to blame, and would listen to no explanation, but sent large bodies of Mogul soldiery to environ the "English House," and stop all trade, cutting off all food and water, until a sufficient fine or ransom had been paid.

Trade on the eastern coast.

About 1620 the East India Company established another factory at Masulipatam, on the eastern side of India. The Hindus along the coast of Coromandel were famous for painting muslins and calicoes, and there was a growing demand for such goods amongst the eastern islands, whilst valuable cargoes of nutmegs and other spices could be obtained in exchange. But Masulipatam was seated in Mohammedan territory. A Sultan of the Deccan, reigning at Golconda, had extended his dominion eastward to the coast of Coromandel, and established the port of Masulipatam for the importation of horses from the Persian Gulf. The traders at the British factory were therefore cramped and worried by the Mohammedan authorities, and yearned to effect a settlement on the territories of some Hindu Raja further south, where they could fortify a factory and mount it with British cannon without the interference of local authorities.

British territory and fortress at Madras, 1639.

§ 3. In 1639 a British merchant named Day bought a strip of territory on the Coromandel coast, about 300 miles to the south of Masulipatam. It was within the dominions of a Hindu Raja, and was about six miles long and one mile inland. It included a small island, which faced the sea and was defended on the land side by a river. Mr. Day agreed to pay the Raja a rent of 500*l.* a year in native coin known as pagodas, and the transaction

CHAP. I. was duly engraved on a plate of gold. A factory of brick was built upon the island, and mounted with cannon, and called Fort St. George. The Raja was perfectly content. He was too glad to get a rent of 500*l.* a year to raise any difficulty as regards fortifications or cannon.

Fort St. George and Black Town.

This factory was the germ of the city of Madras, on the coast of Coromandel. Weavers, washers, painters, and hosts of other Hindu artisans, flocked to the spot and eagerly entered the service of the British, and began to set up their looms and to weave, wash, and paint their cotton goods in the open air beneath the trees. Villages of little huts of mud and bamboo soon grew up on the sandy soil to the north of the island and factory. Each avocation formed a caste, which generally had its own quarters and its own head-man. In this manner a Hindu settlement grew up by the side of Fort St. George and was known as Black Town; and the whole locality, including Fort St. George and Black Town, was called Madras, and was the first territory acquired by the East India Company in India.

Despotic rule.

The transition of the British traders from a factory under Mohammedan control to an independent settlement of their own must have been a grateful change. The President and Council at Fort St. George were *de facto* rulers of the whole settlement, native as well as European, with all the powers of despotic princes and with no interference from without. They acted as a supreme court of judicature for Englishmen in all cases civil and criminal; no Englishman, however, could be condemned to death unless convicted of piracy, which was regarded as the most heinous of crimes. On all other capital

CHAP. I.

charges the Englishman was sent to England for trial.[1]

Portuguese and Dutch neighbours.

Four miles to the south of Fort St. George was the Portuguese town of St. Thomé; but the Portuguese were now friends with the English. Their power was being overshadowed by that of the Dutch, who had founded a town and fortress at Pulicat, nearly thirty miles to the northward of Fort St. George.

Dutch trade in India.

The Dutch settlements in India were the outcome of the hostility of Spain. For centuries the Dutch had been the carriers of Europe, from the Mediterranean to the Baltic. In the period which preceded the sixteenth century they had bought Indian commodities at Genoa, Naples and Venice.

[1] The authorities for the present chapter, which deals with the rise and early development of British rule in India, are somewhat numerous. The most important are the Government records at Madras, in which the weekly transactions of the Governor and Council are entered at full length in a series known as "Consultations." Every year a copy of the "Consultations" was sent to the Court of Directors, together with a summary of the affairs of the year as a "General Letter;" and every year a "General Letter" was received from the Court of Directors, reviewing the "Consultations," and conveying instructions and orders thereon. The Madras records have been closely investigated by the author from 1670 to 1748; and printed extracts were published at Madras in 1860–62, in three volumes small quarto, under the title of *Madras in the Olden Time.* To them may be added Bruce's *Annals of the East India Company;* Sir Thomas Roe's *Journal of a Mission to the Great Mogul in* 1616-18; and the travels of Pietro della Valle, Tavernier, Thevenot and Fryer; as well as Orme's *History of Hindustan,* Stewart's *History of Bengal,* Faria y Souza's *History of Portuguese Asia,* and Shaw's *Predecessors of the High Court at Madras.* Further authorities will be found cited in the author's *History of India from the Earliest Ages,* and in his *Early Records of British India.*

CHAP. I. After the Portuguese established a trade in India, the Dutch went every year to Lisbon to buy Indian commodities for the European markets. In 1580 they threw off the yoke of Spain, and founded the United Provinces. That same year Spain and Portugal were formed into one kingdom under Philip II. In an evil hour for Portuguese interests in India, Philip thought to punish the Dutch by shutting them out of Lisbon. The Dutch revenged themselves by sailing round the Cape and buying what they wanted in the islands of the Eastern Archipelago. In 1600 they built a factory in Java, which grew into the city of Batavia. In 1610 they built a square fort on the Pulicat Lake, which grew into the town of Pulicat and threatened to become the capital of Dutch ascendency in India.

Right and Left Hands. The Indian quarter at Madras was almost entirely Hindu. Scarcely a Mohammedan took up his abode within the Company's bounds. Accordingly one of the earliest acts of the President and Council was to divide the streets of Black Town into those of the right and left hand. All over Southern India, the lower castes of Hindus are divided into Right and Left Hands, and yet no one can account for the distinction, or satisfactorily define the respective rights of each Hand.

The so-called Hands are, however, intensely jealous of each other. For generations each Hand in the towns of Southern India has had its own streets and its own pagoda. At Madras, if one Hand passed in religious procession along the streets of the other Hand, or if the members of one Hand chanted Hindu hymns or mantras before the pagoda of the other, a fray would break out in Black Town, which could only be suppressed by British soldiers, and then would be followed by a strike of weavers or painters, or the flight of all the members of one Hand to the Portuguese settlement at St. Thomé. These conflicts, which more than once brought the settlement to the brink of ruin, reached a climax in Governor Pitt's time, as will appear hereafter. CHAP. I.

Meanwhile, the country round about Madras was in a state of turmoil. The Mohammedan army of the Sultan of Golconda was advancing against the Hindu Rajas of the south, and formed a camp in the neighbourhood. The Raja who had sold the territory to the East India Company fled away to the interior, and was never heard of more. The Mohammedan army captured the Portuguese town of St. Thomé, dismantled the walls of the fortress, and carried off the cannon to Golconda; and they would have treated Fort St. George in like fashion, had not the British stoutly resisted, and quieted the Sultan by engaging to pay him the rent which they had previously paid to the Raja. **Mohammedan invasion.**

About 1670, or some thirty years after the foundation of Madras, the state of affairs was complicated by Charles II.'s unholy alliance with France against the Dutch. A French fleet attacked St. Thomé and drove out the Mohammedans. A Dutch fleet from Pulicat recaptured St. Thomé, drove out the French, and restored the place to the Sultan of Golconda. The British settlement was in sore peril; but in 1674 there was peace between Great Britain and Holland, and the danger was over. **Troubles with Dutch and French, 1670.**

These troubles brought many strangers to Madras, and the population, white and black, was largely increased. Many Portuguese families from St. **Increase of population.**

CHAP. I. Thomé took refuge in Madras, and added to the strength of the European settlement, known as White Town, by building houses under the protection of the factory guns. The British factors and soldiers of the garrison married the daughters of the Portuguese, much to the horror of the English chaplain of Fort St. George, as the marriages were accompanied by numerous conversions of bridegrooms to the Catholic faith. At the same time wealthy Hindu traders and bankers began to build substantial houses in Black Town for the sake of British protection. Many invested their money in trading voyages; some acted as brokers or banyans for the supply of Indian commodities to the Company's servants; others bought European goods at the public auctions, and supplied the native dealers up country.

Fort St. George, 1670–86.

§ 4. Within forty years of the building of the British factory, Madras was the pride and glory of the East India Company. Fort St. George, or White Town, was a European city in miniature. The primitive factory in the centre was replaced by a stately mansion with a dome, which was known as the Governor's House, but included a town-hall, a council-chamber, and sundry offices. It was seated in an open square, having a strong wall along each of its four sides, guards' houses, and bastions at each corner mounted with cannon. Outside the fortification were little streets, paved with pebbles, containing about fifty European houses. There was also a Protestant church for the English inhabitants, and a Catholic chapel for the Portuguese residents. The whole of White Town was environed by an outer

CHAP. I.

wall, sufficiently fortified to keep off an Indian army. None but Britons, or Europeans under British protection, were permitted to reside in White Town. The garrison consisted of two companies of European soldiers, and a large number of native guards, who were known as peons.

Hindu town under British rule.

At this time the population of the native town was estimated at 300,000 souls, but was probably half that number, and an attempt was made to introduce something like a representative government. Whenever the Governor and Council desired to know the wishes of the people generally, or to act with their consent, they summoned the head-men of castes, and consulted them accordingly. Justice, however, was administered by two English gentlemen, who sat twice a week in Black Town in a building known as the Choultry. The Justices of the Choultry tried all offences and disputes amongst the Hindus, and fined, flogged, or imprisoned at discretion. The old English punishments of the stocks, the pillory, and the gallows were also in full force in Black Town, but no Hindu was executed without the confirmation of the Governor and Council. The Justices of the Choultry were bound by no code of laws; they were simply instructed by the Directors of the Company in England to decide all cases, civil and criminal, according to "equity and good conscience," guided by English law and their own experiences of Hindu customs and usages.[1] A Hindu superintendent of police was appointed under the title of "Pedda

[1] The Mofussil Courts, and the High Court in Appeals from the Mofussil Courts, are still required to decide, according to "equity and good conscience." See the "High Court amended Charters" granted in 1866.

CHAP. I. Naik," or "elder chief;" and he was bound to maintain a certain number of constables known as peons, and keep the peace of the town. He was expected to prevent theft and burglary, and either to recover stolen property, or to pay the value to the owner. In return, the Pedda Naik was allowed to cultivate a few fields rent free, and to levy a small octroi duty, or toll, on articles of Hindu consumption.

Protection of Hindus.

The main difficulty at Madras was to keep the peace between the European soldiers of the garrison and the Hindu population. Any European soldier who remained outside the Fort at night time was set publicly in the stocks for a whole day. Any European who attempted to get over the Fort walls, was imprisoned in irons for one entire month, and kept on rice and water. Any soldier who threatened to strike a Hindu was whipped. Any European who took an article out of a shop or bazaar, under pretence of buying it at his own price, was sentenced to pay treble the value to the party aggrieved.

Question of taxation.

Another difficulty was to keep the streets of Black Town clean and wholesome. The Governor and Council summoned the heads of castes, and proposed to levy a small tax on every house. The heads assented to the measure, but offered to carry out the work themselves, and to raise the necessary funds in the same way that they levied contributions from their respective castes for defraying the cost of public festivals. All this, however, was a blind on their part to delude the British Governor and Council. Nothing was done by the heads of castes, no money was collected, and the streets were dirtier than ever.

Meanwhile Madras was threatened by the Sultan of Golconda, and the Directors in England instructed the

CHAP. I.

Contumacy of heads of castes.

Governor and Council at Madras to build a wall round Black Town, and meet the cost by levying a small ground-rent from each householder. In this case no difficulty was anticipated. The Hindus might ignore the importance of sanitation, but they could scarcely refuse to contribute towards the defence of their lives and property, to say nothing of their wives and families. The heads of castes, however, raised strong objections, but found that the Governor was bent on carrying out the orders of the Court of Directors. The heads of castes were told that the rents must be paid, and that those who refused to pay must be prepared to sell their houses and leave the British settlement. At this threat they all promised to pay, but secretly prepared for a general uprising.

Hindu rebellion, 1686.

Suddenly, one Sunday morning, the 3rd of January, 1686, it was known in Fort St. George that the Hindu population of Black Town were rebelling in Asiatic fashion. Under the orders of the heads of castes, the Hindu servants of the Company had thrown up their duties, bazaar dealers had shut up their shops, and provisions and grain were kept out of the town. The Governor in Fort St. George sent a detachment of the British garrison to guard the entrances to Black Town and suppress the tumult. Proclamation was made by beat of drum that unless the heads submitted before sunset, their houses would be pulled down on the following morning, the sites sold by auction, and the rebels and their families banished for ever. Hindus who failed to return to their duties would be discharged from the Company's service; dealers who kept their shops closed would be heavily fined and all their goods confiscated. These peremptory orders had the desired effect. The heads of castes seemed to be

CHAP. I. completely cowed. Before sunset they appeared at the Fort and begged pardon for their rebellion, and were told to put an end to the tumult in Black Town.

Wholesome despotism. Next morning the heads of castes returned to the Fort and presented a petition, begging to be relieved from the payment of the ground-rent. Each man was asked in turn whether he would leave the town, and each in turn said that he would submit, and then the whole body declared with one voice that they would not pay the tax. Proclamation was at once made by beat of drum that the orders of Sunday would be immediately put in execution. The Hindus bent to the storm. They saw that they were at the mercy of their British rulers. The shops were opened, provisions were brought into the town, and all the artisans and servants of the Company returned to their duties. The ground-rents were collected without demur, and later on the scavenger-tax was raised without difficulty.

Mayor, aldermen, and burgesses, 1688. § 5. When the news of these disturbances reached England, the Directors in Leadenhall Street, or rather their once celebrated chairman, the great Sir Josiah Child, devised a scheme for rendering municipal taxation acceptable to the native population. A charter was obtained from James II. for founding a corporation in Madras, consisting of a mayor, twelve aldermen, and sixty burgesses; but it was suggested by the Court of Directors that the heads of Hindu castes, as well as Britons, might be appointed aldermen and burgesses, and it was hoped that the corporation would be willing to tax themselves and the inhabitants generally, for keeping the town clean, improving the public health, building a guild-hall and hospitals, and establishing schools for teaching the English tongue to Hindus, Mohammedans, and other Indian children. Before the Governor and Council at Madras could offer a single suggestion, they received instructions cut and dried. The mayor and three senior aldermen were always to be covenanted British servants of the East India Company, and they alone were to be Justices of the Peace. The remaining nine might belong to any nationality, and included Portuguese, Hindu, and Jewish merchants having dealings with the Company at Madras. Thirty burgesses were named in the charter, but they were all Englishmen; and the remainder were to include the heads of all the castes, so as to induce the whole of the Hindu inhabitants to contribute cheerfully to the public works already specified. The mayor and aldermen were to wear red silk gowns, and the burgesses white silk gowns, and maces were to be carried before the mayor. In a word, all the paraphernalia of an English municipality in the seventeenth century were sent to Madras to be adopted by the new corporation.

Corporation festivities.

The new municipality was inaugurated with much pomp and ceremony in 1688, the year of the glorious Revolution. The Governor of Madras was outside the corporation, but the mayor and three senior aldermen were members of council. On Saturday, the 29th of September, 1688, the Governor received the mayor, aldermen, and burgesses in the council-chamber at Fort St. George. The members of the new corporation then took the oaths and sat down to a corporation dinner; and after a while they all marched to the town-hall in their several robes, with the maces before the mayor. Nothing, however, is

CHAP. I. said about the heads of castes, and nothing more about the burgesses.

Failure of municipal rule The mayor and aldermen were to be a Court of Record, with power to try all causes, criminal and civil, in a summary way, according to "equity and good conscience," and such laws and orders as might be made by the Company. The corporation were authorised to levy taxes for building a guild-hall, a public jail, and a school-house for teaching English, arithmetic, and merchants' accounts to Indian children, and for payment of the necessary salaries. Henceforth, two aldermen sat as justices of the Choultry; but the corporation raised no tax and founded no institution, and eventually died out from sheer want of vitality.

Slavery under Hindu rule. § 6. All this while the slave trade was an institution in Madras, and indeed, throughout Southern India. In most of the Hindu kingdoms of the Peninsula, the farm-labourers were slaves or serfs attached to the soil; they were probably aboriginal populations who had been reduced to slavery by their conquerors. Prisoners of war, male and female, were also compelled to serve the conquerors as domestic servants, and treated as slaves of the family.

Mohammedan slavery. When Turks and Afghans introduced Mohammedan rule, slavery was recognised, but Hindu slaves might raise their condition by embracing Islam, and the converts might become important personages in the household, and marry female members of the family. The favourites of a grandee or Sultan might even marry a daughter, and rise to the rank of steward of the household or minister of state, like Joseph in the court of the Pharaohs.

When the Moguls established their dominion over Northern India there was a change for the better. It was a fundamental law of the Moguls that no subject should be enslaved, but only captives taken in war. This law was still enforced when the Moguls became Mohammedans, for they always looked upon the slavery of subjects with horror, whatever might be their race or religion. Foreign slaves, male and female, provided they were not Mohammedans, were sold by private dealers, or in the public bazaar.[1]

CHAP. I.

Mogul restrictions.

Unfortunately, the Portuguese and other nations of Europe had not as yet awakened to the iniquity of slavery and the slave trade. During the Portuguese wars in Africa, Moors and Negroes were carried off as prisoners of war and sold as slaves in Lisbon. In India the Portuguese established depots for the purchase of slaves. At Goa female slaves were to be found in every Portuguese household, and sometimes were sent into the streets to sell sweetmeats and confectionary, and earn money for their masters in other ways.

Portuguese slave trade.

For many years large numbers of Hindu slaves were brought from Bengal. The Portuguese had been permitted to build a factory at Hughly, on the river

Kidnapping from Bengal.

[1] This was notoriously the case at Surat, where female slaves might be purchased by Europeans. There was a Dutch factory at Surat of the same stamp as the British factory, and its married inmates were in like manner forbidden to bring their wives from Holland. But when the Dutch got possession of Java, they offered grants of land to married Dutchmen, and, according to Pietro della Valle, there was a sudden change in domestic arrangements. Dutch bachelors were in such a hurry to go to Java, that they married Armenian Christians, or went off to the bazaar and bought female slaves and baptised them and married them without loss of time.

CHAP. I. Hughly, about 120 miles from the sea. During an interval of civil war they fortified this settlement and landed numerous cannon, whilst a native town grew up in the neighbourhood. Meanwhile, the scum of Goa and other Portuguese towns, chiefly military deserters and apostate monks, had established themselves on the islands near the mouths of the Ganges, built a fleet of galleys, and led the lives of pirates, brigands, and kidnappers. These men were the pest of the Sunderbunds. They scoured the waterways of the delta of the Ganges, carried off whole villages into slavery, and especially delighted in capturing marriage processions, with the bride and bridegroom and all their kinsfolk and acquaintance in the bravery of silks and jewels. The Portuguese at Hughly were base enough to deal with these villains, to buy the poor wretches who had been kidnapped, and to ship them to Goa, where they were sold as slaves at the daily auctions on the Exchange, together with other commodities from all parts of the world. The rascally kidnappers at the mouths of the Ganges, and the pious traders at Hughly, alike quieted their consciences by baptising their victims, and boasting of having saved their souls from hell.

Vengeance of the Great Mogul.

Such a state of things aroused the Great Mogul to take action. The very existence of a Portuguese fortress and cannon within his dominions had given mortal offence, and this unholy slave trade sealed the fate of the Portuguese at Hughly. The settlement was environed by a Mogul army. There was a rush of ladies and children to the shipping, but the river was low and the vessels ran aground. There was absolutely no way of escape; all provisions were cut off, and the Portuguese were starved into surrender. Five or six hundred prisoners, many of noble birth, were sent to Agra. Some saved their lives by turning Mohammedans; others, mostly priests, perished as martyrs; the choicest of the lads and maidens were sent to the palace of the Great Mogul, and the remainder were distributed amongst the mansions of the Mohammedan grandees. For generations afterwards the doom of the Portuguese at Hughly was likened to the Babylonian captivity of the Hebrews.

Slave trade at Madras.

Hughly was captured in 1632. Seven years later the British built their factory at Madras, on the coast of Coromandel. At every Portuguese settlement in Southern India the slave trade was still in full swing, for the sway of the Great Mogul had only been extended over the northern part of the Deccan, and was as yet far away from the Peninsula. Accordingly the British traders at Madras connived at the exportation of slaves by sea. Some restraints, however, were placed upon kidnapping by insisting on the registration of every slave bought or sold in Madras, together with the names of the seller and purchaser, in order that the information might be given in the event of any inquiry by kinsfolk or acquaintance, and also that a fee might be levied on the registration of every slave.

Great Mogul conquers the Deccan.

In 1688 the British rulers of Madras abolished the slave trade by public proclamation. The Great Mogul, the once famous Aurangzeb, was engaged in conquering the Sultans of the Deccan. Unlike his predecessors, Aurangzeb was a bigoted Sunni, or a zealous believer in the four Caliphs who succeeded Mohammed. The Sultans of the Deccan were Shiahs

CHAP. I. who damned the first three Caliphs as usurpers, and swore that Ali, and Ali only, the son-in-law of the Prophet, the husband of Fatima and the father of Hassan and Hosein, was the rightful successor of Mohammed. Under such circumstances Aurangzeb was impelled by pious zeal for the interest of the Sunni religion to conquer and slay the heretic Sultans of the Deccan and annex their dominions to the Mogul empire. He next prepared to march his army further south into the Peninsula, with the view of conquering the Hindu Rajas and compelling their idolatrous subjects to accept the religion of the Koran.

Stoppage of the slave trade.

The British at Madras were greatly alarmed at the threatened approach of the Great Mogul. They were naturally afraid of sharing the fate of the Portuguese at Hughly. Accordingly they abolished the slave trade by proclamation, and sent numerous petitions to Aurangzeb, tendering their submission to the Great Mogul, praising his imperial majesty to the skies, imploring his protection as though he had been another Cyrus or Darius, and engaging to pay the old rent of 500*l.* per annum in pagodas. Matters were finally arranged, but it is grievous to add that the pious Aurangzeb was not so careful of the welfare of the Hindus as his liberal and tolerant predecessors. He preferred the laws of Mohammed to those of his Mogul ancestor, Chenghiz Khan; and within a few years the slave trade at Madras was as brisk as ever.

British toleration.

§ 7. The Mogul conquest of the Sultans of the Deccan drove many Mohammedans to settle at Madras. The British traders protected the lives and property of

Hindus and Mohammedans, and permitted them to worship as they pleased. In early days, the Directors had repeatedly pressed their servants at Madras to convert the Hindu worshippers of idols to the truths of Christianity, and no one in the British Isles seems to have doubted the possibility or expediency of the work. The British traders at Madras, however, deprecated any interference whatever. They described a terrible riot that broke out at St. Thomé because of some interference with a Hindu procession, and they urged that the frays between the Right and Left Hands were sufficient proof that it was best to leave the Hindus alone. As for Mohammedans, they were the subjects of the Great Mogul, and interference with the dominant religion in India was out of the question.

Flourishing private trade.

During the latter years of the seventeenth century, the British settlement at Madras had grown into a principality, independent, and self-contained. At the same time it presented rare attractions to traders, Asiatic as well as European. The Company's servants were paid very small salaries, but were allowed the privilege of private trade in the eastern seas, so long as they paid customs and did not interfere with the European trade. Every Company's servant in Madras, from the Governor to the youngest writer, engaged more or less in trading ventures. The number of traders was swelled by private individuals who came from England, under the licence of the Court of Directors; as well as by Hindu, Mohammedan, and Armenian merchants, who often took shares with the Company's servants. Moreover, this private trade increased the demand for European commodities which were sold by public

CHAP. I. auction in Fort St. George, and swelled the revenue of the East India Company which was derived from the sea customs.

Decay of Surat. Meanwhile the British situation at the Mogul port of Surat had become intolerable. The religious fanaticism of Aurangzeb had stirred up hatred and discontent amongst Christians and Hindus. The factors at the English House were more oppressed than ever. On the north their trade was cut off by the Rajput princes of Western Hindustan, who were revolting against the Great Mogul and stopping the caravans between Surat and Agra. On the south they were exposed to the Mahrattas of the Western Deccan, who attacked and plundered Surat, and would have plundered the English House had not the factors surreptitiously landed some cannon, and called in the British sailors from the shipping, and manfully beaten off their assailants.

Bombay, 1661–85. Fortunately, the British had taken possession of the island of Bombay, which Charles the Second had obtained from the King of Portugal as part of the dowry of the Infanta Catharine, and made over to the East India Company. Bombay was nearly two hundred miles to the south of Surat, and hedged around by the Mahrattas, but being an island it was well protected, and included both a fortress and a town. Moreover, it had a magnificent harbour, and the valuable trade with the Persian Gulf, the Red Sea, and the Mozambique could be better carried on from this harbour than over the bar of Surat at the mouth of the river Tapty. Accordingly the East India Company secretly resolved on leaving Surat for ever, and removing the British factors and their trade to the island of Bombay.

In Bengal the East India Company had established a factory at Hughly, hard by the dismantled Portuguese fortress; but were exposed to so much insolence and extortion from the Mogul authorities that they were prepared to leave Bengal rather than tamely submit to further oppression. The trade was enormously profitable, and had helped to defray the cost of the fortifications at Madras and Bombay. Saltpetre had been in large demand ever since the breaking out of the civil war between Charles the First and his parliament. Raw silk and opium were equally marketable, and all three products could be brought from Patna to Hughly by the river Ganges. At Dacca, the old capital of Bengal to the eastward of the Ganges, muslins were manufactured of so fine a texture that a piece sufficient for a dress might be passed through a wedding ring; and every young lady in the British Isles who aspired to be a bride was equally anxious to be led to the altar in a cloud of Dacca muslin. Aurangzeb, however, stopped the supply of saltpetre, because the Sultan of Turkey complained that it was used by Christians in their wars against true believers; whilst the Nawab of Bengal, who resided at Dacca, was most overbearing, and on one occasion ordered that Mr. Job Charnock, the chief of the Hughly factory, should be imprisoned and scourged, and his orders were literally obeyed by the Hughly officials.

Bengal trade, 1640-85.

§ 8. Sir Josiah Child, the chairman of the Court of Directors, was endowed with real political genius, but he was imperious and headstrong. He resolved to make war upon the Great Mogul, and compel him to make reparation for the misdeeds of the Nawab of

Plans of Sir Josiah Child, 1685.

CHAP. I. Bengal, and to cede sufficient territory for the establishment of a fortress and a town corresponding to the settlements at Madras and Bombay. He proposed to coerce the Great Mogul by sending out the Company's cruisers from Bombay to capture the Mogul ships going to Mecca, until Aurangzeb came to terms. He also persuaded James II. to send a Royal fleet to Bengal to ensure the success of his scheme. Should his plans fail, should Aurangzeb prove obstinate and impracticable, it was intended to form an alliance with the Raja of Arakan, on the eastern side of the Bay of Bengal, and promise to help him in his wars against the Great Mogul, provided he ceded the required territory at Chittagong. In short, Sir Josiah Child proposed to overawe the Mogul and establish British trade with India on a lasting basis for the future by means of three great fortresses—one at Madras, a second at Bombay, and a third in Bengal or at Chittagong.

Elements of mischief. Unfortunately Sir Josiah Child was unable to cope with the craft and capacity of Aurangzeb. That keen-witted sovereign had spies in all directions, and was gifted with such a power of divining what was going on that he was often suspected of employing supernatural agency. Meanwhile, Sir Josiah Child was maintaining such profound secrecy that no Englishman on the Bengal side knew what was going on at Surat or Bombay, and no Englishman on the Bombay side knew what was going on in the Bay of Bengal, whilst the British at Madras knew nothing whatever of the plans in operation.

The blundering that followed was most disastrous. Whilst the Company's cruisers were capturing Mogul

Blunders and disasters.

ships as lawful prize, Aurangzeb drew the Surat factors into his clutches, and threatened to put them to death unless the prizes were restored and vast sums paid by way of ransom. Meanwhile, the Royal fleet arrived in Bengal, and made its way up the river Hughly, under the command of a certain Captain Heath, who would listen to no advice and regarded Asiatics with contempt, whilst he was ready to make war on anybody. He brought away Mr. Job Charnock and the British factors from Hughly, with all their goods and records. He captured all the Mogul ships he encountered in the Hughly river. He bombarded a Mogul town at the mouth of the river. Meanwhile, the Nawab of Bengal was in a panic of fear at Dacca, willing to make any terms provided only that the terrible admiral would leave Bengal and solemnly promise never to return.

A hot-headed admiral.

The Royal fleet sailed to Arakan and frightened the Raja into a state of utter bewilderment. The Raja could make nothing of the offer of the admiral to help him against the Great Mogul, nor of the demand for the cession of Chittagong, and he naturally vacillated, prevaricated, and procrastinated. The admiral was blind with rage and mortification, and would have captured Chittagong by force of arms; but the place was too strong for him. Accordingly, he sailed away to Madras in a towering fury, and landed Mr. Charnock and the British factors at Madras, swearing that he had heard nothing but deceit and lies since he first entered the Bay of Bengal.

Humiliation.

The East India Company submitted to the Great Mogul, but the great Josiah Child must have found it a bitter pill. The prizes were restored, a vast fine

CHAP. I. was paid, and pardon was humbly implored before the Surat factors were restored to liberty.

Calcutta founded, 1690. Meanwhile, the Moguls had learned to respect the British. The fugitives from Hughly were invited to return to Bengal, and permitted to purchase a strip of land on the eastern bank of the Hughly river, about twenty miles nearer the sea than their old factory. It was three miles long and one mile inland, and included the three native villages of Chutanutti, Govindpore, and Kali Ghat, which grew into a native town resembling that of Madras. Later on, the Hindus round about revolted against Mogul oppression, and the British took advantage of the general alarm to convert their factory into a fortress and to give it the name of Fort William, in honour of the Prince of Orange. The native settlement was known by the name of Calcutta, after the village of Kali Ghat, or the "landing place of the goddess Kali." Thus the dream of Josiah Child was realised, and British trade in India was protected by three fortresses and three towns—Madras, Bombay, and Calcutta.

Indian calm, 1700-40. From the end of the seventeenth century to the middle of the eighteenth the Company's settlements were for the most part shut out from the Indian world. The British had learned their lesson and kept quiet, and the Moguls were busy fighting the Mahrattas, and left them very much alone. The Mogul conquests in the Deccan were made over to a Mogul Viceroy known as the Nizam, whilst those in the eastern Peninsula round about Madras were placed in charge of a Nawab who was known as the Nawab of the Carnatic. Meanwhile, the Moguls kept the Mahrattas quiet by the payment of a yearly black-mail known as chout, or "*chauth*," which was reckoned at one-fourth of the land revenue, but was often commuted for a lump sum. Thus India was to all outward appearance in a state of calm, but it was the calm that precedes a storm.

Typical Madras Governors.

§ 9. Although the administration of Madras was carried on by a Governor and Council, yet each Governor had a strong personal influence and individuality. Two of these Governors, an Englishman and a Scotchman, may be brought under notice as types of all.

Governor Pitt, 1698-1709.

THOMAS PITT, grandfather of the Earl of Chatham, was Governor of Madras from 1698 to 1709. In 1702 the Nawab of the Carnatic was staying at St. Thomé, trying to squeeze some 50,000*l.* out of the British at Madras. He boasted loudly of his friendship for the British whilst his troops were plundering their outlying villages. He was entertained at dinner with great pomp at Fort St. George, and gratified with presents; but shortly afterwards he environed the whole settlement with his army. Pitt held out for months, getting his supplies by sea. At last Pitt offered two or three thousand pounds in rupees, and a peace was patched up, and the Nawab went away.

Imperious rule.

Governor Pitt was as lofty and mysterious in his way as his illustrious grandson. He was much irritated by a protracted quarrel between the Right and Left Hands. He set up stones to mark the boundaries between the streets, but they were carried away at night time. The bulk of the Right Hands fled to St. Thomé, and the Hindu populations in all the country round about were in great commotion. Pitt threatened to send a body of European soldiers to St. Thomé, and put the deserters to the

CHAP. I. sword. At this crisis, the Mogul officer at St. Thomé turned the malcontents out of the town. They went back to Madras submissive and crestfallen, and begged to be forgiven. From this time, however, the distinction between the Right and Left Hands was abolished as far as the streets were concerned, and all streets were opened to both Hands. But the old strife is still burning in the hearts of the Hindus of Southern India. They can be prevented from fighting with swords and clubs, but they carry the battle into the law-courts, where disputes are frequently brought to a decision as regards the right of either Hand to worship at a particular shrine and in a particular way.[1]

Hasty temper.

Pitt was severe on native offenders. Some thieves went off with boat-loads of cotton goods, and the gunner at Fort St. George was ordered to fire upon them. The thieves escaped, but two peons who connived at the robbery were whipped and put in the pillory, whilst Governor Pitt thrashed the native overseer with his own hands.

Pitt diamond.

During the siege of Madras Pitt managed to buy a wonderful diamond from a Golconda jeweller at a small price. In after years he sold it to the Regent of France for 135,000*l.*, and it was known as the Pitt diamond. The matter created some scandal at the time, but is now only remembered in connection with Pope's lines :—

> "Asleep and naked as an Indian lay,
> An honest factor stole his gem away."

[1] Abbé Dubois, who lived many years in Southern India, could not account for the distinction between the two Hands; Dr. Fryer was told about 1676 that the antagonism was planned by the Brahmans to keep the lower castes in subjection.

CHAP. I.

Governor Macrae, 1725-30.

JAMES MACRAE, a Scotch celebrity, was Governor of Madras from 1725 to 1731. He carried out a general survey of Madras and its suburbs for the better collection of the quit-rents and scavenger-tax. The population of Madras numbered 200,000. The expenses of Fort St. George amounted to 20,000*l.* a year, whilst the revenue from the sea customs was under 5,000*l.*

Mayor's Court.

The Mayor's Court was re-organised in Governor Macrae's time under the charter of 1726. It was to consist of a mayor and nine aldermen for the trial of all civil causes. Seven of the aldermen were to be Englishmen, and the remaining two of any nation, provided they were Protestant. The new court was inaugurated in a style which seems inexpressibly absurd in the present day. The new mayor and aldermen were sworn in with much ceremony, and then left Fort St. George in a grand procession of soldiers with kettledrums and trumpets, dancing girls with the country music, court attorneys with all the chief gentry on horseback, and passed through Black Town to the Company's garden in the suburbs, where they were received by the Governor and Council and duly *fêted.*

Breaking up of the Mogul empire.

Meanwhile, the Mogul empire was breaking up. Aurangzeb died in 1707. Within thirty years after his death the power of the Great Moguls had died out; the name and prestige remained, but very little more. The successors of Aurangzeb were *Roisfainéants* shut up in palaces with wives and concubines, whilst all real power was exercised by the Ministers of State and the Viceroys of the provinces. In 1738-39 the British at the three Presidencies were startled by the news that Nadir Shah had invaded India with a

CHAP. I. large Persian army from the north-west, and had plundered the city and palaces of Delhi and carried away the spoil of Northern India. The payment of the Mahratta "chout" was stopped at the Mogul treasury, and armies of Mahratta horsemen were making up the loss by the plunder of the Carnatic and Bengal.

War with France, 1745.

§ 10. In 1745 news reached India that war had been declared between Great Britain and France. This was alarming news for the British traders at Madras, as the French had established a flourishing town and settlement at Pondicherry, on the coast of Coromandel, about a hundred miles to the south of Madras, and a collision might be expected at any moment between the two settlements. Moreover, the Governor of Pondicherry was a certain M. Dupleix, a Frenchman of large capacity and restless ambition, who hated the British with all the ardour of the typical Frenchman of the eighteenth century. The same year a British fleet appeared off the coast of Coromandel and threatened Pondicherry; but the Nawab of the Carnatic declared that he would have no wars between European nations within his territories, and the British fleet sailed away.

Madras captured, 1746.

In 1746 a French fleet appeared off Madras, but the Nawab was not inclined to interfere; he had, in fact, been bought over by M. Dupleix, the French Governor of Pondicherry. The French bombarded Fort St. George; the native inhabitants fled from Madras; and the British inhabitants were carried in triumph to Pondicherry as prisoners of war.

The Nawab of the Carnatic affected to be very angry at this bombardment of Madras. He demanded

French defeat the Mogul army.

that the settlement should be transferred to his authority, and sent an army of 10,000 Moguls to take possession of the town and fortress. To his utter amazement the army of 10,000 Moguls was utterly routed by a battalion of 800 Frenchmen. From that day it was felt throughout Southern India that no Mogul army could stand against the rapid firing of disciplined Europeans. In 1748 the war between Great Britain and France was over for a while, and Madras was restored to the British.

Brilliant success of Dupleix.

Later on, the death of the Nizam of the Deccan threw the whole country into confusion. Rival kinsmen began to fight for the throne of the province without any reference to the Great Mogul. Dupleix plunged at once into the fray. He saw that a French force might turn the scale of victory, and he moved a French army, under the command of Bussy, to help a victorious candidate as occasion served, without the slightest regard to the rightness or wrongness of his claim. In 1751 he had realised his dream of ambition. He had placed a Nizam on the throne at Hyderabad, and he was rewarded with the cession of a territory stretching 600 miles along the coast, for the maintenance of a French standing army. To crown all, he induced the Nizam to appoint him Nawab of the Carnatic; and, in spite of Dupleix being a Frenchman and a Catholic, the appointment was actually made under the seal of the Great Mogul. Meanwhile, the British had supported the claim of a Mogul prince named Mohammed Ali to the throne of the Carnatic, but had been circumvented at every turn, and were now called upon to acknowledge the superior authority of their bitter enemy Dupleix.

CHAP. I.

Triumph of Robert Clive.

British rule in Southern India was at its last gasp. If Dupleix could only have got hold of Mohammed Ali, he might have been master of the Carnatic; Madras might have been a French settlement, and a French Governor and Council might have taken the place of the British in Fort St. George. As it was, Mohammed Ali was very nearly surrendering. He had fled away to seek the help of the Hindu Rajas of the south, and was being closely besieged by the French in the city of Trichinopoly, 180 miles to the south of Arcot. At this crisis Robert Clive saved the East India Company. He left Madras with a small force, and after a march of seventy miles into the interior, threw himself into the city of Arcot, the capital of the Carnatic, where the Nawabs of the Carnatic had held their court for more than half a century. The native garrison fled at his approach, and the inhabitants, numbering 100,000, offered no resistance. The French were aghast at hearing that the capital of the Carnatic was in the hands of the British. They despatched a large force from Trichinopoly, but failed to recover Arcot. In the end they raised the siege of Trichinopoly, and Mohammed Ali was delivered out of their hands and placed by the British in possession of the Carnatic, to the exclusion of Dupleix and ruin of his ambitious schemes.

Tragedy at Calcutta, 1756.

British and French were now anxious for peace, and agreed to make Dupleix their scapegoat. They threw the whole blame of the war upon the unfortunate Frenchman, who returned to France and died in poverty. In 1755 a treaty was patched up at Pondicherry, but was never executed. In 1756, on the eve of the Seven Years' War, terrible news arrived from

Bengal. The Nawab had captured the settlement at Calcutta; and a hundred and twenty-three English prisoners had been thrust into a barrack cell, and perished most miserably of heat and suffocation. CHAP. I.

§ 11. The tragedy was appalling, but the causes were intelligible. About the beginning of the eighteenth century, a Nawab of Bengal, Behar, and Orissa, territories considerably larger than the United Kingdom, had removed his capital from Dacca to Murshedabad, about a hundred miles due north of Calcutta. Here he founded a dynasty, which reigned in peace for some forty years. About 1742 a usurper seized the throne of Murshedabad, and reigned as Nawab. He died of extreme old age in April, 1756, and was succeeded by a grandson, a young man timid and suspicious, surrounded by foes eager to take his life and throne. The new Nawab heard that Governor Drake was sheltering one of his enemies at Calcutta, and strengthening the fortifications; and he ordered the British to surrender the refugee and stop further defences. Governor Drake replied that he knew nothing of any enemies of the Nawab; that he was ready to obey the Nawab in all things; and that he was repairing the defences on the river to prevent being surprised by the French, as Madras had been surprised ten years before. The Nawab was in a fury at this message, and set off for Calcutta in the heats of June with an army of fifty thousand men.

Threats of the Nawab of Bengal.

For half a century the British had paid little or no attention to their defences. Fort William had been deemed a sufficient protection on the side of the river, and on the land side the native inhabitants

Defences at Calcutta.

CHAP. I. had begun to dig a ditch as a defence against the Mahratta horsemen; but the Mahrattas were paid chout to go away, and the ditch was never finished. The Europeans dwelt in houses and gardens along the bank of the river Hughly, on either side of Fort William; and an English Church, the Mayor's Court and some other buildings, covered Fort William on the land side. The native quarter, including a large bazaar, adjoined the Mahratta ditch, and avenues of trees led from the native quarter to Fort William and the European buildings.

Neglected precautions.

Had Governor Drake or any member of his Council possessed a spark of military genius, they might have held Fort William against the Nawab in spite of his superior numbers. There was a garrison of two hundred European soldiers in the Fort. The European residents should have abandoned their houses on the river, and repaired to the Fort with their wives and children. The neighbouring buildings should have been demolished to prevent the Nawab's troops from approaching under cover. The enemy should have been harassed with shells all day and sallies all night, until the Nawab raised the siege. Moreover, the beginning of the south-west monsoon was daily expected. With it would come the ships of the season from Europe. Could the besieged have held out for ten days, they might have been rescued by the ships, just as Charnock and the factors were carried away from Hughly some seventy years before.

Weak preparations.

Whilst the Nawab's army was approaching Calcutta, the native population were flying *en masse* to the neighbouring villages. There was also a large population of Portuguese half-castes, which should have been left to do the same, as they would have been in no manner of danger. Unfortunately, two thousand of these black women and children were admitted into the Fort, and the overcrowding and confusion were fatal. Meanwhile, batteries and breastworks were constructed in the avenues leading to the Fort, in the wild hope of protecting the whole European quarter; but they were too far away to be supported by reinforcements from the European garrison. CHAP. I.

Siege of Fort William.

At noon on Wednesday, the 16th of June, the Nawab's army poured into the settlement through the unfinished portion of the Mahratta ditch. They set fire to the native bazaar, and, after meeting obstinate resistance, they captured the batteries and breastworks in the avenues. The European gunners spiked their cannon and fell back upon the Fort; but the Nawab's artillerymen drilled the cannon and turned them round towards the Fort; whilst bodies of the Nawab's matchlockmen occupied the buildings outside the Fort which ought to have been demolished, and opened fire upon the ramparts and bastions.

Escape of women and children.

The fighting lasted all Thursday and Friday. On Friday night the English ladies and children were placed on board the single ship which lay before the Fort. On Saturday the firing was hotter than ever. Hopeless efforts were made to place the Portuguese women and children on board the ship, but they would have been safer in the neighbouring villages, for the overcrowding was such that many boats were sunk and numbers were drowned. Governor Drake, however, got on board, and the ship moved slowly down the river, leaving the British soldiers and others to their fate.

CHAP. I.

Loss of Fort William.

Throughout Saturday night the garrison fired rockets for recalling the ship. At sunrise they waved flags, but without effect. A Mr. Holwell, a member of Council, was elected Governor in the room of Drake. But resistance was useless. The British soldiers broke into the arrack-room and got hopelessly intoxicated. Late in the afternoon a mob of the Nawab's troops advanced to the Fort with ladders. In a few moments they were swarming over the walls, whilst the drunken European soldiers ran to the back of the Fort and broke down the gates leading to the river. But the Fort was closely environed by the Nawab's troops, and whilst some of the fugitives may have escaped to the boats or been drowned in the river, the bulk were brought back into the Fort as prisoners of war.

Black Hole tragedy.

By this time the Nawab had taken possession of Fort William, but was terribly disappointed at finding very little money and only a poor stock of merchandise. The season ships to Europe had carried off all the Indian exports to escape the south-west monsoon, and the ships from England were waiting for the monsoon to carry their European cargoes up the river. There were 146 prisoners, and no place of security except the barrack cell, known as the Black Hole, which rarely held more than two or three prisoners, and was only eighteen feet square. In this horrid hole they were driven with clubs and swords, and next morning only twenty three were taken out alive.

Such was the close of the first act of the East India Company's rule. Within a very brief space of time the British traders entered upon a new era of conquest and dominion; but the tragedy at

Calcutta in June, 1756, has never been forgotten, and to this day there is not an English man or woman in India who does not occasionally call up a painful memory of the Black Hole.[1]

CHAP. I.

End of the first period.

[1] Since the foregoing chapter was in type, Professor Terrien de Lacouperie has kindly pointed out that a division between right and left hands has existed from a remote period in Central and Eastern Asia. Among the Turkish Hiung-nu on the north-west of China, the officers were arranged into two divisions, a left- and a right-hand side, both before and after the Christian era. The Burut-Kirghiz are still divided into two wings, viz., *on* of the right and *sol* of the left.

In China the task of keeping a daily chronicle of "words" and "facts" was entrusted to two officers, one on the left-hand of the emperor and the other on his right. The officer on the left recorded all speeches and addresses, whilst that on the right recorded all facts and events. This last division, however, is a mere title in Chinese administration; the left-hand being more honourable than the right, and taking the precedence.

The distinction between the right and left hands in Southern India, is, as already seen, a caste antagonism, and it is impossible to say whether it has or has not any connection, however remote, with that in Central Asia or China. The Dravidian populations of Southern India certainly immigrated from the region beyond the Himalayas in some unknown period, but all historical links are wanting save the evidence of language. Professor Terrien de Lacouperie, in his lectures on "Indo-Chinese Philology," has pointed out that the Dravidian group forms the fourth division of the Kueonlunic branch of Turanian languages.

CHAPTER II.

SECOND PERIOD: BENGAL PROVINCES.

1756—1798.

§ 1. From Calcutta to Plassy, 1757–58. § 2. Nawab Rule under British Protection. § 3. British Arrogance: Massacre at Patna. § 4. Lord Clive's Double Government, 1765–67. § 5. Warren Hastings, 1772–85: Life and Career. § 6. British Rule: Treatment of Bengal Zemindars. § 7. British Collectors and Magistrates: Circuit Courts and Sudder. § 8. Innovations of Parliament. § 9. Collisions in Calcutta Council: Trial and Execution of Nundcomar. § 10. Clashing of Supreme Court and Sudder. § 11. Mahratta War: Goddard and Popham. § 12. Triple Alliance against the British: the Mahrattas, the Nizam, and Hyder Ali. § 13. Parliamentary Interference: the Two India Bills. § 14. Charges against Warren Hastings. § 15. Lord Cornwallis, 1786–93: Perpetual Settlement and Judicial Reforms. § 16. Sir John Shore, 1793–98: Non-Intervention.

Madras politics.

In June, 1756, Calcutta was lost; the news reached Madras in August. War with France was trembling in the balance. An army of Europeans and sepoys, under Colonel Clive, was waiting to attack the French in the Deccan. A Royal fleet, under Admiral Watson, was waiting to bombard the French at Pondicherry. But the news from Calcutta outweighed all other considerations; and Clive and Watson were dispatched to the river Hughly with 900 Europeans and 1,500 sepoys.

Calcutta recaptured.

§ 1. The force appears small in modern eyes, but it was irresistible against Asiatics. The ships of war, with their tiers of cannon, were sufficient to create a panic.

The expedition reached Calcutta on the 1st of January, 1757. The Mogul commandant at Fort William fled away in terror, and next morning the British flag was hoisted over the factory. The Company's merchandise, which had been reserved for the Nawab, was lying untouched, but every house in the town, Asiatic as well as European, had been plundered by the Mogul soldiers. CHAP. II.

Nawab accepts terms.

At this moment, news arrived that war with France had begun. Clive and Watson were anxious to make peace with the Nawab in order to fight the French. The Nawab, on his part, was frightened at the British fleet, and was ready to promise anything if the ships and cannon would only go away. He agreed to reinstate the British in all their factories and privileges, and to pay full compensation for all the plunder that had been carried away from Calcutta, so that nothing further was wanted but the execution of these terms.

Treachery and intrigue.

The Nawab, however, never seems to have intended to fulfil his promises. He vacillated, procrastinated, and lied egregiously. He signed a treaty, but evaded every application for the money. He worried Clive and Watson with fresh promises and excuses until they were wild with the delay. At last they discovered that he was intriguing with the French for their destruction. But the Nawab himself was environed with dangers of all kinds. His own grandees were plotting against him, and opened up a secret correspondence with Clive. Englishmen, Mohammedans, and Hindus became entangled in a web of conspiracy and craft, from which it was difficult to escape with an unsullied reputation. Eventually, the Nawab sent an army to Plassy, on the route to Calcutta, as if to overawe the British settlement. The army was commanded by

CHAP. II. Mir Jafir, the head of the conspiracy for dethroning the Nawab. Shortly afterwards, the Nawab himself followed Mir Jafir to Plassy, and the whole force was estimated at 50,000 men and forty pieces of cannon.

Battle of Plassy, June, 1757. Clive advanced from Calcutta to Plassy with 3,000 men and nine pieces of cannon. The battle of Plassy was fought on the 23rd of June, 1757, just a year and three days after the Black Hole tragedy. It was more of a British cannonade than an action between two armies. Clive was expecting to be joined every moment by Mir Jafir. The Asiatic plotter had sworn to be faithful to both parties, and was mortally afraid of both the Nawab and the British. He dared not desert the Nawab, and he dared not fight the British. For hours he did nothing. At last, towards the close of the day, he moved his forces from the field, and made off towards Murshedabad. Clive advanced to charge the Nawab's camp, but the Nawab saw that he was deserted and betrayed, and fled in abject terror. The days of the fugitive were numbered. He hid himself for a while with a favourite wife and his choicest jewels, but was then taken prisoner and brutally murdered by a son of Mir Jafir. Such was the end of the once notorious Suraj-ad-daula, better known to British soldiers and sailors as "Sir Roger Dowler."

Over-flowing riches. Colonel Clive marched on to Murshedabad, and installed Mir Jafir on the throne as Nawab of Bengal, Behar, and Orissa. Clive, and Clive alone, was the lord paramount of the hour, the hero of Plassy, the invincible warrior. The money and jewels in the treasury at Murshedabad were lavished by Mir Jafir on Colonel Clive and his party. The British officers of the army and fleet received large donations One million sterling was given to the East India Company, another million sterling to the inhabitants of Calcutta—European and Asiatic. A hundred boats loaded with silver went down the river from Murshedabad to Calcutta, followed by the curses of the grandees; whilst the sight of the boats approaching Calcutta was hailed with the joy of men who had escaped shipwreck. "For once," says a contemporary, "and only for once, the people of Calcutta were all friends." CHAP. II.

§ 2. The battle of Plassy was a British triumph, but it entailed enormous responsibilities. Colonel Clive had raised up a Nawab to be absolute ruler of territories larger than Great Britain and Ireland, and far more populous. Bengal, including the delta of the Ganges, was one of the most fertile regions in the world, whilst the inhabitants were most submissive and easily governed. For centuries the Bengalis had been oppressed by foreigners—Turk, Afghan, Abyssinian and Mogul. The revenues, however, had been collected by Hindu officials, as being at once more exacting in their demands, and more easily stripped of their ill-gotten gains. Terrible responsibilities.

Nawab Mir Jafir was most subservient to the British and most anxious to please them, but was otherwise as dissolute and worthless as any Turkish pasha. In his younger days, when the Mahrattas were harrying Bengal, Mir Jafir might have been a good soldier, but since then he had degenerated into a worn-out voluptuary, spending all the money he could get on jewels and dancing-girls, whilst his own troops were in mutiny for want of pay, and his British supporters and protectors were demanding Wretched rule of Mir Jafir

CHAP. II. further supplies for the payment of their own forces. To make matters worse, the Nawab was removing the old Hindu officials and placing his Mohammedan kinsmen in their room.

Delhi affairs: flight of the Prince Imperial.

Suddenly, a new vista opened out to Clive through the territory of Oudh, on the north-west, to the remote capital of the Great Mogul at Delhi. The Great Mogul was a mere pageant in the hands of the Vizier, who exercised what remained of the imperial authority. The Prince Imperial, the son and heir of the Great Mogul, was afraid of being murdered by the Vizier, and fled away into Oudh, and threw himself on the protection of the Nawab.

Invasion of the Nawab of Oudh.

The Nawab of Oudh had long desired to get possession of the Bengal provinces, and thought to secure them by making the Prince Imperial a cat's paw. He proclaimed that the Prince Imperial had been invested by his father with the government of Bengal, Behar, and Orissa. He then sent the Prince forward with a large force to enforce the proclamation, whilst he himself remained behind in Oudh and awaited events.[1] To make matters worse, the Hindu officials in the Bengal provinces, who had been dispossessed, or were expecting to be dispossessed, were preparing to join the invaders.

[1] The three provinces of Bengal, Behar, and Orissa are known to Europeans by the one name of Bengal. Bengal proper includes the delta of the Ganges and Brahmaputra. Behar is the frontier province towards Oudh, having its capital at Patna. Orissa lies to the south of Behar and Bengal proper, but Cuttack and the hilly country to the south and west had been ceded to the Mahrattas. The Orissa of the period comprises little more than Midnapore; but the high-sounding title was still retained of Nawab of Bengal, Behar and Orissa. After the Mahratta wars of 1803, the British took possession of Cuttack and remaining portions of Orissa, in order to hold the sea-board against invasion.

Clive's difficulty.

Mir Jafir was in a panic of fear at the appearance of the Prince Imperial, and proposed to pay him a sum of money to go away. Clive would not listen to the suggestion. He ignored the Prince Imperial and the Great Mogul, and soon routed the invading army. The Prince Imperial then became a suppliant to the British, and implored Clive for help; but Clive had been requested by the Vizier at Delhi to arrest the fugitive, and would not commit himself. He, however, sent a bag of 500 mohurs, about 800*l.* sterling, to relieve the immediate necessities of the Prince Imperial, and the money was gladly received by the impoverished fugitive.

Wanted, a British army.

Meanwhile, Clive was at his wits' end for money. The Bengal provinces could be held against any enemy in India by a standing army of Europeans and sepoys. Such an army could be maintained for half a million sterling per annum, and the public revenue amounted to three or four millions; but the Nawab refused to disband his own rabble soldiery, and pretended that he could not pay the Europeans.

Solution.

At this crisis Clive received a secret and startling proposal from the Vizier at Delhi, that he should accept the post of Dewan to the Great Mogul for Bengal, Behar, and Orissa. In the palmy days of the Mogul empire, every province was governed by two officials, the Nawab and the Dewan. The Nawab kept the peace and administered justice; the Dewan kept the public purse, received the revenues, paid all salaries, and sent the surplus as tribute to the Great Mogul. The later Nawabs had become their own Dewans, and spent the revenue as they pleased, without sending any tribute to the Great Mogul. Had Clive closed with the offer, it would have involved a mortal struggle

CHAP. II. with Mir Jafir, for it would have deprived the Nawab of all power over the public purse. But it would have removed every financial difficulty, as the Vizier would have been satisfied with a yearly tribute of half a million sterling, or even less, whilst Clive would have had the whole remaining surplus at his own disposal.

Clive's offer to Pitt, 1759.

Clive would not accept the post of Dewan, either for himself or for the East India Company. But he wrote privately to the British premier, the first William Pitt, and proposed that the British Crown should act as Dewan to the Great Mogul. Under such an arrangement, the Crown might have taken over the Bengal revenues, sent half, or a quarter of a million a year to Delhi, spent another half million on a standing army, and devoted another half million to the salaries of the Nawab and his officials; and then might have secured a surplus of two millions a year towards the payment of the national debt. William Pitt, however, was already alarmed at the growing power of the Crown, and he declined taking over the proposed income lest it should endanger the liberties of the British nation.

Turmoils in the north-west.

In 1760 Colonel Clive returned to England, and in 1761 the war with France was over. India might now have been at peace, but the north-west was in a turmoil. The Great Mogul was murdered by his Vizier. The Afghans had slaughtered 200,000 Mahrattas on the fatal field of Paniput, and established their ascendency at Delhi. The fugitive Prince Imperial was proclaimed Padishah, or Emperor, by the Nawab of Oudh, who assumed the title of Nawab Vizier; and the Padishah and his Nawab Vizier invaded Behar and threatened Patna.

Change of Nawabs.

§ 3. The British at Calcutta were now in sore peril, and there was no Clive to guide them. They deposed Mir Jafir on their own authority, and set up his son-in-law, Mir Kasim, as Nawab of Bengal, Behar, and Orissa. The new Nawab was unquestionably a better man than the deposed Mir Jafir; but the transfer of a throne by a Governor and Council of British merchants was somewhat startling. There was, however, no one to resist the Calcutta traders, and Mir Jafir yielded to his kismet, retired from his post as Nawab, and removed to Calcutta, as a safer residence than Murshedabad.

Mastery of the British.

Mir Kasim agreed to all the British demands. He was bound over to pay half a million sterling for the maintenance of the British army; but he averted money disputes with the Company's servants by ceding three districts in the immediate neighbourhood of Calcutta, which yielded the same amount of revenue, and the British could collect the money for themselves. Above all, the new Nawab agreed, as Mir Jafir had done before him, to free the Company's servants from the payment of all inland transit duties within the Bengal provinces.

Dealings with the Padishahs

Mir Kasim, accompanied by a British force, took the field against the young Padishah and the Nawab Vizier. The invaders were soon defeated; the Nawab Vizier fled back to Oudh, but the young Padishah remained at Patna. Accordingly, the British determined to get his sanction to their proceedings, and thus to justify their appointment of a new Nawab in the eyes of the people of India and the European nations trading with Bengal. He was without territory or revenue. His throne and capital at Delhi were in the hands of the Afghans. Yet he had been proclaimed

CHAP. II. Padishah in India, and was legally the Great Mogul. Accordingly, the British determined to recognize his sovereignty, and arrange for the appointment of Mir Kasim as Nawab of Bengal, Behar and Orissa, under his imperial seal and commission.

British set up a Great Mogul. It was somewhat audacious for a handful of British traders to set up a Great Mogul for themselves as lord paramount of India. It was still more audacious to carry out the ceremony of installation in a building sacred to silk and saltpetre. Nevertheless, the work was done. The Company's factory at Patna was converted into a Mogul palace; the centre room into a hall of audience; the dining-tables into an imperial throne. The Padishah was carried in procession to the factory, and enthroned on the dining-tables as the Great Mogul. Mir Kasim paid homage to the sovereign, and was invested with the post of Nawab of the Bengal provinces. In return, the Nawab was bound over to pay a yearly tribute to the Great Mogul of a quarter of a million sterling.

Enthronement at Patna. The installation of the Great Mogul, and the formal appointment of the Nawab of Bengal, were established facts, but no party was satisfied. The Padishah was disgusted, because the British would not conduct him to Delhi and place him on the throne of Aurangzeb. The Nawab was disgusted at paying a heavy tribute when the Padishah might have been forced by a little pressure to sell the appointment for a bag of rupees. He was apparently bent on breaking off all relations with the British, and there was no objection to his doing so. He moved his court from Murshedabad, which was only a hundred miles from Calcutta, to Monghyr, which was more than three hundred miles. Here he formed an army of picked men, and employed a European deserter, known as Sombre or Sumru, to drill the troops in British fashion, and began to manufacture muskets and cast guns. CHAP. II.

No one satisfied.

The quarrel began about the right of the British servants of the Company, under the treaty with Mir Kasim, to carry their commodities through the Bengal provinces free from the payment of all transit duties. The British at Calcutta twisted the privilege of non-payment into a right to carry such native commodities as salt, tobacco, opium, betel, sugar, and oil, without payment; whilst all Bengali dealers were compelled to pay a duty at every station. The British were thus able to undersell native dealers, and monopolise the whole trade of the country. The Nawab protested against this interpretation, and insisted on collecting the duties, unless the goods were bought for exportation by sea. Then ensued quarrels, misunderstandings, frays and reprisals; the Nawab complaining of the loss of duties, whilst the British set him at defiance, and resisted all attempts to collect the duties by force of arms.

Quarrel with Mir Kasim.

Mir Kasim cut away the British monopoly by abolishing all inland transit duties. The Bengali dealers were thus placed on the same footing as the Company's servants. The Company's servants were blind with wrath at this measure. They insisted that they enjoyed a certain privilege under the treaty with Mir Kasim, and that this privilege was rendered valueless by the general abolition of duties. Accordingly, they proposed sending two of their number to Monghyr to argue the matter with the Nawab.

Fresh exasperations.

The city of Monghyr is situated on the river Ganges, three hundred miles above Calcutta and a

CHAP. II. hundred miles below Patna. The two British envoys were received and entertained by the Nawab, but told there was nothing to settle; he had ceased to collect duties from his own subjects and the British had nothing to do with the matter. At this very moment a boat arrived at Monghyr on its way to Patna with a cargo of firelocks from Calcutta for the garrison at the British factory. The Nawab at once suspected that the British were preparing for war. He confiscated the firelocks, and kept one of the envoys as a hostage, but permitted the other to return to Calcutta. The latter man was doomed. On his way down the river he was fired upon by the troops of the Nawab, and brutally murdered.

Mir Jafir restored.

When the news of this catastrophe reached Calcutta, the Company's servants seem to have lost their heads. In vain they were told that the British at Patna, and those at another factory, were at the mercy of the Nawab. They swore that they would be avenged although every Briton up country was slaughtered; and they wrote out a declaration to that effect, and each man signed it. The Governor and Council of Calcutta then went in a body to the house of Mir Jafir, and restored him to his post as Nawab of Bengal, Behar, and Orissa, on the condition that he once again levied the duties from Bengali traders. Mir Jafir readily promised, and indeed would have promised anything to recover his lost throne.

Peril's at Patna.

Meanwhile, the British at Patna were in extreme danger. They had a European garrison at the factory, but the factory was untenable. They made a desperate effort to seize the town of Patna, and for a few hours were successful. The Mogul commandant was taken by surprise and fled with most of his troops; but the Mogul fortress still held out. The British ought to have stormed the fortress, but delayed on account of the heat. The result was fatal. The European soldiers went to the bazaar for drink, whilst the sepoys plundered the shops and houses, and within a very short time the whole force was utterly demoralised.

British prisoners.

Suddenly, the Mogul commandant met with reinforcements, and returned and recovered the town. The British fled back to the factory, but saw that they were being environed by the Nawab's troops. They hurriedly embarked in boats, in the hope of escaping up the stream into Oudh, but the enemy closed around them. Had they resisted to the last, some might have escaped. As it was they surrendered as prisoners, and were taken to Monghyr, where they found that the British inmates of another factory had been arrested and imprisoned in like manner.

British advance: massacre at Patna, 1763.

An avenging army was soon on its way from Calcutta. Murshedabad was captured, but not without a stout resistance, for the drilled troops of the Nawab were vastly superior to the rabble hosts that had fought at Calcutta and Plassy. The British force, however, overcame every obstacle, and pushed on to Monghyr, whilst the Nawab fled to Patna, carrying his prisoners with him to the number of a hundred and fifty souls. At Patna the Nawab heard that Monghyr was taken by the British, and resolved on exacting a terrible revenge. His prisoners were shut up in a large square building with a courtyard in the centre. He ordered Sombre to slaughter the whole, and the miscreant environed the building with sepoys. The British assembled in the courtyard, bent

CHAP. II. on fighting for their lives. The sepoys climbed to the roof, but were assailed with a storm of brickbats and bottles from the courtyard. Sombre ordered them to fire on the prisoners, but they hung back, declaring that they were sepoys and not executioners, and would not fire on men without arms in their hands. Then Sombre grew furious and violent; struck down the nearest sepoys with his own hands, and threatened and bullied the rest into obedience. The sepoys yielded to their European master. Successive volleys were fired into the courtyard, until it was strewed with dead bodies. Not a single prisoner escaped that horrible slaughter.

Mir Kasim and the Nawab Vizier.

The massacre at Patna sealed the doom of the Nawab. He fled away into Oudh with his family and treasures, but the avenging Furies were at his heels. The Nawab Vizier received him with ostentatious hospitality, but only that he might strip him of his treasures. The Nawab Vizier declared war against the British for the restoration of Mir Kasim, but it was only that he might eventually get the Bengal provinces into his own hands.

Battle of Buxar, 1764.

The war lasted many months, but was brought to a close in 1764 by the battle of Buxar. The victory gained by Sir Hector Monro at Buxar on the Behar frontier was as decisive as that of Plassy. The Nawab Vizier fled away in terror to the Rohilla Afghans beyond his north-west frontier, leaving his dominions at the absolute disposal of the British; and Sir Hector Monro marched on to the capital at Lucknow and took possession of the whole of Oudh.

British triumph

The triumph of the British was complete. Mir Kasim lost his treasures and died in obscurity. The Nawab Vizier was a helpless fugitive; neither

Rohillas, nor Mahrattas, nor any other power could help him against the British. The Great Mogul was once more a suppliant in their hands. The British were *de facto* masters of the bulk of the old Mogul empire, and might have taken possession of the whole of Northern India in the name of the Great Mogul. As it was they proposed making over Oudh to the Afghans, and restoring the Great Mogul to the throne of his fathers at Delhi. Before, however, the Governor and Council at Calcutta could change the map of India, the Court of Directors upset their plans by sending out Clive for the last time with the authority of a dictator.

Lord Clive Dictator, 1765.

§ 4. The Directors of the East India Company had been alternately infuriated and terrified at the news from Bengal. They were extremely angry at the quarrel about the private trade, especially as they had not shared in the profits; but the massacre at Patna filled them with grief and despair. Accordingly Clive, who had been raised to the peerage, was sent to Bengal as Governor, with full power to act as he thought proper.

Settlement of Oudh.

When Lord Clive landed at Calcutta Mir Jafir was dead, and the existing Governor and Council had sold the throne of the three provinces to an illegitimate son for 200,000*l.* and divided the money amongst themselves. Lord Clive was extremely wroth, but could do nothing. The offenders retired from the service of the Company and returned to England. Meanwhile Lord Clive stopped the expedition to Delhi, restored Oudh to the Nawab Vizier, and secured a handsome sum out of the transaction for the benefit of the East Indian Company.

CHAP. II.

Company acquire Bengal, Behar, and Orissa, 1765.

But the crowning event in Lord Clive's life was the acceptance of the post of Dewan to the Great Mogul in the name of the East India Company. Henceforth, the Governor and Council at Calcutta took over the revenues of Bengal, Behar, and Orissa from the Nawab's revenue officers, and provided for the military defence of the three provinces. A quarter of a million sterling was paid to the Great Mogul, and half a million to the Nawab at Murshedabad for the salaries of himself and his officials; but all interference on the part of the British with the administration of the Nawab and his ministers and servants was strictly forbidden, as contrary to the policy of non-intervention. Accordingly, the Nawab and his officials were left to govern the country in their own fashion, without a revenue and without an army.

Sorrows of the Great Mogul.

The Great Mogul, however, was not content. He would not live in the Bengal provinces; he wanted to go to Delhi, and he was sulky because the British would not take him there. He set up his little court at Allahabad, half-way between Calcutta and Delhi, and lived like a prince; but he was unhappy. A British brigade was posted hard by, and the officer in command would not allow him to support his imperial dignity by beating the imperial kettle-drums, because of the noise.

Agony of Bengal, 1765–72.

The arrangements as regards the Bengal provinces, known in India as the acquisition of the Dewanny, were carried out in 1765. In 1767 Lord Clive returned to England, and the Bengal provinces were reduced to greater misery than ever. There was no one to control the native officials, and they accumulated riches at the expense of the masses. The wealth which the old Nawabs had lavished on their pleasures was at least spent within the three provinces; whereas it was now sent to China to buy tea and silk for the East India Company, or was remitted to England as the private fortunes of the Company's servants. Bengal was drained of its silver, and the masses loudly complained that the British ought to protect them against their oppressors. But non-intervention was the cry both in Bengal and in the British Isles, and nothing was done. CHAP. II.

British supervisors.

Meanwhile the revenue had rapidly declined. Before Lord Clive left Bengal he was compelled to do something in spite of his policy of non-intervention. He sent a British civil servant to every district in the Bengal provinces, under the name of Supervisor. The supervisors were to watch and report what was going on, but not to interfere with the Bengali officials.[1] They were to collect statistics respecting the land, its produce and capacity; the authorised amount of land revenue and the illegal exactions; the administration of justice and the regulation of trade. The British supervisors could only report what they saw, and what the native officials chose to tell them. One thing was certain: the people were terribly oppressed and the administration was in utter confusion; and so long as the British played at non-intervention it was impossible to apply a remedy.

Famine, 1770-71.

At last the dreadful famine of 1770-71 desolated and depopulated the whole country. Terrible reports

[1] In the present day there are forty-five districts in the Bengal provinces, namely, thirty-seven regulation and eight non-regulation. The distinction between the two classes of districts will be explained hereafter.

CHAP. II. reached England that the Company's servants had leagued with the native officials to buy up all the grain and sell it at famine prices. Meanwhile the revenue had rapidly declined, and the blame was thrown on the Bengali officials. Accordingly the Court of Directors resolved to dismiss the Asiatic officials, and to appoint covenanted British servants in their room; and they selected Warren Hastings to be Governor of Bengal, with peremptory orders to carry out the necessary reforms.

Restricted authority of Lord Clive.

§ 5. The change from Lord Clive to Warren Hastings was most momentous. Lord Clive was a soldier born to command. Warren Hastings was emphatically an administrator born to rule. From the first Lord Clive had shirked all political responsibility. He was content to place the East India Company in the position of Dewan, with the additional duty of maintaining a standing army for the defence of the country, but without attempting to invest it with the ruling powers of a Nawab. So long as the Company took over the revenue, the Nawab and his officials were left to govern the people, and administer law and justice, according to their own will and pleasure For himself, Lord Clive was content to rule the Company's settlement and some small cessions of territory of no account, and to leave the outside masses in utter darkness.

Vast dominion of Hastings.

Warren Hastings went to Calcutta as absolute ruler over the three provinces. He was a prince amongst princes; the equal if not the superior of any Hindu or Mohammedan ruler within the Himalayas and the two seas. As President of the Council his authority was not confined by the Mahratta ditch, but stretched far away over territories as large, if not larger, than Great Britain and Ireland. He united the powers of British Governor, Nawab, and Great Mogul. He was destined to strip the Nawab of every vestige of authority; to cut down his yearly income from half a million sterling to 160,000*l*., and to reduce him to the condition of a private Mohammedan grandee dwelling at Murshedabad. As for the Great Mogul, he had vanished from the scene. In 1771 he had quitted Oudh and returned to Delhi with the Mahrattas, and thereby forfeited his pension and empty suzerainty as far as the British were concerned. Later on, the Mahrattas demanded payment of the yearly tribute, but were flatly refused by Warren Hastings.

Career of Hastings *ante* 1772.

In 1772 Warren Hastings was forty years of age, with very large experiences. He had landed at Calcutta at the age of eighteen, and served as a clerk and warehouseman in the factory at Calcutta. In 1757, after the battle of Plassy, he was Resident at the court of Nawab Mir Jafir at Murshedabad. Later on, during the quarrel with Mir Kasim, he was a member of the Council at Calcutta, and one of the very few who took the part of the Nawab. In 1764 he went to England and became poor. In 1769 he returned to India and was appointed member of the Council at Madras. In 1772 he proceeded to Calcutta to become Governor of Bengal, Behar, and Orissa, in other words —to govern territories covering an area of 150,000 square miles, or one-tenth of the great continent of India. Henceforth his dominion extended from the mouths of the Ganges to the foot of the Himalayas, and from the frontier at Oudh to the frontiers at Assam and Bhutan.

CHAP. II.

Two portraits.

Warren Hastings must be regarded in two different aspects. In 1766, whilst residing in England, his portrait was painted by Sir Joshua Reynolds, and represents a mild, benevolent, and intelligent English gentleman. Twenty years afterwards another portrait was painted, which represents a stubborn and vindictive official, from whom all traces of the mild gentleman had disappeared.[1]

British rule in Bengal provinces.

§ 6. The first task of Warren Hastings was to introduce British administration into the Bengal provinces. The work had been easy enough when dealing with the population of towns, who were dependent on the East India Company for employment and protection. But dealing with provinces having a population of twenty or thirty millions of Hindus and Mohammedans, who knew very little of the British, and very little of their laws or ways, was a very different matter, and demanded extreme tact and caution.

Land revenue.

Warren Hastings began the work of government with the reform of the land revenue—the backbone of all administration in India. In those days the task was beyond the strength of any Englishman or body of Englishmen. During the Mahratta invasions and sudden changes of Nawabs the collection of the revenue had fallen into utter confusion, and it was impossible for Europeans to understand local rights or wrongs.

Zemindars and ryots.

The bulk of the land revenue in Bengal was collected by middle men, known as zemindars, from tenant farmers known as ryots. The zemindar was half a landlord and half a revenue collector. He

[1] The first portrait of Warren Hastings was exhibited at the Grosvenor Gallery in 1883. The second portrait is still hanging in the Council Chamber at the India Office at Westminster.

generally possessed some hereditary land which was the family demesne; but outside the demesne were the landholders or ryots, from whom he collected the rents. The zemindar was not a landlord in the eyes of the ryots, because under Mogul law he could not raise the rents. Still he was a great man within his zemindary. He was magistrate, judge, and controller of the village police; and he had armed followers in his pay, who helped the village police in pursuing robbers and collecting rents. He had the right of hunting, fishing, and cutting wood, throughout his zemindary. Moreover, he levied irregular cesses, benevolences or aids, from the ryots, to defray the expenses of a birth or marriage within his own family, or to meet the demands of the Nawab in an emergency like a Mahratta invasion.

British zemindar at Calcutta.

The changes in the status of Bengal zemindars may be gathered from what is known of old Calcutta. Before the battle of Plassy the East India Company itself was nothing more than a Bengal zemindar, and held the settlement at Calcutta on a zemindary tenure. The Company was pledged to pay to the Nawab a fixed yearly royalty for their little territory. A British civil servant was appointed to represent the Company as zemindar, to bear the name and fulfil the duties of the post; and he collected the ground-rents within the Company's bounds and paid the yearly royalty to the Nawab. He could not raise the rents, for that was forbidden by Mogul law, but otherwise he was all powerful. He administered justice, criminal and civil, like the Justices of the Choultry at Madras. He also raised an additional income by farming out certain trades as monopolies, levying octroi duties on provisions, and taking fees

CHAP. II. for the registration of marriages, and sale of houses, boats, and slaves.

Auction sales of Calcutta lands.

After Plassy the British zemindar at Calcutta cared nothing for Mogul law. He raised the rents within the Company's bounds by the simple process of putting the leases up to auction; and the eagerness of the Bengalis to hold lands and sub-let them to under-tenants led to much competition and a large advance of rents. The zemindar who carried out this innovation was no other than Mr. Holwell, the same gentleman who was accepted as Governor of Calcutta on the morning of the day that ended in the Black Hole disaster. During that terrible night Mr. Holwell seems to have imbibed hatred and contempt for Moguls and Nawabs. Whilst Clive was shilly-shallying with Mir Jafir, Holwell was urging the deposition of the Nawab, the annexation of the Bengal provinces, and the radical measure of putting up all the zemindaries to public auction.[1] This scheme was ignored at the time as the dream of a madman; but nevertheless, within fifteen years, or half a generation, it was seriously considered by Warren Hastings.

Mogul revenue records.

The revenue records of the Moguls had always been singularly complete down to the minutest detail. The holding of every ryot and the area of every zemindary had been measured and remeasured; the average value of the yearly produce of every field had been calculated; and the yearly rents payable by the ryots and the yearly revenue payable by the zemindar had been fixed in each case on the basis of the average harvests. All these details had been entered at length in the Mogul records. But the revenue records which contained all the details respecting the

[1] See Holwell's *Historical Events in Bengal*.

land in the Bengal provinces had mysteriously disappeared when they were most wanted. A Mohammedan contemporary says that they were all destroyed when Mir Kasim fled into Oudh. Possibly they may have been thrown into the Ganges and carried out to sea.

CHAP. II.

Mysterious disappearance.

British collectors.

Warren Hastings did perhaps the best he could under the circumstances. By the stroke of a pen he converted the British supervisors into British collectors of revenues; and thus brought the new collectors into direct contact with the zemindars, who collected yearly rents from the ryots or tenant farmers. The next work would have been to remeasure all the lands and to make fresh estimates of the average yearly value of the produce of each field. This work had been carried out within the Company's zemindary at Calcutta, and many frauds and errors had been discovered and corrected. But what was possible in an estate, was impossible in a territory considerably larger than the British isles. Warren Hastings had no means at his disposal for re-measuring the lands and revaluing the yearly produce, and it was utterly impossible to get at the actual facts as regards rents and revenues. Not only were the records lost, but the revenue administration was in utter confusion; the ministers exacted what they could from the zemindars, and the zemindars in their turn oppressed the ryots. Moreover, no reliable information could be obtained from ryots or zemindars, who were alike suspicious of British intentions and mortally terrified by the British invasion. The new British collectors, with the help of native officials, arrived at some approximate estimate of the rents paid by the ryots in each zemindary, and then

CHAP. II. every zemindar in possession was called upon to pay a certain lump sum as yearly revenue for the whole during a term of five years. If he accepted a lease for the five years, well and good. If he refused, the lease was sold to the highest bidder, with no other reserve than that of requiring him to give the necessary security for the yearly payment to the British collectors.

Disastrous results. The experiment proved a failure. The revenue demands had been fixed too high. Such was the passion for local influence, that many zemindars had agreed to pay a larger revenue than could be realised from the rents. Vast amounts were lost as arrears that could not be realised. Many zemindaries were sold by auction, and were bought up by native speculators who were ruined in their turn. When the five years' leases had run out no attempt was made to renew them; but zemindaries were let on yearly leases until some permanent system could be devised, and this arrangement continued in force until the end of Warren Hastings's administration.

Auction sales of zemindaries.

Judicial reforms: Mohammedan criminal courts. § 7. The system of judicial administration introduced by Warren Hastings was equally cautious and experimental. Bengal zemindars ceased to act as magistrates or judges. The British collector became magistrate and civil judge.[1] As magistrate he made over all prisoners for trial to a Mohammedan court, which was created in each district, but over which he maintained some degree of control. A cazi

[1] The control over the country police was also transferred from the zemindars to the new magistrates and collectors. This measure was good in itself, but attended with disadvantages, which will be brought under review hereafter.

sat as judge and tried the prisoners, whilst muftis and mulvis expounded or interpreted Mohammedan law; but the British collector was present to see that trials were properly conducted, and perhaps to intercede when the punishment awarded was barbarous or cruel. This was little more than a reform of the existing system—such a reform as might have been carried out by an Akbar or Aurangzeb. For centuries Mohammedan law had been the common law of Northern India, and Hindu criminal law, with its hideous severities as regards caste, had been ignored by Mogul rulers, although, no doubt, caste laws were often enforced by the Hindus themselves.

Mixed civil courts: collectors, cazis, pundits.

Civil justice was administered more directly by the British collectors. In civil disputes, especially as regards inheritance and marriage, the parties concerned were necessarily guided by their own laws. Accordingly the collector sat as judge, but was assisted by Mohammedan lawyers in deciding cases between Mohammedans, and by learned Brahmans, or pundits, in deciding cases between Hindus. Under most circumstances the cazi or pundit must often have been the real judge, whilst the British collector was only the representative of the supreme authority.

Courts of circuit and appeal.

Courts of circuit and appeal were also appointed to travel through different areas, and sit as British judges of assize in both criminal and civil courts. Here was that same mixture of British and Asiatic judges as in the collectors' courts. But many changes were made from time to time in the judicial system, and the whole question will be better considered hereafter when dealing with the reforms of Lord Cornwallis, who eventually succeeded Warren Hastings as Governor-General.

CHAP. II.

Chief Court or Sudder.

Meanwhile the Governor and Council still formed the chief court at Calcutta, and confirmed all capital sentences, or heard appeals in important civil cases, as in the old times when British authority was bounded by the Mahratta ditch. From time to time they passed regulations for the guidance of collectors, and eventually Warren Hastings drew up a clear and concise criminal code with his own hands. This chief court was known as the Sudder. It had a civil and a criminal side, and lasted as an institution down to the latest days of the East India Company.[1]

Patriarchal justice.

Under such circumstances British ideas of justice gradually superseded Mohammedan usages. Indeed it was impossible to maintain the criminal law of the Mohammedans in courts controlled more or less by British judges. Under Mohammedan law theft was punished by mutilation, adultery was punished by death, or not punished at all unless four eye-witnesses could be produced; whilst the most atrocious murderer might escape from justice by the payment of a blood fine to the kinsmen of his victim. Cazis and muftis might be nominally independent, but practically they yielded to British influences; and British judges administered justice in a patriarchal fashion, which

[1] The old Sudder Courts at Calcutta, Madras, and Bombay finally disappeared in 1862, when they were amalgamated with the Supreme Courts, which will be described hereafter, and which, up to that date, were exclusively composed of barrister judges. In the present day they are forgotten by all but lawyers familiar with a past generation, yet the Sudder Courts played their part in the history of the past. In the beginning of the nineteenth century, when the Marquis of Wellesley was Governor-General, three civilians were appointed judges in the Sudder, one being a member of Council and the Chief Judge in the room of the Governor-General.

might be condemned by trained lawyers, but was far better suited to the condition of the masses than British courts of law in the last century. CHAP. II.

New members of Council and barrister judges.

§ 8. Whilst carrying out these reforms Warren Hastings was taken somewhat aback by the appointment of three English gentlemen, not in the service of the Company, to seats in the Calcutta Council. At the same time four barrister judges, equally independent of the Company, were sent out from England to form a Supreme Court of Judicature at Calcutta for the administration of English law, civil and criminal. The jurisdiction of the Supreme Court was to extend to all British subjects, and to all Asiatics who were servants of the Company or had dealings with British subjects. The Chief Justice was Sir Elijah Impey, who was known to Hastings, as the two had been schoolfellows together at Westminster. The three other barristers were puisne judges.

Regulating Act of 1773.

The three new members of Council and the four new Supreme Court judges had been appointed, not by the East India Company, but by Parliament and the Crown. The public mind in England had been greatly stirred by reports of maladministration, and in 1773 a "Regulating Act" had been passed to bring the administration of merchant rulers under some control independent of that of the East India Company. No offence was intended to Warren Hastings; on the contrary, he was raised by the same "Regulating Act" to the post of Governor-General, with a controlling power over Madras and Bombay on all questions of war and peace. He filled the chair as President of the Council, but besides him there was only Mr. Barwell, who

CHAP. II. belonged to the Company's service. The three remaining members were the three strangers and outsiders—General Clavering, Colonel Monson, and Mr. Philip Francis, the reputed author of the *Letters of Junius.*

Warren Hastings and Philip Francis.

§ 9. From the very first there were jealous suspicions in the Council between the two gentlemen in the service of the Company and the three gentlemen appointed by the Crown. In one direction Warren Hastings had laid himself open to an attack. In an evil hour he had lent the services of a British brigade to the Nawab Vizier of Oudh, and the Nawab Vizier had employed the brigade against the Rohilla Afghans on the north-west in a quarrel with which the British had no concern. The Rohilla Afghans were defeated by the British brigade, and then plundered and brutally ill-treated by the cowardly troops of the Nawab Vizier. Warren Hastings could only defend himself by saying that money was urgently required by the East India Company, and that the Nawab Vizier had paid heavily for the brigade.

Charges against Hastings.

Whilst Philip Francis and his two independent colleagues were denouncing this transaction, the idea spread amongst the Bengalis that the three new members of Council had been sent by the King of Great Britain to redress the wrongs of natives. Petitions against Warren Hastings were poured into the Calcutta Council, and seriously investigated by Philip Francis and his two colleagues, whilst Hastings and Barwell formed a minority and could not override their proceedings. Hastings was charged with having taken a bribe of 100,000*l.* from the

Nawab Vizier of Oudh. Then it was said that the public auctions of zemindaries were shams; that the native servants of Hastings and others had succeeded in getting large estates at low leases, and that Hastings had shared in the gains. Finally, a Brahman, named Nundcomar, a man of notoriously bad character, charged Hastings with having taken bribes for certain lucrative appointments in the household of the Nawab at Murshedabad.

Nundcomar executed.

Warren Hastings might have rebutted the charges by producing his accounts, and allowing his steward and other servants to be examined before the Council. But he preferred standing on his dignity and refusing to answer the charges brought forward by Nundcomar, who was notorious for perjury, for forging other people's seals, and for carrying on secret correspondence with the enemies of the British. Suddenly Nundcomar was arrested on a charge of forgery, and tried in the Supreme Court by a full bench, comprising Chief Justice Impey and the three puisne judges, and, after a fair summing up, was found guilty by a British jury, and hanged accordingly.

Inaction of Hastings: extenuating circumstances.

Nundcomar was a Brahman, and in those early days no Brahman, under Hindu law, could be put to death; whilst killing a Brahman, even by accident or unavoidable circumstances, was regarded by Hindus as the most horrible crime that could be committed by man. Forgery was a capital offence under English law, but not under Hindu or Mohammedan law. Hastings might have reprieved Nundcomar, but would not interfere. Philip Francis and his two allies, Clavering and Monson, were insolent and aggressive in the extreme. They had pushed Hastings into a corner from

CHAP. II. which he could not escape without damaging his position as Governor in the eyes of the Bengali population. They were equally insolent towards Sir Elijah Impey and the Supreme Court. They demanded, in arrogant language, that every respect should be paid to the caste feelings of Nundcomar during his imprisonment; and whilst the trial was proceeding they addressed the Chief Justice in the language of reprimand, as though they had been his superiors. Sir Elijah Impey went so far as to consult Hindu pundits on the proper treatment of a Brahman under confinement, and to act in accordance with their suggestions. Indeed he seems to have regarded the pretensions of a Brahman to be above English law, to be as deserving of respect as the old "Benefit of Clergy," which was still in existence in England, although taken away by statute from several offences. The execution was delayed for more than a month after conviction, and Nundcomar would probably have been reprieved altogether, but for the arrogance of Philip Francis and his two allies, and the additional perjuries and forgeries which were committed in the course of the trial. Had Sir Elijah Impey submitted further to the dictation of Francis, the Supreme Court would have lost all authority in the eyes of the people of Bengal. The abstract justice in executing Nundcomar for the crime of forgery may be open to question, but Sir Elijah Impey, as Chief Justice of the Supreme Court, was bound to follow English law, without making any exception in favour of a Brahman.

§ 10. Meanwhile there was a collision between the Supreme Court and the Sudder. The Supreme Court began to exercise jurisdiction over zemindars and other Asiatics throughout the Bengal provinces, and to override the decisions of the Company's Courts. Its powers had not been clearly defined, and on one occasion it had been called upon to arbitrate in a quarrel between Warren Hastings and General Clavering, thus assuming a superior authority by deciding differences between the Governor-General and a member of his Council. Again, the judges of the Supreme Court were qualified lawyers appointed by the Crown, and they ignored the decisions of the Company's servants, who were not lawyers.

Collision between the Supreme Court and the Sudder.

The collision, however, was entirely due to the false position which the East India Company had taken up. The servants of the Company had as yet received no authority from Parliament or the Crown to act as judges, or to make laws. They affected to treat the Nawab as a sovereign, and to act in his name; but the Nawab was a fiction set up to hide the territorial power of the East India Company from the British nation. Warren Hastings pleaded that the Bengal zemindars were servants of the Nawab, over whom the Supreme Court had no jurisdiction. The judges replied that the Nawab was a puppet, a phantom, as unsubstantial as a king of the fairies. Unfortunately, the maintenance of this phantom Nawab for the benefit of the East India Company has been for more than a century a dead weight on the revenues of Bengal.

Points in dispute.

In 1781 another Act of Parliament was passed which put everything to rights. It authorised the Governor-General and Council of Bengal to make regulations which should have the force of laws, and it restricted the jurisdiction of the Supreme Court

Parliamentary settlement, 1781.

CHAP. II. to the old bounds of the settlement between the Mahratta ditch and the river Hughly. But the state of Englishmen—that is, of British born subjects of the Crown—was exceptional. They could not be tried by any of the Company's Courts, or under any of the Bengal regulations. A British born subject who committed a criminal offence in any part of the Company's territories in Bengal could only be tried by the judges in the Supreme Court, in accordance with English law, and could only be convicted by a jury of his own countrymen.

Alleged corruption of Impey.

Whilst the struggle was going on between the Supreme Court and the Sudder, Warren Hastings appointed Sir Elijah Impey to be chief judge in the Sudder, on a salary of 7,000*l.* per annum, in addition to his post as chief justice in the Supreme Court. Philip Francis denounced this arrangement as a bribe to Impey; possibly it may have been so, but in itself the appointment was admirably suited to the exigencies of the time. As an experienced lawyer, Sir Elijah Impey was far better fitted than Warren Hastings to act as chief judge in the Sudder, to hear appeals from the Company's Courts up-country, and to control the judicial administration of the Company's judges, who could not pretend to any legal training. But the malice of Philip Francis was as obvious in the case of Impey as in the case of Hastings. Francis had been cast in heavy damages by the Supreme Court as a co-respondent; and he was bent on the ruin of Impey. The result was that Impey was recalled to England and impeached.[1]

[1] The defence of Sir Elijah Impey has been thoroughly investigated from a legal point of view, in the *Story of Nuncomar and the Impeachment of Sir Elijah Impey*, by Sir James Fitzjames Stephen.

CHAP. II.

Origin of the Mahratta power.

§ 11. Meanwhile the British had been drawn into a war with the Mahrattas. For a hundred years the Mahrattas had been the terror of India. Between 1660 and 1680, Sivaji, the hero of the Mahrattas, founded the Mahratta kingdom in the Western Deccan, between Surat and Goa. The head-quarters of the family of Sivaji had been at Poona, about seventy miles to the south-east of Bombay, and Sivaji's early life and exploits were associated with Poona. Subsequently, in consequence of Mogul aggressions, the Mahratta capital was removed to Satara, about seventy miles to the south of Poona.

Rise of the Peishwas, 1748.

In 1748 there was a revolution. The last descendant of Sivaji was shut up in a fortress at Satara, whilst the Brahman minister, known as the Peishwa, removed to Poona, the ancient seat of Sivaji's family, and cradle of his dynasty. The imprisonment of the sovereign at Satara, and the reign of a Brahman minister at Poona, hardened into an institution; and whenever a Peishwa died, his successor went to Satara to be invested with the office of minister by his imprisoned sovereign.[1]

Peishwa and his feudatories: Sindia, Holkar, &c.

The Mahratta kingdom covered the greater part of the area of the Mahratta-speaking people. But the Peishwa sent his lieutenants to collect chout, or black-mail, in Northern India; and one of these lieutenants, Mahadaji Sindia, became a greater man than his master. Sindia always professed to be the loyal servant of the Peishwa, and yet he managed to exercise a commanding influence at Poona.

[1] Two centuries have passed away since the death of Sivaji, yet in June, 1885, a public meeting was held at Poona to take steps for repairing his tomb. His admirers styled him the Wallace of the Deccan.

CHAP. II. It was Mahadaji Sindia who carried off the Great Mogul to Delhi in 1771 and established a dominion in Hindustan, extending from the Gwalior territory northward over the valleys of the Jumna and Ganges. The other lieutenants were only beginning to play their parts in history; they included Holkar of Indore, the Gaekwar of Baroda, and the Bhonsla Raja of Berar in the Deccan, immediately to the northward of the Nizam.

British relations with Berar.

Very soon after the battle of Plassy, the British at Calcutta came into contact with the Bhonsla Raja of Berar. It was the Bhonsla Raja who compelled the later Nawabs of Bengal to pay chout, and to cede Cuttack; and when Lord Clive had concluded his settlement with the Great Mogul and the Nawab Vizier of Oudh, he advised the Court of Directors to pay chout on condition of getting back Cuttack. But the Directors did not want Cuttack and would not pay black-mail; and the Bhonsla Raja pressed his demand at convenient intervals, but wisely abstained from invading the Bengal provinces.

Bombay and the Peishwas.

Meanwhile, the British at Bombay had come into contact with the Mahrattas at Poona. For years the East India Company had been anxious to hold two important positions close to Bombay harbour, namely, the little island of Salsette and the little peninsula of Bassein. But the Mahrattas had wrested Salsette and Bassein from the Portuguese, and would not part with them on any terms. A civil war, however, had broken out in the Mahratta country. A Peishwa had been murdered. An uncle ascended the throne, but was banished on suspicion of being the murderer. He applied for help to the British at Bombay, and offered to cede the coveted positions if the British at Bombay would restore him to the Mahratta capital. The Governor and Council at Bombay closed with the offer, and the war began. CHAP. II.

Disastrous retreat.

After some successes, the British at Bombay met with disaster. Mahadaji Sindia appeared at Poona with a large army to act against the banished Peishwa. A British force advanced from Bombay towards Poona, but took alarm at the report of Sindia's army, and suddenly halted, and beat a retreat. During the return march, the British force was environed by the Mahrattas, and finally surrendered to Sindia under what is known as the "Convention of Wurgaum."

Successes of Warren Hastings.

Warren Hastings condemned the war from the outset; as, however, the Company was committed to a war, he exerted himself, in the teeth of Francis, to maintain British prestige in India. He sent an expedition, under Colonel Goddard, from Bengal to the Mahratta country, and detached another force under Captain Popham to capture Sindia's fortress at Gwalior. The success of these exploits electrified half India. The war was brought to a triumphant close, but all conquered territories, excepting Salsette and Bassein, were restored to the Mahrattas. Indeed, Warren Hastings was not a conqueror like Clive; he acquired no territory during his régime, excepting that of Benares, which was ceded to the Company by the Nawab Vizier of Oudh.

Three Asiatic powers in India.

§ 12. During the Mahratta war secret negotiations were carried on between the Indian powers for a confederation against the British. The two great powers of the Deccan—the Mahrattas on the west representing the Hindus, and the Nizam on the east representing the Mohammedans—had hated one

CHAP. II. another for the greater part of a century. A third power, that of a Mohammedan adventurer named Hyder Ali, was becoming formidable further south on the western tableland of the peninsula. Hyder Ali is said to have once served as a sepoy in the French army. Later on, he entered the service of the Hindu Raja of Mysore, and eventually ousted the Raja, usurped the sovereign authority, and conquered the countries round about.

Hyder Ali of Mysore.

For many years Hyder Ali was the Ishmael of the Deccan and peninsula. His hand was against every man, and every man's hand was against him. He invaded alike the territories of the Mahrattas and the Nizam in the Deccan, and those of the Nawab of the Carnatic up to the suburbs of Madras and Fort St. George. At the same time, he more than once exasperated the British by his secret dealings with the French at Pondicherry.

Invasion of the Carnatic, 1780: breaking up of the confederation.

About 1779 Warren Hastings was warned that the three powers—the Mahrattas, the Nizam, and Hyder Ali—were preparing for simultaneous attacks on Bengal, Bombay, and Madras, and that a large Mahratta army was already on the move from Berar territory for the invasion of the Bengal provinces. In 1780 Hyder Ali desolated the Carnatic with an army of a hundred thousand men, but he was the only one of the three allies that kept to his engagement, and was eventually driven back by Sir Eyre Coote, one of the half-forgotten warriors of the eighteenth century. The Nizam did nothing; he probably waited to see what the others would do. The Mahrattas of Berar encamped in great force in the hills and jungles of Orissa, but only appear to have wanted a money present; and after wasting several months they were induced by Warren Hastings to return to Berar. No movement of any kind was undertaken against Bombay; and thus the strange confederation of Mohammedans and Mahrattas melted away. CHAP. II.

§ 13. The quarrels, the wars, and the irregularities of Warren Hastings induced the British Parliament to attempt radical changes. The antagonism between Philip Francis and Warren Hastings had led to a duel, in which Francis was wounded; and he returned to England to pour his bitter prejudices against Warren Hastings into the ears of Burke and Fox. The result was that a bitter animosity was excited, not only against Warren Hastings, but against the East India Company; and Parliament was called upon to decide whether the control of the administration of British India ought not to be transferred from the Court of Directors to the British Crown. The main question was one of patronage. The patronage of Indian appointments would render the Crown too powerful, as the elder Pitt had foreseen in the days of Clive; and George III. was already straining his royal prerogative over Parliament and Ministers to an extent which was exciting alarm. Parliament interferes.

In 1783, when the coalition ministry of Charles James Fox and Lord North was in power, Fox brought forward a bill for abolishing the Court of Directors, and transferring their authority and patronage to seven Commissioners nominated by Ministers. The bill was passed by the Commons, but George III. opposed it, and it was rejected by the Lords. Fox's India Bill, 1783.

In 1784 William Pitt the younger brought in another bill, which left the Directors in full possession

CHAP. II. of their power and patronage, but brought them under the strict supervision of a Board of Control, consisting of six privy councillors nominated by the Crown. Henceforth the President of the Board of Control, who was always a member of the Cabinet, was the centre of all authority, and was strictly responsible to Parliament for the conduct of Indian affairs.

Pitt creates a Board of Control, 1784.

Trial of Warren Hastings.

§ 14. Warren Hastings returned to England in 1785 to find that the minds of Burke, Fox, and other leading statesmen had been poisoned against him by Philip Francis. Eventually he was impeached by the Commons and tried by the Lords in Westminster Hall. Hastings was certainly responsible for the Rohilla war, and also responsible for the execution of Nundcomar; but the crowning charge against him was that he had connived at the torture of the servants of the Oudh Begums by the Nawab Vizier of Oudh. The charge was painted in terrible colours by Sheridan, and it may be as well to sum up the actual facts.

Case of the Oudh Begums.

A Nawab Vizier of Oudh died in 1775, leaving treasure to the value of some two or three millions sterling in the public treasury at Lucknow. The son and successor of the deceased ruler naturally assumed possession on the ground that the money was state property; but his mother and grandmother, known as the two Begums, claimed it as private property, which the late Nawab Vizier had made over to them as a gift. Warren Hastings declined to interfere. Philip Francis, however, insisted that the British Government ought to interfere; and eventually the money was made over to the Begums on the condition that they paid some quarter of a million towards the State debt due to the East India Company.

Did Hastings connive at torture?

During the Mahratta war money was urgently required. The Nawab Vizier owed large arrears to the Company, but could not pay up unless he recovered possession of the State treasures. Philip Francis had returned to England. Accordingly Warren Hastings abandoned the Begums to the tender mercies of the Nawab Vizier, and connived at the imprisonment of their servants. It subsequently appeared that the Nawab Vizier tortured the servants until the money was surrendered, but there is no evidence to show that Warren Hastings connived at the torture.

Services of Hastings.

Warren Hastings was undoubtedly a man of great abilities and marvellous energy. His services to the East India Company, and to British interests in India, are beyond all calculation. But he was exposed to great temptation in times when public virtue was less exalted than it has been in the present generation, and he was hedged around with enemies who were spiteful and unscrupulous enough to misrepresent any and every transaction. His errors were those of his time, but his genius is stamped for ever on the history of British India. His misdeeds cannot be entirely overlooked, but he paid a bitter penalty. For many months he was threatened by the proceedings which culminated in his trial at Westminster Hall. Eventually he was acquitted of all charges, but his trial was protracted over seven long years and ruined his private fortunes and public career.

After the lapse of a hundred years, the flaws in the character of Warren Hastings may be condoned in

CHAP. II.

Merits as an administrator.

consideration of his merits as an administrator. He found the Bengal provinces in chaos, and introduced light and order. He converted British traders into revenue collectors, magistrates, and judges, but he established Courts of Appeal to supervise their proceedings; and if his magistrates and judges had no legal training, they were at any rate Britons with a national sense of justice, and their decisions were infinitely better than those of Bengal zemindars, without law, or justice, or control. Warren Hastings kept a watchful eye on British interests as well as on the welfare of the people under his charge. He sent a mission to Tibet, which shows his anxiety for the extension of trade. He recorded a touching tribute to the memory of Augustus Cleveland, a young Bengal civilian who had done much to humanise and elevate the rude Sonthals of the Rajmahal hills, which sufficiently proves his sympathy with the well-being of the masses. Altogether, if Warren Hastings is not so free from blame as he is represented by his friends, he certainly was not so black as he has been painted by his enemies.

Lord Cornwallis. 1786–93.

§ 15. In 1786 Lord Cornwallis, an independent peer, was appointed Governor-General. This event marks a change in British rule. Lord Cornwallis was the first British peer, and the first Englishman not in the service of the East India Company, who was appointed to the post of Governor-General. He carried out two measures which have left their mark in history, namely, the perpetual settlement with the Bengal zemindars, and the reform of the judicial system.

The settlement with the Bengal zemindars was still

awaiting a decision. Lord Cornwallis was anxious to arrange the land revenue of the Bengal provinces on English lines. He abandoned the yearly leases, and concluded leases for ten years, with the view of eventually declaring the settlement to be perpetual. Mr. John Shore, a Bengal civilian, pressed for a preliminary inquiry into the rights of the ryots, for the purpose of fixing the rents. But Lord Cornwallis was opposed to any further delay. In 1793 he proclaimed that the ten years settlement would be perpetual; that the tenant-rights of ryots would be left to future inquiry; and that henceforth the Bengal zemindars would be invested with the proprietary rights enjoyed by English landlords, so long as they paid the fixed yearly revenue to Government and respected all existing rights of ryots and cultivators.

Perpetual settlement.

The judicial system introduced by Warren Hastings was modified by Lord Cornwallis. The British collector, as already seen, was also magistrate and civil judge. Lord Cornwallis decided that a collector ought to have no judicial duties under which he might be called on to adjudicate in revenue questions. Accordingly a regulation was passed under which the duties of revenue collector were separated from those of magistrate and judge, and the magistrate and judge was to be the head of the district, whilst the revenue collector was his subordinate. It is difficult to understand the merits of this measure. Since then the two offices have been sometimes united and sometimes separated. Eventually the two offices of magistrate and collector were united in the same person.

Judicial Reforms.

Four provincial Courts of Circuit and Appeal were created by Lord Cornwallis, and remained without alteration for a period of forty years. One Court

Non-intervention.

CHAP. II. was at Calcutta, a second at Dacca, a third at Murshedabad, and a fourth at Patna. Each Court consisted of three civilian judges and three Asiatic expounders of the law, namely, a Mohammedan cazi and mufti, and a Hindu pundit. The judges sat in their respective cities to hear appeals in civil cases; and they went twice a year on circuit to try the prisoners who had been committed by the district magistrates within their respective jurisdictions.

Munsifs and darogahs.

Lord Cornwallis also created a class of Hindu civil judges named munsifs, and a new body of Asiatic police under the name of darogahs. These changes are best dealt with in connection with modern reforms which will be brought under review in a future chapter.

First war against Tippu.

Lord Cornwallis was engaged in two campaigns against Tippu of Mysore, the son and successor of Hyder Ali. The war is a thing of the past. Tippu had invaded the territory of the Hindu Raja of Travancore, who was under British protection; and a triple alliance was formed against him as a common enemy by the British Government, the Peishwa of the Mahrattas, and the Nizam of Hyderabad. In the end Tippu was reduced to submission and compelled to cede half his territories, which were distributed amongst the three allies. The confederation, which only lasted to the end of the war, is memorable for suggesting the idea of maintaining the peace of India by a balance of power, which for a brief interval dazzled the imaginations of Anglo-Indian statesmen.[1]

[1] Lord Cornwallis carried out important reforms in the Bengal army, and thus enabled his successors to build up the larger Indian empire. The British army in India, Asiatic and European, will be brought under review in Chapter V., which deals with the sepoy revolt of 1857–58.

In 1793 Lord Cornwallis was succeeded by Sir John Shore, the Bengal civilian who pressed Lord Cornwallis to settle the rights and rents of the ryots before proclaiming the perpetual settlement with the zemindars. He is better known by his later title of Lord Teignmouth. He was the first British ruler who suppressed a Hindu institution. He put a stop to "sitting in dharna," a Hindu usage which was subversive of all justice and all law. It was based on the superstitious belief that the life of a Brahman was as sacred as that of a sovereign, and that killing a Brahman, or being in any way implicated in his death, was the most hideous crime that could be committed by mortal man. Any Brahman might ruin a Hindu, either for private revenge or to avenge another, by sitting at his door and refusing to take food. The victim was as helpless as a bird under the fascination of a serpent. He dared not eat so long as the Brahman fasted. He dared not move lest the Brahman should injure himself or kill himself—a catastrophe which would doom the victim to excommunication in this life and perdition in the next. The terrors of this superstition were removed by a British regulation passed in 1797; and although "sitting in dharna" is still a crime under the Penal Code, the memory of the usage is passing away.[1]

CHAP. II.

Shore, 1793-98; abolition of "dharna."

Sir John Shore strictly adhered to the old policy of

[1] The abolition of "sitting in dharna" by Sir John Shore was the first great social reform which was carried out in India under British rule. In 1802 Lord Wellesley abolished the still more horrible practice of sacrificing living children by throwing them to the alligators at the mouth of the Ganges; whilst the once famous rite of suttee, or the burning of living widows with their dead husbands, was practised under British rule down to 1829, when it was abolished by Lord William Bentinck.

CHAP. II. non-intervention, which amounted to political isolation. Meanwhile the Mahratta powers united to demand enormous arrears of chout from the Nizam; and the Nizam was utterly defeated, prostrated and paralysed. All hope of a balance of power for the maintenance of the peace of India was thus cast to the winds. Finally, as if to show beyond all question the absurdity of the idea, the Mahratta powers were at war with each other for the mastery at Poona. Such was the state of affairs in 1798 when Lord Mornington, better known by his later title of Marquis of Wellesley, succeeded Sir John Shore as Governor-General, boasting, as he left Europe, that he was going to govern India from a throne with the sceptre of a statesman, and not from behind a counter with the yard measure of a trader.

CHAPTER III.

THIRD PERIOD: IMPERIAL GOVERNMENT.

1798—1836.

§ 1. Lord Mornington (Marquis of Wellesley), 1798—1805: last war against Tippu, 1799. § 2. Carnatic confiscated and annexed to Madras Presidency. § 3. Wellesley's scheme of a paramount power. § 4. Second Mahratta war: successes of Arthur Wellesley and Lake. § 5. Disastrous war with Holkar. § 6. Return to non-intervention. § 7. Sepoy mutiny in Madras army. § 8. Lord Minto, 1807—13: wars and alliances against France. § 9. Evils of non-intervention in Rajputana: troubles in Nipal. § 10. Lord Moira (Marquis of Hastings), 1813—23: war with Nipal, 1814—15. § 11. Revival of the paramount power: Pindhari and Mahratta wars, 1817—18. § 12. Lord Amherst, 1823—28: wars with Burma and Bhurtpore. § 13. Lord William Bentinck, 1828—35; abolition of Suttee. § 14. Suppression of Thugs. § 15. Administrative reforms. § 16. North-West Provinces: Joint Village Proprietors. § 17. Madras and Bombay Presidencies: Ryotwari Settlements. § 18. Changes under the Charter of 1833. § 18. Sir Charles Metcalfe, 1835—36.

French menaces, 1798.

IN 1798 British India was confronted on all sides by France or Frenchmen. An army of sepoys, drilled and commanded by French officers, was maintained by the Nizam in the Deccan. Another French officered army was maintained by Sindia in Western Hindustan, between the Jumna and the Ganges. Napoleon Buonaparte was invading Egypt, and threatening to conquer the world.

Asiatic aspirations of Napoleon.

The successes and crimes of the French Revolution had filled Europe with indignation and despair. Napoleon Buonaparte had risen, like another Chenghiz Khan or Timour, to take the world by storm. He had driven the British from Toulon, conquered Italy,

CHAP. III. wrested the Netherlands from Austria, threatened to invade the British Isles, and then had landed in Egypt, won the battle of the Pyramids, and proclaimed himself to be a follower of the Prophet. Not a man in Europe or Asia could penetrate the designs of the young Corsican. Alexander of Macedon had invaded Egypt as a prelude to the conquest of Persia and India. Napoleon might follow in his footsteps after the lapse of twenty-two centuries. He might restore the Caliphat of Bagdad on the banks of the Tigris, or resuscitate the sovereignty of the Great Mogul over Northern India, from the banks of the Indus to the mouths of the Ganges.

Tippu's alliance with France.

§ 1. The first duty of Lord Mornington was to get rid of the French sepoy battalions in the Deccan and Hindustan, and to provide for the defence of India against France and Napoleon. Within three weeks of his landing at Calcutta the note of alarm was sounded in Southern India. Tippu, Sultan of Mysore, had formed a hostile alliance with France against Great Britain. It appeared that Tippu had been groaning under his humiliation by Lord Cornwallis, and burning to be revenged on the British government. He hesitated to ally himself with the Mahrattas or the Nizam, and coveted an alliance with a European power. Accordingly he secretly sent emissaries to the French governor of Mauritius, to conclude a treaty with France and Napoleon against Great Britain. The idea fired the imagination of the French at Mauritius, and the fact of the treaty was published in the *Mauritius Gazette*, and republished in the Calcutta newspapers for the edification of the new Governor-General.

Explanations demanded.

Lord Mornington naturally concluded that Tippu was in collusion with Napoleon, and that a French fleet might soon be sailing from Egypt down the Red Sea to help Tippu in the invasion of the Carnatic, or to help Sindia to restore the supremacy of the Great Mogul over Oudh and Bengal. In the first instance he called upon Tippu for an explanation, and proposed to send an envoy to Seringapatam to arrange for a better understanding between the two governments.

Tippu dumbfoundered.

Meanwhile Tippu was amazed and bewildered. To have his secret designs suddenly published in successive newspapers, and then to be called upon for an explanation, seems to have stupefied him. He replied that the French were liars, and refused to receive an envoy from Lord Mornington. To have overlooked the offence would have been sheer madness. Accordingly Lord Mornington determined to revive the old alliance with the Nizam and the Mahrattas against Tippu, and meanwhile to get rid of the French sepoy battalions.

French battalions disbanded at Hyderabad.

The Nizam welcomed a British alliance as offering a means of escape from the crushing demands of the Mahrattas. He was glad enough for the British to disband his French sepoy battalions, which drained his resources, and were threatening to mutiny for arrears of pay. A British force was moved to Hyderabad, the disbandment was proclaimed, and a battle was expected. Suddenly, the French sepoys raised an uproar, and the French officers rushed into the British lines for protection. It was the old Asiatic story of mutiny for want of pay, and when the British advanced the money, the sepoys went away rejoicing, and the French officers were thankful for their deliverance.

CHAP. III.

Mahrattas evade a British alliance.

Lord Mornington next began his negotiations with the Mahrattas, but they raised up a host of difficulties. The Peishwa at Poona was a young Brahman, sharp and suspicious. He was jealous of the British alliance with the Nizam, which boded no good as regarded future payments of chout, but he was anxious to keep on good terms with the British. Accordingly he promised to send a contingent to join the British in the war against Tippu, but at heart he had no intention of doing anything of the kind. With him an alliance with the Christian or the Mohammedan was a mere question of money. He was anxious to sell his alliance to the highest bidder. Accordingly he entertained Tippu's envoys at Poona in the hope that the Sultan might eventually offer higher terms than the British for the services of a Mahratta army.

Destruction of Tippu, 1799.

In 1799 Lord Mornington began the war against Mysore. A British army from Madras, under the command of General Harris, invaded it from the east, whilst another force from Bombay invaded it from the west. The two armies soon closed round Tippu. He saw that he was environed by his enemies, and that resistance was hopeless. He sued for terms, but was told to cede the half of his remaining dominions and pay up two millions sterling. He refused to surrender on such crushing conditions, and retired to his fortress at Seringapatam, resolved to die sword in hand rather than become a servant or a pensioner. In May, 1799, Seringapatam was taken by storm, and the dead body of Tippu was found in the gateway.

Cruelty of Tippu.

The fate of Tippu might have been regretted but for his cruel treatment of British prisoners in former wars. At Bangalore, British captives were chained together, starved, threatened, and tormented until some were driven to become Mohammedans. The consequence was, that during the advance on Seringapatam British soldiers were burning for revenge, and Sir David Baird, one of the greatest sufferers, begged for the command of the storming party as a relief to his outraged feelings. When the war was over, the death and downfall of the tyrant was celebrated in songs which were reverberated from India to the British Isles, and the old strains are still lingering in the memories of some who are yet living.[1]

Hindu Raj restored.

Lord Mornington annexed part of Mysore territory to the Madras Presidency, and gave another share to the Nizam; and he proposed, as will be seen hereafter, to give a third share to the Mahrattas; but he converted the remainder into a Hindu kingdom. Accordingly an infant scion of the Hindu Raja, who had been deposed by Hyder Ali some forty years previously, was placed on the throne of Mysore in charge of a British Resident and a Brahman Minister until he should attain his majority. The subsequent career of the Raja will be brought under review hereafter.

Annexation of the Carnatic.

§ 2. Soon after the capture of Seringapatam a clandestine correspondence was discovered in the palace

[1] The following fragment preserves something of the feeling of the time:—

"Fill the wine-cup fast, for the storm is past,
The tyrant Tippu is slain at last,
And victory smiles
To reward the toils
Of Britons once again.

"Let the trumpet sound, and the sound go round
Along the bound of Eastern ground;
Let the cymbals clang
With a merry-merry bang,
To the joys of the next campaign."

CHAP. III. between the Nawab of the Carnatic and the deceased Tippu. The treachery was undeniable. At the same time the discovery enabled the British to get rid of a dynasty that had oppressed the people and intrigued with the enemies of the East India Company for half a century. Nawab Mohammed Ali, whom the British had placed on the throne of the Carnatic in opposition to the French, had died in 1795. His son and successor had followed in the steps of his father, but no complaints reached him, for he was smitten with mortal disease. Lord Mornington, now Marquis of Wellesley, waited for his death, and then told the family that their rule was over. The title of Nawab was preserved, and pensions were liberally provided, but the Carnatic was incorporated with the Madras Presidency, and brought under British administration like the Bengal provinces.

Scandals of Nawab rule.

The annexation of the Carnatic delivered Madras from a host of scandals which had been accumulating for some forty years. The old Nawab had removed from Arcot to Madras, and carried on costly intrigues with the Company's servants in India, and with influential persons in the British Isles, in the hope of getting the revenues into his own hands, and leaving the East India Company to defend his territories out of their own resources. He loaded himself with debt by bribing his supporters with pretended loans, which existed only on paper, bore exorbitant interest, and were eventually charged on the public revenue. All this while, he and his officials were obstructing British operations in the field by withholding supplies, or treacherously informing the enemy of the movements of the British army. Since the annexation of the Carnatic in 1801 all these evils have passed into oblivion, and the public peace has remained undisturbed. CHAP. III.

Wellesley's political system.

§ 3. The war with Tippu taught Lord Wellesley that it was impossible to trust the Mahrattas. They would not join the British government against a common enemy unless paid to do so; and they were always ready to go over to the enemy on the same terms. Accordingly Lord Wellesley proposed to maintain the peace of India, not by a balance of power, but by becoming the sovereign head of a league for the prevention of all future wars.

Subsidiary alliances.

With these views Lord Wellesley proposed that neither the Nizam nor the Mahrattas should take any French officers into their pay for the future; that neither should engage in any war or negotiation without the consent of the British government; and that each should maintain a subsidiary force of sepoys, drilled and commanded by British officers, which should be at the disposal of the British government for the maintenance of the peace of India.

Nizam accepts.

The Nizam accepted the subsidiary alliance. He provided for the maintenance of a Hyderabad Subsidiary Force by ceding to the British government all the territories which he had received on account of the Mysore wars. By this arrangement all money transactions were avoided, and the subsidiary force was paid out of the revenues of the ceded districts.

Mahrattas refuse.

The Mahratta rulers utterly refused to accept subsidiary alliances in any shape or form. They did not want British protection, and they would not permit any interference by mediation or otherwise with their claims for chout against the Nizam. The Peishwa would not maintain a subsidiary force, but he was

CHAP. III. willing to take British battalions of sepoys into his pay, provided he might employ them against Sindia or any other refractory feudatory. He would not pledge himself to abstain from all wars or negotiations without the consent of the British government. He was willing to help the British in a war with France, but he would not dismiss the Frenchmen in his service.

Sindia refuses British alliance against Afghans.

Sindia was still more obstinate and contemptuous. Mahadaji Sindia was dead. His successor, Daulat Rao Sindia, was a young man of nineteen, but already the irresponsible ruler of a large dominion in Western Hindustan. He was all-powerful at Delhi, and was bent upon being equally all-powerful at Poona. He collected chout from the princes of Rajputana, and, with the help of his French-officered battalions of sepoys, he had established a supremacy over the valleys of the Jumna and Ganges from the banks of the Sutlej to the frontier of Oudh at Cawnpore. Lord Wellesley would not venture to offer a subsidiary alliance to a prince so puffed up with pride as young Sindia. The Afghans, however, were threatening to invade India, and Lord Wellesley invited Sindia to join in an alliance against the Afghans. But Sindia would not hamper himself with a British alliance. He was not afraid of the Afghans. At any rate he waited for the Afghans to appear before taking any steps to prevent their coming.

British fears of France and Russia.

Lord Wellesley was not afraid of Afghans alone, but of French or Russians, who might make their way through Persia, join the Afghans, resuscitate the Great Mogul, and establish a European empire in his name as the rightful representative of Aurangzeb. Accordingly Lord Wellesley sent the once famous Sir

John Malcolm on a mission to Persia to persuade the Shah to bar out the French and prevent the Afghans from invading India. Meanwhile, he anxiously waited some turn in Mahratta affairs which would bring their rulers into a more compliant mood towards the British government. CHAP. III.

Lord Wellesley, however, determined that the Nawab Vizier of Oudh should contribute something further towards the defence of India against invasion. The Nawab Vizier maintained a rabble army that was costly and useless, and he depended entirely on British troops for his defence against Afghans and Mahrattas. He was urged to disband his rabble army and replace it by battalions of sepoys trained and commanded by British officers; but he was impracticable, and Lord Wellesley got over the difficulty by taking half his territory for the maintenance of the required battalions. This was an arbitrary proceeding, but it was justified on the score of state necessity and self-preservation. It pushed the British frontier westward to Cawnpore on the Ganges, where it was close to Sindia and his French sepoy battalions, and would be face to face with any foreign invasion from the north-west. The new territories were called "ceded provinces," and eventually were incorporated with what are now known as the North-West Provinces.[1] Provinces taken from Oudh.

Meanwhile the Mahratta empire was falling into the hands of Sindia. This ambitious feudatory tried to pose as the protector of his suzerain the Peishwa. Sindia master of Holkar.

[1] There was also some show of treaty rights in appropriating the territory, but the question is obscure and obsolete. In 1775 the Nawab Vizier had ceded the revenues of the territory for the maintenance of a British force in Oudh, and Lord Wellesley is said to have only closed the mortgage by taking over the country.

CHAP. III. The two, however, were perpetually plotting against each other; the soldier and the Brahman were each trying to be master. About this time Holkar died, and Sindia hastened to Indore and put an imbecile son of Holkar on the throne, as a preliminary step to appropriating the territory and revenues.

Rise of Jaswant Rao Holkar.

At this moment a bandit prince appeared at Indore with an army of predatory horsemen,—brigands and outlaws, the scum of Central India. He was a bastard son of the deceased Holkar, and was known as Jaswant Rao Holkar. He was routed by Sindia's French battalions, but the scattered horsemen soon rallied round his banners, and he went off to the south to threaten Poona and the Peishwa.

Flight of the Peishwa.

The Peishwa was wild with terror. Under his orders a brother of Jaswant Rao Holkar had been dragged to death by an elephant through the streets, and he had reason to believe that Jaswant Rao was bent on revenge. His army was reinforced by Sindia, but the united forces were utterly routed by Jaswant Rao outside the city of Poona. Accordingly he fled away to the coast, and embarked on board a British ship for the port of Bassein, about twenty miles to the north of Bombay.

Peishwa accepts subsidiary alliance, 1802.

The Peishwa was ready to make any sacrifice to procure British help. Accordingly he accepted the subsidiary alliance on the condition that the British restored him to Poona. The terms were soon arranged, and the treaty was signed at Bassein on the last day of December, 1802. The Peishwa ceded territories for the maintenance of a Poona Subsidiary Force, and sacrificed his position as suzerain of the Mahratta confederacy. For the future he was bound to abstain from all wars and negotiations, even with his own feudatories, excepting by the knowledge and consent of the British government. CHAP. III.

Surprise of the Mahratta feudatories.

§ 4. The Mahratta feudatories were bewildered and stupefied by the treaty of Bassein. In a single day the British government had become their suzerain in the room of the Peishwa; the Christian governor of Calcutta was lord over the Brahman Peishwa of Poona. True, the Peishwa was restored to his throne at Poona, but only as the creature of the British government, not as the suzerain of the Mahrattas. Sindia's hope of ruling the Mahrattas in the name of the Peishwa was shattered by the treaty. The Raja of Berar was equally down-hearted. The Gaekwar of Baroda accepted the subsidiary alliance, and ceased to play a part in history. Jaswant Rao Holkar was out of the running; he was an outlaw and an interloper.

Vacillations of Sindia and the Bhonsla.

The whole brunt of the struggle against the British supremacy, if there was to be any struggle at all, thus fell on Daulat Rao Sindia of Gwalior and the Bhonsla Raja of Berar. Meanwhile the two Mahratta princes moved restlessly about with large armies, drawing nearer and nearer to the Nizam's frontier as if to enforce their claims to chout. They would not accept a subsidiary treaty, and they would not break with the British government. They tried to tempt Jaswant Rao to join them, but the young brigand only played with them. He got them to recognise his succession to the throne of Indore, and then returned to his capital, declaring that he must leave Sindia and the Bhonsla to fight the British in the Deccan, whilst he went away north to fight them in Hindustan.

Wellesley's campaign in the Deccan, 1803.

Lord Wellesley was well prepared for an outbreak. His younger brother, Colonel Arthur Wellesley, was watching Sindia and the Bhonsla in the Deccan, whilst General Lake, commander-in-chief of the Bengal army, was watching the French sepoy battalions of Sindia in Hindustan. Sindia was vacillating and irresolute, but his language was growing more hostile. He said he was waiting for Jaswant Rao Holkar; he talked of collecting chout in the Nizam's territory; and he expressed doubts whether there would be peace or war. At last he was told that he was breaking the public peace, and must take the consequences.

British victory at Assaye.

The battle of Assaye was fought on the Nizam's frontier on 23rd September, 1803. It was the old story of a British army of five thousand men fighting an Asiatic army of fifty thousand. The Mahratta artillery worked terrible execution on the British army, and one-third of its European force was left dead or wounded in the field. But the Bhonsla Raja fled at the first shot, and Sindia soon followed his example. General Wellesley's victory at Assaye crushed the hopes of the Mahrattas. Sindia especially took his lesson to heart. It was followed by the capture of fortresses and another victory at Argaum; and by the end of 1803 the campaign in the Deccan was over, and Sindia and the Bhonsla came to terms.

General Lake's campaign in Hindustan.

Meanwhile, General Lake had fought a brilliant campaign in Hindustan. Directly he heard that war had begun in the Deccan he left Cawnpore, on the British frontier, and pushed his way to Delhi. He defeated the French sepoy cavalry and captured the fortress at Alighur. Next he defeated the French sepoy infantry and entered Delhi in triumph. He was received with open arms by the poor old Padishah,

Shah Alam, who once again threw himself upon British protection. He left Delhi in charge of Colonel Ochterlony, marched down the right bank of the river Jumna, captured the city of Agra, and brought the campaign to a close by a crowning victory at Laswari, which broke up the French sepoy battalions for ever, and placed the British government in possession of the relics of the Mogul empire in Hindustan. CHAP. III.

British power paramount.

The campaigns of Wellesley and Lake established the British government as the paramount power in India. Sindia was driven by Wellesley to the northward of the Nerbudda river, and by Lake to the southward of the Jumna. The Bhonsla Raja was deprived of Berar on one side and Cuttack on the other, and was henceforth known only as the Raja of Nagpore. The British government had acquired the sovereignty of the Great Mogul and that of the Peishwa of the Mahrattas. It took the princes of Rajputana under its protection, and prepared to shut out Sindia and Holkar from Rajput territories. Only one Mahratta prince of any importance remained to tender his submission, and that was Jaswant Rao Holkar of Indore.

Relations with Holkar.

§ 5. The British government was not responsible for the usurpation of Jaswant Rao Holkar. It was willing to accept him as the *de facto* ruler of the Indore principality, and to leave him alone, provided only that he kept within his own territories, and respected the territories of the British and their allies.

Holkar's pretensions.

Jaswant Rao Holkar, however, was a born freebooter, a Mahratta of the old school of Sivaji. He was not ambitious for political power like Sindia, and

CHAP. III. he wanted no drilled battalions. He was a Cossack at heart, and loved the old free life of Mahratta brigandage. Like Sivaji, he was at home in the saddle, with spear in hand, and a bag of grain and goblet of water hanging from his horse. He and his hordes scoured the country on horseback, collected plunder or chout, and rode over the hills and far away whenever regular troops advanced against them. Indore was his home and Western India was his quarry; and never perhaps did he collect a richer harvest of plunder and chout than he did in Rajputana during the latter half of 1803, when Lake was driving Sindia and the French out of Hindustan, and Wellesley was establishing peace in the Deccan.

Difficulties as regards "chout." Jaswant Rao Holkar looked at the British government from his own individual point of view. He was no respecter of persons; he despised the Peishwa, and had got all he wanted from Sindia and the Bhonsla. The British government was his *bête noire;* it had grown in strength, and was opposed to the collection of chout. He wanted it to guarantee him in the possession of Holkar's principality, and to sanction his levying chout after the manner of his ancestors; and he refused to withdraw from Rajputana until these terms were granted. If his pretensions were rejected, he threatened to burn, sack, and slaughter his enemies by hundreds of thousands. Such was the ignorant and refractory Mahratta that defied the East India Company and the British nation.

Lake attacks Holkar. The reduction of Jaswant Rao Holkar was thus a political necessity. In April, 1804, General Lake entered Rajputana, and drove Jaswant Rao Holkar southward into Indore territory. In June the rains were approaching, and General Lake left Colonel Monson to keep a watch on Holkar, with five battalions of sepoys, a train of artillery, and two bodies of irregular horse, and then withdrew to cantonments. Colonel Monson pushed on still further south into Indore territory, but in July everything went wrong. Supplies ran low. Expected reinforcements failed to arrive. Jaswant Rao turned back with overwhelming forces and a large train of artillery. In an evil hour Monson beat a retreat. The rains were very heavy. The British guns sunk in the mud and were spiked and abandoned. Terrible disasters were incurred in crossing rivers. The Rajputs turned against him. His brigade was exposed to the fire of Holkar's guns and the charges of Holkar's horse. About the end of August only a shattered remnant of Monson's brigade managed to reach British territory.

CHAP. III. Disastrous retreat of Monson, 1804.

Reaction against British supremacy.

For a brief period British prestige vanished from Hindustan, and Jaswant Rao Holkar was the hero of the hour. Sindia forgot his wrongs against Jaswant Rao, and his defeats at Assaye and Argaum, and declared for Holkar. Fresh bodies of bandits and outlaws joined the standard of Holkar to share in the spoil of his successes. With Mahratta audacity Jaswant Rao pushed on to Delhi, to capture Shah Alam and plunder Hindustan in the name of the Great Mogul. He was beaten off from Delhi by the small garrison under Colonel Ochterlony, but the Jhat Raja of Bhurtpore received him with open arms in that huge clay fortress, the stronghold of the predatory system of the eighteenth century, which to this day is the wonder of Hindustan. Holkar left his guns in the fortress and went out to plunder; and Lake, instead of following him up, wasted four months

CHAP. III. in a futile attempt to capture the Bhurtpore fortress without a siege train.

Reversal of Lord Wellesley's policy, 1805.

§ 6. The retreat of Monson was not only a disastrous blow to British prestige, but ruined for a while the reputation of Lord Wellesley. Because a Mahratta freebooter had broken loose in Hindustan, the Home authorities imagined that all the Mahratta powers had risen against the imperial policy of the Governor-General. Lord Wellesley was recalled from his post, and Lord Cornwallis was sent out to take his place, to reverse the policy of his illustrious predecessor, to scuttle out of Western Hindustan, to restore all the ceded territories, to surrender all the captured fortresses, and to abandon large tracts of country to be plundered and devastated by the Mahrattas, as they had been from the days of Sivaji to those of Wellesley and Lake.

Death of Lord Cornwallis.

Before Lord Cornwallis reached Bengal the political outlook had brightened. Jaswant Rao Holkar was flying into the Punjab from General Lake, and was soon brought to bay. Daulat Rao Sindia was repenting his desertion from the British alliance. The Jhat Raja of Bhurtpore had implored forgiveness and paid a heavy fine. But Lord Cornwallis was sixty-seven years of age, and had lost the nerve which he had displayed in his wars against Tippu; and he would have ignored the turn of the tide, and persisted in falling back on the old policy of conciliation and non-intervention, had not death cut short his career before he had been ten weeks in the country.

Sir George Barlow, a Bengal civilian, succeeded for a while to the post of Governor-General, as a provisional arrangement. He had been a member of Council under both Wellesley and Cornwallis, and he halted between the two. He refused to restore the conquered territories to Sindia and the Bhonsla, but he gave back the Indore principality to Holkar, together with the captured fortresses. Worst of all, he annulled most of the protective treaties with the Rajput princes on the ground that they had deserted the British government during Monson's retreat from Jaswant Rao Holkar.

Sir George Barlow's half measures, 1806.

Non-intervention: sad results.

For some years the policy of the British government was a half-hearted system of non-intervention. Public opinion in the British Isles, as expressed by Parliament and Ministers, was impressed with the necessity for maintaining friendly relations with the Mahrattas, and for abstaining from any measure which might tend to a renewal of hostilities. The fact was ignored that Mahratta independence meant plunder and devastation, and that British supremacy meant order and law. Accordingly the Mahratta princes were left to plunder and collect chout in Rajputana, and practically to make war on each other, so long as they respected the territories of the British government and its allies. The result was that the Peishwa was brooding over his lost suzerainty; Sindia and the Bhonsla were mourning over their lost territories; and Jaswant Rao Holkar was drowning his intellects in cherry brandy, which he procured from Bombay, until he was seized with delirium tremens, and confined as a madman. All this while an under-current of intrigue was at work between Indian courts, which served in the end to revive wild hopes of getting rid of British supremacy, and rekindling the old aspirations for war and rapine.

CHAP. III.

Sepoy revolt at Vellore, 1806.

§ 7. In 1806 the peace of India was broken by an alarm from a very different quarter. In those days India was so remote from the British Isles that the existence of the British government mainly depended on the loyalty of its sepoy armies. Suddenly it was discovered that the Madras army was on the brink of mutiny. The British authorities at Madras had introduced an obnoxious head-dress resembling a European hat, in the place of the old time-honoured turban, and had, moreover, forbidden the sepoys to appear on parade with earrings and caste marks. India was astounded by a revolt of the Madras sepoys at the fortress of Vellore, about eight miles to the westward of Arcot. The fallen families of Hyder and Tippu were lodged in this fortress, and many of Tippu's old soldiers were serving in the garrison; and these people taunted the sepoys about wearing hats and becoming Christians, whilst some secret intriguing was going on for restoring Mohammedan ascendency in Southern India, under the deposed dynasty of Mysore.

Slaughter of British officers.

The garrison at Vellore consisted of about four hundred Europeans and fifteen hundred sepoys. At midnight, without warning, the sepoys rose in mutiny. One body fired on the European barracks until half the soldiers were killed or wounded. Another body fired on the houses of the British officers, and shot them down as they rushed out to know the cause of the uproar. All this while provisions were distributed amongst the sepoys by the Mysore princes, and the flag of Mysore was hoisted over the fortress.

Fortunately the news was carried to Arcot, where Colonel Gillespie commanded a British garrison. Gillespie at once galloped to Vellore with a troop

Suppression of mutiny: recall of Bentinck.

of British dragoons and two field guns. The gates of Vellore were blown open; the soldiers rushed in; four hundred mutineers were cut down, and the outbreak was over. The Home authorities wanted a scapegoat; and Lord William Bentinck, the governor of Madras, and Sir John Craddock, the commander-in-chief of the Madras army, were recalled. Fifty years afterwards, when the Bengal army broke out in mutiny on the score of greased cartridges, many an old officer wished that a Gillespie, with the independent authority of a Gillespie, had been in command at Barrackpore.

Lord Minto, 1807—13: lawless condition of Bundelkund.

§ 8. In 1807 Lord Minto succeeded Barlow as Governor-General. He broke the spell of non-intervention. South of the river Jumna, between the frontiers of Bengal and those of Sindia and Holkar, are the hills and jungles of Bundelkund. For centuries the chiefs of Bundelkund had never been more than half conquered. They never paid tribute to Mogul or Mahratta unless compelled by force of arms; and they kept the country in constant anarchy by their lawless acts and endless feuds.

British conquest.

When the Peishwa accepted the British alliance, he ceded Bundelkund for the maintenance of the Poona Subsidiary Force. Of course the cession was a sham. The Peishwa ceded territory which only nominally belonged to him, and the British were too happy in concluding a subsidiary alliance to inquire too nicely into his sovereign rights over Bundelkund. The result was that the chiefs of Bundelkund defied the British as they defied the Peishwa, and Sir George Barlow sacrificed revenue and ignored

CHAP. III. brigandage rather than interfere with his western neighbours. Lord Minto found that there were a hundred and fifty leaders of banditti in Bundelkund, who held as many fortresses, settled all disputes by the sword, and offered an asylum to all the bandits and burglars that escaped from British territory. Lord Minto organised an expedition which established for a while something like peace and order in Bundelkund, and secured the collection of tribute with a regularity which had been unknown for centuries.

Dangers in the Punjab.

Lord Minto's main work was to keep Napoleon and the French out of India. The north-west frontier was still vulnerable, but the Afghans had retired from the Punjab, and the once famous Runjeet Singh had founded a Sikh kingdom between the Indus and the Sutlej. As far as the British were concerned, the Sikhs formed a barrier against the Afghans; and Runjeet Singh was apparently friendly, for he had refused to shelter Jaswant Rao Holkar in his flight from Lord Lake. But there was no knowing what Runjeet Singh might do if the French found their way to Lahore. To crown the perplexity, the Sikh princes on the British side of the river Sutlej, who had done homage to the British government during the campaigns of Lord Lake, were being conquered by Runjeet Singh, and were appealing to the British government for protection.

Mission to Runjeet Singh, 1808—9.

In 1808–9 a young Bengal civilian, named Charles Metcalfe, was sent on a mission to Lahore. The work before him was difficult and complicated, and somewhat trying to the nerves. The object was to secure Runjeet Singh as a useful ally against the French and Afghans, whilst protecting the Sikh states on the

British side of the Sutlej, namely, Jhind, Nabha, and Patiala.

Runjeet Singh was naturally disgusted at being checked by British interference. It was unfair, he said, for the British to wait until he had conquered the three states, and then to demand possession. Metcalfe cleverly dropped the question of justice, and appealed to Runjeet Singh's self-interest. By giving up the three states, Runjeet Singh would secure an alliance with the British, a strong frontier on the Sutlej, and freedom to push his conquests on the north and west. Runjeet Singh took the hint. He withdrew his pretensions from the British side of the Sutlej, and professed a friendship which remained unbroken until his death in 1839; but he knew what he was about. He conquered Cashmere on the north, and he wrested Peshawar from the Afghans; but he refused to open his dominions to British trade, and he was jealous to the last of any attempt to enter his territories.

Missions to Persia and Afghanistan.

About the same time Lord Minto sent John Malcolm on a second mission to Persia, and Mountstuart Elphinstone on a mission to Cabul to provide against French invasion. Neither mission was followed by any practical result, but they opened up new countries to European ideas, and led to the publication of works on Persia and Afghanistan by the respective envoys, which have retained their interest to this day.

Capture of Mauritius and Java.

Meanwhile the war against France and Napoleon had extended to eastern waters. The island of the Mauritius had become a French depôt for frigates and privateers, which swept the seas from Madagascar to Java, until the East India Company reckoned its losses by millions, and private traders were brought to the brink of ruin. Lord Minto sent one expedition, which

CHAP. III. wrested the Mauritius from the French; and he conducted another expedition in person, which wrested the island of Java from the Dutch, who at that time were the allies of France. The Mauritius has remained a British possession until this day, but Java was restored to Holland at the conclusion of the war.

Anarchy in Rajputana.

§ 9. During the struggle against France difficulties were arising in Western Hindustan. The princes of Rajputana had been engaged in wars and feuds amongst themselves from a remote antiquity, but for nearly a century they had been also exposed to the raids and depredations of Mahratta armies. Lord Wellesley had brought the Rajput princes into subsidiary alliance with the British government, but the treaties had been annulled by Sir George Barlow, and war and pillage were as rampant as ever. The evil had been aggravated by the rise of Afghan adventurers, who had conquered territories and founded new kingdoms in central India amidst the prevailing anarchy; whilst a low class of freebooters, known as Pindharies, plundered the villagers in the skirts of the Mahratta armies, or robbed and pillaged the surrounding territories, with a savage ferocity which rendered them a pest and terror.

The Rana, or suzerain.

The hereditary suzerain of the Rajputs was a prince known as the Rana of Oodeypore. The Rana claimed descent from Rama, the hero of ancient Oudh, and incarnation of Vishnu or the Sun, whose mythical and divine glory is celebrated in the Ramayana. Unfortunately the living Rana was a weak and helpless prince, who was the dependent of his own feudatories, whilst his territories were at the mercy of Mahrattas and Afghans. He had a daughter who was regarded as a prize and treasure, not on account of her beauty or accomplishments, for she was only an immature girl, but because her high birth would ennoble her bridegroom and her future sons or daughters.

War for the Rana's daughter.

From 1806 to 1810 the Rajas of Jeypore and Jodhpore were fighting for the hand of this daughter of the Rana. The girl herself had no voice in the matter. In Rajput traditions a princess is supposed to choose her own bridegroom in an assembly of Rajas, by throwing a garland round the neck of the happy lover. But in modern practice the "choice" has fallen into disuse, and a gilded cocoa-nut is sent by the father of the princess to some selected Raja as typical of an offer of her hand. The cocoa-nut for the Oodeypore princess had been sent to a Raja of Jodhpore, but he died before the marriage, and the cocoa-nut was sent to the Raja of Jeypore. Then followed a contention. The new Raja of Jodhpore claimed the princess, on the ground that the offer had been made, not to the individual, but to the throne of Jodhpore. The Raja of Jeypore, however, had accepted the cocoa-nut, and insisted on his rights. The contention became a war to the knife, and nearly every prince in Rajputana took a part in the contest. Strange to say, the Rana himself, the father of the princess, looked on as a neutral whilst Jeypore and Jodhpore were fighting for his daughter. Meanwhile his territories, known as the garden of Rajputana, were ravaged by Sindia and an Afghan adventurer named Amir Khan, until nothing was to be seen but ruined harvests and desolated villages.

Amidst this terrible turmoil, the princes and chiefs of Rajputana implored the British government to

CHAP. III. interfere. They asserted that there always had been Non-intervention. a paramount power in India; that such a power had been formerly exercised by the Great Mogul; that the East India Company had acquired that power; and that the British government was bound to stop the war. The Rana of Oodeypore offered to cede half his territories if the British government would protect the other half. Jeypore and Jodhpore offered to submit their claims to British arbitration, and pledged themselves to abide by the decision. Lord Minto had only to declare which bridegroom he recognised, and his dictum would have been accepted. But Lord Minto shrunk from the exercise of a sovereignty which would have been a violation of the sacred dogma of non-interference, and have carried British influence outside British territories. Accordingly, the war was stopped by a tragedy. The Rana settled the marriage dispute by poisoning his daughter. The young princess is said to have drunk the fatal draught with the courage of a heroine, knowing that it would save her father; but the unhappy mother was overpowered by grief, and died broken-hearted.

Ghorka conquest of Nipal. Meanwhile war clouds were gathering on the southern slopes of the Himalayas. Down to the middle of the eighteenth century, the territory of Nipal had been peopled by a peaceful and industrious race of Buddhists known as Newars, but about the year 1767, when the British had taken over the Bengal provinces, the Newars were conquered by a Rajput tribe from Cashmere, known as Ghorkas. The Ghorka conquest of Nipal was as complete as the Norman conquest of England. The Ghorkas established a military despotism with Brahmanical institutions, and parcelled out the country amongst feudal nobles known as Bharadars. CHAP. III.

Ghorka rule.

Ghorka rule in Nipal was for many years distracted by tragedies in the royal family, and civil wars between the Bharadars for the post of minister. The Newars were more down-trodden than the Anglo-Saxons under the Norman kings. The Ghorka army was all-powerful, but plots and assassinations were common enough in the court and capital at Khatmandu, and the deposition of a minister or a sovereign might be the work of a day.

Ghorka aggressions.

During the early years of the nineteenth century the Ghorkas began to encroach on British territory, annexing villages and revenues from Darjeeling to Simla without right or reason. They were obviously bent on extending their dominion southward to the Ganges, and for a long time aggressions were overlooked for the sake of peace. At last two districts were appropriated to which the Ghorkas had not a shadow of a claim, and it was absolutely necessary to make a stand against their pretensions. Accordingly, Lord Minto sent an ultimatum to Khatmandu, declaring that unless the districts were restored they would be recovered by force of arms. Before the answer arrived, Lord Minto was succeeded in the post of Governor-General by Lord Moira, better known by his later title of Marquis of Hastings.

Lord Moira—Marquis of Hastings, 1813—23.

§ 10. Lord Moira landed at Calcutta in 1813. Shortly after his arrival an answer was received from the Ghorka government, that the disputed districts belonged to Nipal, and would not be surrendered. Lord Moira at once fixed a day on which the districts were to be restored; and when the day had passed

CHAP. III. without any action being taken by the Ghorkas, a British detachment entered the districts and set up police stations.

Ghorka council of war. Meanwhile the Ghorkas had been alarmed by the letter of Lord Moira. A great council of Bharadars was summoned to Khatmandu, and the question of peace or war was discussed in a military spirit. It was decided that, as the British had been unable to capture the mud fortress of Bhurtpore, which was the work of men's hands, they could not possibly capture the mountain fortresses on the Himalayas, which were the work of the Almighty. Accordingly, the council of Bharadars resolved on war, but they did not declare it in European fashion. A Ghorka army suddenly entered the disputed districts, surrounded the police stations, and murdered many of the constables, and then returned to Khatmandu to await the action of the British government in the way of reprisals.

Ghorkas superior to Mahrattas. The war against the Ghorkas was more remote and more serious than the wars against the Mahrattas. The Mahrattas fought in the plains, and trusted in their artillery; but when their gunners were shot or bayoneted, as in the battle of Assaye, they seemed to have lost all life and energy, and were broken up into loose bodies of runaways. The Ghorkas, on the other hand were resolute and hardy mountaineers, with a Rajput pride, and military instincts like the ancient Spartans. Their nerves had not been enfeebled by opium, and they exulted in the strength of their mountain fortresses, which they deemed impregnable against all the world.

Difficult invasion of Nipal. Those who have ascended the Himalayas to Darjeeling or Simla may realise something of the difficulties of an invasion of Nipal. The British army advanced in four divisions by four different routes. They had first to make their way through a belt of marsh and jungle at the foot of the mountains. They had then to climb precipices and shelves which would have daunted the army of Hannibal. Moreover, it was impossible to storm the fortresses without artillery; and dragging up eighteen-pounders in the teeth of snow-storms and mountain blasts, opening up roads by blasting rocks, and battering down obstructions with field guns, were tasks which would have tested the genius of the ablest commanders. CHAP. III.

Successes of Ochterlony, 1814—15.

The operations of 1814 nearly proved a failure. One general took fright at the jungle, and galloped back to the plains, leaving his division behind. General David Ochterlony, who advanced his division along the valley of the Sutlej, gained the most brilliant successes. He was one of the half-forgotten heroes of the East India Company. He had fought against Hyder Ali in the days of Warren Hastings, and beaten back Holkar from the walls of Delhi in the days of Lord Wellesley. For five months in the worst season of the year he carried one fortress after another, until the enemy made a final stand at Maloun on a shelf of the Himalayas. The Ghorkas made a desperate attack on the British works, but the attempt failed; and when the British batteries were about to open fire, the Ghorka garrison came to terms, and were permitted to march out with the honours of war.

Peace with Nipal, 1816.

The fall of Maloun shook the faith of the Ghorka government in their heaven-built fortresses. Commissioners were sent to conclude a peace. Nipal agreed to cede Kumaon in the west, and the southern belt of forest and jungle known as the Terai. It also agreed to receive a British Resident at Khatmandu.

CHAP. III. Lord Moira had actually signed the treaty, when the Ghorkas raised the question of whether the Terai included the forest or only the swamp. War was renewed. Ochterlony advanced an army within fifty miles of Khatmandu, and then the Ghorkas concluded the treaty, and the British army withdrew from Nipal. The Terai, however, was a bone of contention for many years afterwards. Nothing was said about a subsidiary army, and to this day Nipal is outside the pale of subsidiary alliances; but Nipal is bound over not to take any European into her service without the consent of the British government.

Imperial policy of Lord Hastings.

§ 11. Lord Moira, now Marquis of Hastings, next turned his attention to the affairs of Malwa, the homes of Sindia and Holkar, between Bundelkund and Rajputana. Before leaving the British Isles, he had a strong sense of the danger of Lord Wellesley's policy, and a strong faith in the wisdom of non-intervention. But a brief experience of the actual condition of India compelled him to recant. The hordes of Pindharies were swelling into armies. They ravaged the territories of British allies, and threatened those under British rule. Lord Hastings declared that British power would never prosper in India until it assumed the headship of a league like that projected by Lord Wellesley. But the Home authorities were still afraid of the Mahrattas, and Lord Hastings was told that no league was to be formed in India, and no steps taken against the Pindharies, that were likely to be in any way offensive to the Mahrattas.

Pindhari raids.

In 1815-16, the last year of the Ghorka war, the Pindharies extended their raids to British territory. The horrors committed by these miscreants are indescribable. Villages were environed by Pindharies, and the inhabitants robbed and tortured. Fathers piled firewood round their dwellings, and perished in the flames with their wives and families, rather than fall into the hands of Pindharies; whilst in some villages, the whole female population threw themselves into wells to escape a worse fate. George Canning described Pindhari atrocities in a speech which aroused parliament to a sense of its duties and responsibilities; and it was resolved to make war on Sindia, Holkar, or any other power in India, which should attempt to shield the Pindharies from the just resentment of the British nation.

Disaffection of Mahrattas

Meanwhile the Mahratta princes had become unruly and disorganised. Lord Wellesley had bound them to the British government by subsidiary alliances; but these ties had been loosened by his successors, excepting in the case of the Peishwa. Accordingly the Mahratta princes were smitten by a common desire to throw off British supremacy, and return to their old life of war and plunder. The Peishwa was labouring to recover his lost suzerainty, with the help of Sindia, Holkar, Nagpore, and the leaders of the Pindharies. Sindia was more amenable to British authority, and would have been guided by the advice of the British Resident at his court, but, under the policy of non-intervention, the Resident had been told to confine his attention to British interests, and not to interfere with Sindia. The result was that Sindia was secretly negotiating with the Peishwa, the Ghorkas, and even with Runjeet Singh of the Punjab, for joint attacks on the British government. Holkar had died of cherry brandy; the army of Indore was in mutiny for arrears of pay, and its leaders were in

CHAP. III. secret communication with the Peishwa; whilst an infant Holkar and his regent mother had shut themselves up in a remote fortress as a refuge against the disaffected soldiery. Amir Khan the Afghan, the most powerful prince of the period, had established a principality at Tonk, in Rajputana, and commanded a large army of drilled battalions, and a formidable train of artillery.

Contumacy of the Peishwa.

Lord Hastings wanted to crush the Pindharies, but to avoid all collision with the Mahrattas. The Peishwa, however, seemed bent on provoking British interference. A Brahman envoy, from the Gaekwar of Baroda, had been sent to Poona, under a British guarantee, to settle some obsolete dispute about chout, and, in spite of the guarantee, the Brahman had been barbarously murdered, under the orders of the Peishwa and his minister. Lord Hastings accepted the explanation of the Peishwa that he was innocent of the murder, but ordered the Mahratta minister to be imprisoned in the fortress of Thanna, near Bombay. Later on the minister escaped from the fortress with the connivance of the Peishwa, and was secretly protected by the Peishwa, and it seemed impossible to condone the offence.

Elphinstone and Malcolm.

At this crisis Mr. Mountstuart Elphinstone, one of the ablest of the old Bengal civilians, was Resident at Poona; whilst Sir John Malcolm, of the Madras army, was negotiating with the Mahratta princes for their co-operation in the war against the Pindharies. Elphinstone found that the Peishwa was secretly intriguing with his exiled minister, and levying troops to an extent that meant mischief. Accordingly he threatened the Peishwa with the displeasure of the British government, and required him to deliver up three important fortresses as a pledge for his future good behaviour. The Peishwa the artfully invited Sir John Malcolm to come and see him, and so talked him over that Malcolm believed in his good faith, and advised that the fortresses should be given back. Elphinstone had no such confidence in the Peishwa; nevertheless he restored the fortresses, as he would not throw cold water on Malcolm's good intentions.

Pindhari war: Mahratta plots.

By this time Lord Hastings had planned his campaign against the Pindharies. The British force was overwhelming, for it was known that the three predatory powers—Sindia, Holkar, and Amir Khan—were bent on sheltering the Pindharies by enlisting them as soldiers or hiding them in the jungles until the danger had passed away. They had no conception of the scale on which Lord Hastings had planned his campaign. They knew that a force was advancing from the south, and that it would probably comprise an army from Madras, the Hyderabad Subsidiary Force, and the Poona Subsidiary Force; but they fondly imagined that, if the Pindharies were kept out of the way, the British forces would soon return to cantonments, and that the Pindharies would then revenge the attack on their homes by fresh raids on British territories.

Mortification of Sindia.

Lord Hastings, however, was bent on disarming Sindia, Holkar, and Amir Khan before exterminating the Pindhari gangs, and thus guarding against the possible revival of the gangs after the conclusion of the war. Daulat Rao Sindia was suddenly asked to give a friendly reception to the Madras army coming from the south. He hesitated, vacillated, and asked for time to consider the proposition. He was told

CHAP. III. that consideration was out of the question; that he was pledged to co-operate with the British forces against the Pindharies; that a large Bengal army was advancing from the north over the river Jumna, under the direct orders of Lord Hastings in person; and that the Pindharies would be environed and exterminated by the two armies. Sindia was utterly taken by surprise. He knew that it would be sheer madness to fight against the Governor-General. He hastened to receive the Madras army, and was lavish in his professions of loyalty. He was then charged with having violated treaties by carrying on secret negotiations with Nipal and Runjeet Singh. He solemnly protested his innocence, but two of his messengers to Nipal had been arrested on the way, and his own letters addressed to the Ghorka government were placed in his hands in open durbar by the British Resident, who simply stated what they were. The letters in question were damnatory. Sindia had proposed that Ghorkas and Mahrattas should join in a common attack on the British government.

Sindia submits.

Sindia bent to his destiny. He saw that he was checkmated at every turn. He was dumbfoundered, and made no attempt to defend himself. Nothing further was done. Lord Hastings left him in possession of his territories, but took the Rajput princes under British protection, and bound over Sindia to co-operate against the Pindharies, and to prevent the formation of any gangs for the future.

Amir Khan submits.

Amir Khan was growing old, and was glad to make any terms which would leave him in possession of his principality. He disbanded his battalions and sold his cannon to the British government, on condition of being recognised as hereditary ruler of Tonk. No cause for uneasiness remained, excepting the disaffected Peishwa of Poona, the mutinous army of Holkar, and some suspicious movements on the part of the Bhonsla Raja of Nagpore.

Destruction of the Pindharies.

When the rains were over the British armies began to move. There were 120,000 troops under arms, the largest force that had ever taken the field in India under British colours; twice as many as Lord Wellesley assembled in 1803-4, and four times as many as Lord Cornwallis led against Tippu in 1791-92. The Pindharies found themselves abandoned by Sindia and Amir Khan, and environed by the armies from Bengal and Madras. Many were shot down, or put to the sword, or perished in the jungle, or were slain by villagers in revenge for former cruelties. Others threw themselves on British protection, and were settled on lands, and became peaceful and industrious cultivators. Within a few years no traces of the Pindhari gangs were to be found in India.

Hostility of the Peishwa

All this while the Peishwa was at Poona, bent on mischief. He resumed his levy of troops and his secret intrigues with other princes. The Poona Subsidiary Force was called away to the northward to co-operate against the Pindharies, but Mr. Elphinstone obtained a European regiment from Bombay, and posted it at Khirki, about four miles from the British Residency.

Treachery, defeat, flight.

The Peishwa was baffled by the European regiment. He affected to regard it as a menace, and threatened to leave Poona unless it was sent back to Bombay, but he was quieted by its removal to Khirki. He was relying on the support of Sindia and Amir Khan, and was assured that the Bhonsla Raja of Nagpore

CHAP. III. and the army of Holkar were preparing to join him. On the 5th November, 1817, Mr. Elphinstone left the British Residency at Poona, and followed the European regiment to Khirki. That same afternoon the Peishwa attacked the British force at Khirki with an army of 26,000 men, but was beaten back with heavy losses. At night the British Residency was plundered and set on fire, and the magnificent library of Mr. Elphinstone was utterly destroyed. Twelve days afterwards the Subsidiary Force returned to Poona, and the Peishwa was seized with a panic and fled away from his dominions, never to return.

Plottings at Nagpore. The next explosion was at Nagpore. The Bhonsla Raja, who fled from Assaye, was dead, and a nephew named Appa Sahib had succeeded to the throne. Appa Sahib tried to ingratiate himself with the British, but was playing the same double game as Sindia and the Peishwa. Mr. Jenkins was Resident at Nagpore, and when news arrived of the attack on Khirki, Appa Sahib expatiated to him on the treachery of the Peishwa and his own loyalty. All this while, however, he was in secret correspondence with the Peishwa, and levying troops for the coming war against the British.

British preparations. The British Residency was separated from the city of Nagpore by the Sitabuldi hill. On the 25th of November, 1817, eight days after the flight of the Peishwa, all communication with the Residency was stopped by Appa Sahib, and the Raja and his ministers were sending their families and valuables out of the city of Nagpore. Mr. Jenkins foresaw an outbreak, and ordered the Nagpore Subsidiary Force to occupy Sitabuldi hill. There was no European regiment as at Khirki, and only 1,400 sepoys fit for duty, including three troops of Bengal cavalry, and there were only four six-pounders.

Victory on Sitabuldi hill.

At evening, 26th December, 1817, Appa Sahib advanced against the hill Sitabuldi with an army of 18,000 men, including 4,000 Arabs and thirty-six guns. The battle lasted from six o'clock in the evening until noon the next day. The British force was literally overwhelmed by the enemy. The Arabs were closing round the Residency, when Captain Fitzgerald charged them with the three troops of Bengal cavalry. The sudden attack surprised and bewildered the Arabs. The British sepoys on the hill saw the confusion, and rushed down the slope and drove the Arabs before them like sheep. The memory of this victory has been preserved down to our own time. The hill Sitabuldi is a monument to the loyalty and valour of the Bengal cavalry. Every visitor to Nagpore makes a pilgrimage to Sitabuldi to behold the scene of one of the most glorious triumphs of the old sepoy army in India. Appa Sahib fled from Nagpore, but Lord Hastings refused to annex the principality; and an infant grandson of the predecessor of Appa Sahib was placed upon the throne, under the guardianship of Mr. Jenkins.

Defeat of Holkar's army at Mehidpore.

On the 21st December, five days before the battle of Sitabuldi, the army of Holkar had been defeated by Sir John Malcolm at Mehidpore. Holkar's soldiers had received their arrears of pay from the Peishwa, and declared for the Peishwa. Malcolm approached them with the Madras army, and they murdered the regent mother on suspicion of negotiating with the British, and began the battle of Mehidpore by plundering the British baggage. Holkar's army was defeated; the principality of Indore was placed

CHAP. III at the disposal of Lord Hastings. The infant Raja was left on the throne, and Holkar's state was brought into subsidiary alliance with the British government, and required to cede territory for the maintenance of a subsidiary army.

Peishwa at Satara.

Nothing remained to complete the pacification of India but the capture of the Peishwa. He had fled southward to Satara, to strengthen his cause by releasing the captive Raja and setting up the old standard of Sivaji. But British prestige had been effectually restored by Lord Hastings, and the restless movements of the Peishwa were little more than feverish efforts to escape from his British pursuers.

Glorious action at Korygaum.

One glorious battle was fought on New Year's Day, 1818, a victory of Bombay sepoys which is celebrated in Deccan songs of triumph to this day. A detachment of 800 Bombay sepoys was drawn up at the village of Korygaum, on the bank of the river Bhima, near Satara, under the command of Captain Staunton. On the opposite bank was the army of the Peishwa, numbering 25,000 horse and 6,000 Arab infantry, Staunton had but ten British officers and twenty-four British gunners with two six-pounders. Staunton occupied the village, but was environed by the Peishwa's army, and cut off from all supplies and water. The Mahrattas were mad to capture the village. Three times they tried to storm it with rockets, but were beaten back by sheer pluck and desperation. Raging with hunger and thirst, Bombay sepoys and British officers and gunners fought like heroes, whilst the Peishwa looked on in anger and despair from a neighbouring hill. Staunton lost a third of his sepoys and eight out of his ten officers, but the Mahrattas left six hundred killed and wounded on the field. Next morning the Mahrattas refused to renew the fight, and the army of the Peishwa moved away. CHAP. III.

Such a humiliation must have taken away all hope from the Peishwa. For six months longer he kept out of the reach of his pursuers, but was at last environed by British troops under Sir John Malcolm. He threw himself on the mercy of the British government, and eventually talked over Sir John Malcolm, as he had done a year or two previously in the matter of the three fortresses. From feelings of pity for an Asiatic prince who had ruined himself by his own treachery, Malcolm gave his personal guarantee that the British government would pay a pension to the conquered Peishwa of 80,000*l.* a year. Lord Hastings was extremely angry at such a charge upon the yearly revenue, but would not withhold his sanction to Malcolm's guarantee.[1] Since then there has been no Peishwa of the Mahrattas. The ex-ruler lived in idle luxury near Cawnpore, whilst his dominions were incorporated with the Bombay Presidency. A futile attempt was made by Lord Hastings to revive the extinct Raja of Satara, but in the course of years the Raja was intriguing like the Peishwa, and the principality was eventually annexed by Lord Dalhousie.

Extinction of the Peishwa, 1818.

[1] The ex-Peishwa was born in 1775, when Warren Hastings and Philip Francis were beginning to quarrel at Calcutta. He ascended the throne of Poona in 1795. He concluded the treaty of Bassein with Lord Wellesley in 1802. He was dethroned in 1818. He lived at Bithoor, near Cawnpore, until he died, an old man of seventy-seven, in 1853. After his death the notorious Nana Sahib claimed to be an adopted son, and demanded a continuation of the pension of 80,000*l.* The story will be found in Chapter VI., of the present volume, in connection with the massacre at Cawnpore during the sepoy mutinies of 1857.

CHAP. III.

Pacification and protection of Rajputana, 1818.

The crowning event in the administration of Lord Hastings was the renewal of protective treaties with the princes of Rajputana. The raids of the Mahrattas, which had been the curse and agony of Rajputana for nearly a century, were stopped for ever. The territory of Ajmere, in the heart of Rajputana, which had been successively the head-quarters of Mogul and Mahratta suzerainty, was taken over by the British government, and is to this day the head-quarters of the Agent to the Viceroy for the states of Rajputana, and a centre of British supremacy and paramount power.

Lord Amherst, 1823–28: demands of Burma.

§ 12. Lord Amherst succeeded Lord Hastings as Governor-General in 1823. The wars of 1817-18 had established the peace of India, by breaking up the predatory system which had been a terror to Hindus and Mohammedans for more than a century. But the king of Burma, to the eastward of Bengal, was causing some anxiety by demanding the surrender of political fugitives from his dominions who had taken refuge in British territory. The British government refused compliance. Had the refugees been given up, they would have been crucified, or otherwise tortured to death by the Burmese officials. Common humanity forbade the concession, so the refugees were required to keep the peace within British territory, and to abstain from all plots or hostile movements against the Burmese government.

Burmese aggressions.

For years the Burmese officials tried to bully the British government into surrendering these refugees. They knew nothing of the outer world, and treated the British with contempt as a nation of traders, who had paid the Indian sepoys to fight their battles. Conciliation only provoked them to insolence and aggression. They seized an island belonging to the British. They overran the intervening countries of Munipore and Assam, and demanded the cession of Chittagong. Finally, they invaded British territory and cut off a detachment of sepoys, and threatened, with all the bombast of barbarians, to conquer Bengal, and bring away the Governor-General in golden fetters.

Expedition to Rangoon, 1824

At last Lord Amherst sent an expedition under Sir Archibald Campbell to the port of Rangoon, the capital of the Burmese province of Pegu. The Burmese officials were taken by surprise. They sent a mob of raw levies to prevent the British from landing, but the impromptu army fled at the first discharge of British guns. The British landed, and found that all the men, women, and children of Rangoon had fled to the jungle, with all their provisions and grain. The British occupied Rangoon, but the country round about was forest and swamp. The rains began, and the troops were struck down with fever, dysentery, and bad food. No supplies could be obtained except by sea from Madras or Calcutta. Nearly every European in Rangoon who survived the rains of 1824 had reason to remember the Burmese seaport to the end of his days.

British advance to Ava.

Peace.

When the rains were over a Burmese general of great renown approached Rangoon with an army of 60,000 braves, and environed the place with stockades. There was some severe fighting at these stockades, but at last they were taken by storm, and the braves fled in a panic. The British expedition advanced up the river Irrawaddy, through the valley of Pegu. The people of Pegu, who had been conquered by the king of Burma some sixty years before,

CHAP. III. rejoiced at being delivered from their Burmese oppressors, and eagerly brought in supplies. The British expedition was approaching Ava, the capital of the kingdom, when the king of Burma came to terms, and agreed to pay a million sterling towards the expenses of a war which cost more than ten millions. The British were content with annexing two strips of sea-board, known as Arakan and Tenasserim, which never paid the cost of administration; and left the valley of Pegu, and even the port of Rangoon, in possession of the king of Burma. But Assam and Cachar, between Bengal and Burma, were brought under British rule, and eventually made up for the expenditure on the war by the cultivation of tea.

War against Bhurtpore, 1825—26.

Meanwhile, Lord Amherst had some difficulty with the Jhat state of Bhurtpore in Rajputana, which had defied Lord Lake in 1805, but had eventually been brought under British protection. In 1825 the Raja died, and the succession of an infant son was recognised by the British government. An uncle, however, seized the throne, and shut himself up in the mud fortress which had resisted the assaults of Lord Lake. At first Lord Amherst was disinclined to interfere, but all the restless spirits, who had been reduced to obedience by the wars of 1817-18, were beginning to rally round the usurper, who had openly defied the British government. A British force was sent to Bhurtpore, under Lord Combermere. The mud walls were undermined, and blown up with gunpowder. The British soldiers rushed in, the usurper was deposed, and the young Raja was restored to the throne, under the protection of the paramount power.

§ 13. Lord William Bentinck succeeded Lord Amherst in 1828. His administration was emphatically one of progress. He promoted English education amongst Hindus and Mohammedans, and founded a medical college at Calcutta. He laboured hard to establish steam navigation between India and Europe *viâ* the Red Sea, in the place of the old sailing route round the Cape. He encouraged the cultivation of tea in Assam and Cachar. He sought to open a trade with Central Asia up the river Indus, but was foiled by Runjeet Singh, who was still as friendly as ever, but resolutely bent on keeping the British out of his territories.

Lord William Bentinck, 1828—35: peace and progress.

In 1829, the year after the arrival of Lord William Bentinck, he electrified India by the abolition of suttee. In these advanced days it is difficult to understand why British rulers did not suppress this hateful rite the moment they had the power. But for many years toleration and non-intervention were a kind of fanaticism with British administrators; and the Bengalis appeared to exult in the performance of a rite which they knew to be obnoxious to Europeans. As a matter of fact, the number of suttees in Bengal appeared to increase under British rule, and this was most marked in the villages round Calcutta.

Abolition of Suttee 1829

The abolition of suttee by treating it as a capital crime was followed by none of the evils which had been anticipated. There was no rising of the sepoys; no discontent on the part of the masses. British rulers were delivered from the odium of sanctioning a barbarous crime under the plea of religious toleration; whilst the living widow was no longer compelled to immolate herself with her dead husband, nor was her son forced by a sense of duty to apply the torch to

Relief of Hindus.

the funeral pile. The pride of Brahmans and Rajputs may have been wounded when all concerned in the performance of the ancient rite were punished by imprisonment or death, but humanity has triumphed, and suttees have vanished from British India, and from every state owing allegiance to British sovereignty.

Thug atrocities.

§ 14. The suppression of the Thugs was another work of the time. These detestable miscreants appeared to the outer world as honest traders or agriculturists, who occasionally went on pilgrimage or travelled for business or pleasure. In reality they were organised gangs of murderers, having a dialect and signs of their own. They made friends with other travellers going the same way; halted beneath the shade of trees, and suddenly threw their nooses round the necks of their victims, strangled them to death, rifled them of their money and goods, and buried them with a speed which defied detection. Sometimes the unwary traveller was beguiled by a female to a lonely spot, and was never heard of more.

Hereditary Thug gangs.

Every boy born of Thugs was brought up in what may be called the religion of the noose. From his cradle he was taught that he was bound to follow the trade of his forefathers; that, like them, he was the blind instrument of the deity of life and death. At first he acted as a scout; then he was allowed to handle and bury the victim; and finally tried his prentice hand at strangling. Before committing his first murder, one of the elders acted as his Guru or spiritual guide, and initiated him in the use of the noose as a solemn rite associated with the worship of the goddess Durga, Bowani, or Kali, the mythical bride of Siva, the incarnation of the mysteries of life and dissolution, who is often represented with a noose in her hand.[1] Throughout his after career he adored the goddess as a tutelar deity; worshipped her in temples where Thugs officiated as priests; and propitiated her with offerings of flesh meat and strong drinks, which were supposed to be most acceptable to female divinity. CHAP. III.

Suppression.

The Hindus were too fearful and superstitious to suppress the Thugs. The Moguls had no such scruples, and often condemned Thugs to a cruel death; but wealthy Hindus would offer large ransoms to save their lives, or would follow the miscreants to the place of execution and regale them with sweetmeats and tobacco. When, however, the British discovered the secret organisation, they resolved to break up the gangs and put an end to the hereditary association. A department was organised for the suppression of Thugs, and chiefs and princes were called upon to co-operate in the work of extermination. Between 1830 and 1835 two thousand Thugs were arrested, and fifteen hundred were imprisoned for life, or transported beyond the seas, or publicly executed. Many saved their lives by giving evidence against their fellows, but were shut up for the rest of their days to protect them from vengeance, and to prevent their return to a horrible profession which had become an hereditary instinct in Thug families. To this day the children or grandchildren of the old Thug gangs, who were the terror of India within the

[1] Kali, the black goddess, is the tutelar deity of Calcutta. By a strange anomaly, Calcutta is so called after the temple Kali, at the village of Kali ghat, in the suburbs of the British metropolis. The temple enclosure, where kids and goats are sacrificed, is not a pleasant place to look at.

CHAP. III. memory of living men, are manufacturing carpets, or working at some other useful trade, within prison walls.

Civil and judicial reforms.

§ 15. Lord William Bentinck put a finishing touch to the civil and judicial administration which Warren Hastings initiated and Lord Cornwallis reformed. The district was still retained as the unit of Indian administration, with its civil judge, and its collector and magistrate, and necessary establishments of native officials. But the civil judge was invested with the criminal powers of a sessions judge for the trial of prisoners, and henceforth known as the district judge. The four provincial courts of circuit and appeal were swept away, and the supervision of districts was entrusted to commissioners of divisions, each having five or six districts under his control. Henceforth the collector and magistrate was under the control of the commissioner, and was sometimes known as the deputy commissioner.[1]

Lord William Bentinck also introduced an Asiatic

[1] In each district there was a magistrate and collector. The two duties had been separated by Lord Cornwallis, but were generally united in one officer, who was the head of the district and representative of the British government. As magistrate he punished Asiatic offenders with fine and imprisonment, and committed serious cases for trial. He controlled the police, managed the jail, and was generally responsible for the peace and order of the district. As collector he received the revenues of the district, took charge of the treasury, and controlled the district expenditure. If anything went wrong in the district the magistrate and collector was the universal referee and centre of authority.

The civil judge in each district was raised to the rank of a sessions judge. He was the judicial head of the district. He heard appeals from all the subordinate courts, tried all important element into British administration, which was the first real movement in that direction. He appointed natives of India to be "deputy collectors," and created a higher class of native judges to those appointed by Lord Cornwallis. They are known in the present day as "subordinate judges." The further development of these political experiments belong to the later history.

CHAP. III.

Asiatic officials.

§ 16. Hitherto the "North-West Provinces" had been a mere appendage of Bengal. They were known as the Upper Provinces, whilst Bengal, Behar, and Orissa were known as the Lower Provinces. But a territory which extended from Assam to the Punjab was too vast for the supervision of the Governor-General of Bengal in Council. Accordingly the North-West Provinces were separated from Bengal and placed under a Lieutenant-Governor,

North-West Provinces.

civil cases, and held a jail delivery once a month, for the trial of all prisoners committed by the magistrate and collector. Henceforth he was known as the district judge.

Lord William Bentinck abolished the four provincial courts of circuit and appeal which had been established by Lord Cornwallis, declaring that they had become mere resting-places for those civil servants who were unfit for higher duties. In their room he appointed commissioners of divisions, each of whom had five or six districts under his control. Henceforth the commissioner supervised the civil and judicial administration throughout the districts within his division. He was the channel of all communications between the British government at Calcutta and the district officers. Sometimes he heard appeals from the civil and sessions judge, but as a rule such appeals went to the Sudder Courts at Calcutta. In revenue matters he was controlled by the Board of Revenue at Calcutta.

The district officers had European assistants, as well as establishments of Asiatic officials.

CHAP. III. without a Council, but with a separate Sudder Court and Board of Revenue.[1]

Hindu village communities.

The Hindu people in the North-West Provinces are more masculine and independent than those of Bengal. In Bengal the Hindu village communities had nearly faded away under the domination of zemindars. In the North-West Provinces the village communities had survived every revolution, and have been compared to little commonwealths, each having an individual and domestic life of its own, unchanged by the storms and troubles of the outer world. The village community paid a yearly revenue, —a share of the crops or a commutation in money,— to whatever power might be uppermost, Mogul or Mahratta, Mohammedan or Hindu. The members took a keen interest, individually and collectively, in settling the yearly rate to be paid by the whole village to the government of the day. But otherwise they cared not who was the reigning authority, Sindia or Lord Wellesley; nor who was the French general of the sepoy battalions of Sindia, nor who was the British commander-in-chief of the armies of the Governor-General.

The village community was originally a brotherhood, consisting of a tribe, family, or clan, who

[1] The North-West Provinces, which extend from Bengal to the Punjab, were to have been formed into the "Agra" Presidency. The change of name would have been extremely convenient. Later on, when the Punjab was annexed, the term "North-West Provinces" became a misnomer. The Punjab was *de facto* the furthest province on the north-west. Since then Oudh has been annexed to the North-West Provinces, and the term "North-West Provinces and Oudh" has become cumbrous. A single name like "Agra" would be more appropriate.

settled in a particular locality, and distributed the land, or the produce of the land, amongst themselves. The area was called a village, but was more like an English parish. The village community managed its own affairs, and claimed a joint proprietorship in all the land within the village area. They rented out waste lands to yearly tenants, strangers and outsiders, who were treated as tenants, and shut out from the management. Some of these tenants acquired rights of occupancy by prescription or length of possession, whilst others were only tenants at will.

Constitution of Hindu villages.

Hereditary officials and artisans.

The village commonwealth had its own hereditary officials, such as a village accountant, who kept a record of all transactions between the joint proprietors, and all accounts between the joint proprietors and their tenants. There was also a village constable or guide, who watched the crops and looked after strangers. Sometimes, when a brotherhood had decayed, a head man ruled the village in their room; and the headman, with the help of the accountant and constable, managed all the domestic affairs of the village, and conducted its relations with the outer world. To these were added hereditary artisans, such as a carpenter, potter, blacksmith, barber, tailor, washerman, and jeweller. In like manner there was an hereditary schoolmaster, astrologer, and priest, who were generally Brahmans. The higher officials were remunerated with hereditary lands, held rent free; but the others were paid by fees of grain or money. Traces of these institutions are still to be found in Behar and Orissa, but in Bengal proper the village life has died out. Hereditary artisans still remain, but here-

CHAP. III. ditary officials have become the servants of the zemindar.

Land revenue. These village communities contributed a yearly revenue to the government of the day, either as joint proprietors or through a head man. In theory they claimed possession of the land because they had cleared the jungle, and cultivated and occupied a virgin soil. But they paid a revenue to the Raja in return for protection, or to satisfy the superior right of the sovereign, or as black-mail to prevent the Raja from carrying off their crops and cattle.

Talukdars or zemindars. After the Mohammedan conquest the mode of collection differed according to circumstances. Sometimes officials were appointed by the sovereign. Sometimes a local magnate, or a revenue farmer, was employed, who collected the revenue from a group of villages, and paid a yearly block sum to the sovereign. They were middle-men, getting what they could out of the village communities, and paying as little as they could to the government of the day. These local chiefs, or revenue contractors, were known in the North-West Provinces as talukdars. They corresponded to the zemindars of Bengal, and often, like them, assumed the rights of ownership over the villages.

Settlement with joint village proprietors. Lord Wellesley ordered that the land revenue in the North-West Provinces should be settled with the talukdars at fixed rates, like the perpetual settlement with the zemindars in Bengal. Fortunately, there was a preliminary inquiry into the conflicting rights of talukdars and village proprietors, which terminated in favour of the villagers. Lord William Bentinck travelled through the North-

West Provinces, and eventually the land revenue was settled direct with the joint village proprietors. CHAP. III.

§ 17. The Madras Presidency seems to have been originally distributed into village communities of joint proprietors. A Hindu legend has been preserved to this day, which tells the story of old Hindu colonisation. A Raja of the southern country had a son by a woman of low birth. The people refused to accept the prince as their Raja. Accordingly the young man crossed the river Palar with a band of emigrants, and cleared the forest to the northward, near the site of the modern city of Madras. For six years the emigrants paid no share of the crops to the Raja. In the seventh year they were brought under the revenue administration.[1]

Madras villages: Hindu colonisation.

The modern history of this locality is equally interesting. It was ceded by the Nawab of the Carnatic to the East India Company during the wars of the eighteenth century, and was known as the Company's Jaghir. It was found to be in the possession of joint village proprietors of the same constitution as those described in the North-West Provinces, and a settlement of the land revenue was made with these joint proprietors.

Joint village proprietors.

During the latter half of the eighteenth century the rights of the joint village proprietors in Southern India faded away under the tyranny of Asiatic rulers, but the hereditary officials, artisans, and professionals still survived. Few, if any, joint village proprietors in their full entirety could be found in any villages

Disappearance.

[1] See the author's *History of India from the Earliest Ages*, vol. iii., pages 60, 280, etc.

CHAP. III. under the Nawab's officials; whilst those within the Company's Jaghir had been duly respected and preserved by the British officials. Under such circumstances it was proposed to settle the revenue of the Carnatic territory, acquired in 1801, with individual ryots or landholders under what was afterwards known as the ryotwari system.

Perpetual settlement ordered. Lord Wellesley, however, interfered, and ordered that perpetual settlements should be concluded with zemindars. Somehow this zemindari settlement had a fascination for British statesmen of the period. It was believed that the creation of an aristocracy of landlords would guarantee the permanence of British rule in India. Accordingly, Lord Wellesley was deaf to all arguments in favour of a ryotwari settlement, and threatened to remove any public servant in the Madras Presidency who should hesitate to carry out his orders.

No zemindars. Madras had no alternative but to submit. There were zemindars in the Telugu country to the northward, which had been conquered centuries previously by the Mohammedan Sultans of Golconda; and with these zemindars it was easy to conclude a perpetual settlement. But there were no zemindars in the Tamil country to the southward.

Zemindars created. In this extremity there was no alternative but to manufacture zemindars. Accordingly zemindars were created in the Madras Presidency by the old Bengal process of grouping villages together, selling them by auction, and treating the lucky buyer as a zemindar. But the new zemindars failed to pay the stipulated revenue. The groups of villages were again brought into the market, and as Lord Wellesley had left India, the estates were bought in by the Madras government, and the revenue resettled with individual ryots or cultivators.[1]

Military bond-holders.

In Malabar and Canara on the western coast the proprietors of land did not live in villages. They were landholders of the old military type, clinging to their lands with hereditary tenacity, employing serfs or slaves to cultivate them, and paying no revenue except feudal service and homage to their suzerain. Eventually Malabar and Canara were conquered by Tippu of Mysore, and the landholders were compelled to pay revenue, or to surrender their lands.

Thomas Munro: ryotwari settlement.

Thomas Munro is the real author of the ryotwari settlement. He was a cadet in the Madras army, who landed at Fort St. George about the time that Hyder Ali was desolating the Carnatic. In 1792 he was employed in settling the revenue in Malabar and Canara, which had been ceded by Tippu to Lord Cornwallis; and there he formed his ideas of a settlement direct with individual landholders. The con-

[1] The villages in the Company's Jaghir shared the same fate. They were sold by auction in groups, and were mostly bought up by native servants and dependents of the British officials at Madras. In process of time the ryotwari settlement was introduced, and then a very knotty question was raised. Under the ryotwari settlement a certain portion of the waste lands round a village was given to the villagers in common for grazing and other purposes; but the culturable waste lands were taken over by the British authorities, and valued, and rented out accordingly, to such ryots as were willing to bring them under cultivation. The buyers of the villages in the Company's Jaghir claimed, however, to be proprietors of the whole of the waste lands. For many years the demand was referred by the Board of Revenue to the Supreme Court, and by the Supreme Court back again to the Board of Revenue. By this time the question has perhaps been settled.

CHAP. III. troversy between Madras and Bengal raged for years, but in the end Thomas Munro was victorious. He converted the Board of Control and Court of Directors to his views. He was knighted, and appointed Governor of Madras. He died in 1827, after having triumphantly introduced the ryotwari. The zemindars in the Telegu country still retain their estates with the proprietary rights of landlords.

Bombay: Mountstuart Elphinstone.

Meanwhile the Bombay Presidency had been vastly enlarged by the acquisition of the dominions of the Peishwa. Mr. Mountstuart Elphinstone, the contemporary of Sir Thomas Munro, was appointed Governor of Bombay. He introduced the ryotwari settlement into the Mahratta country, and framed a code of laws which remained in force throughout the Bombay Presidency until 1860, when it was superseded by the Penal Code.

Madras collectorates.

Lord William Bentinck's system of commissioners of divisions was introduced into the North-West Provinces and Bombay; but the Madras Presidency was without commissioners or divisions, and was distributed into twenty large districts or collectorates, which on an average are as large as Yorkshire. In Bengal and the North-West Provinces the districts on an average are no larger than Devonshire. In each Madras district there was a collector, who might be described as a proconsul, and a civil and sessions judge, corresponding to those in the other Presidencies. The administration of the Madras Presidency, revenue and judicial, has always been distinguished by a larger element of Asiatic officials than either Bengal, Bombay, or the North-West Provinces.

§ 18. The last and most important changes in the

rule of the East India Company were carried out during the administration of Lord William Bentinck, under the charter Act of 1833. Before, however, dealing with this radical reform, it may be as well to review the successive stages in the relations of the East India Company towards parliament and the crown.

Charter Act of 1833: India thrown open.

Company and Crown, 1600-1688.

During the seventeenth century, the first of the Company's existence, it mainly depended on the favour of the crown. It had obtained a charter of exclusive trade from Queen Elizabeth. It prevailed on James I. to send Sir Thomas Roe as ambassador to India, to propitiate the Great Mogul and secure his good offices for the Company's trade. It sold 600,000 lbs. of pepper to Charles I. on the security of bonds on the customs, and enabled that sovereign to raise £60,000 for the expenses of his war with Parliament. Oliver Cromwell however did not approve of trade monopolies. The Lord Protector was willing to help the English Company to fight the Dutch Company, but he was of opinion that every Englishman had as much right as the Company to trade in the Eastern seas. Charles II. and James II. renewed the Company's original monopoly and privileges, and received presents in return, which however rarely exceeded the modest sum of £1,200 a year.

Parliament interposes, 1688-1708.

Under William of Orange the monopoly of the East Indies was again in danger. Parliament voted that every Englishman might traffic wherever he pleased. The Directors scattered bribes with a lavish hand; but parliament insisted upon searching the books of the Company. Then discoveries were made which were scandalous alike to the Company and the nation.

CHAP. III. Every man in power, from the highest to the lowest, had taken money from the India House. In 1693 about £90,000 had been spent in corruption. The Duke of Leeds was impeached in the House of Commons for taking a bribe of £5,000, and £10,000 was traced to the illustrious William. In this extremity the King prorogued parliament, and proceedings were brought to a close.

The United Company. The parliamentary vote however had abolished for a while the monopoly of the trade with the East Indies. A second East India Company was formed and the two rivals nearly ruined each other. At last the two Companies were united into one, and a large loan was advanced to government by the new corporation. Under this new arrangement the trade monopoly was secured to the united Company throughout the eighteenth century.

Old East India House. In those early days every shop in London exhibited a sign or emblem. The first old East India House was a quaint building with a large entablature in front, bearing three ships in full sail and a dolphin at each end. The business was distributed amongst the Directors, and transacted in committees. All the Directors put their names to the letters sent to India, and signed themselves "Your loving friends." To this day the business of the India Office is conducted by committees, but the "loving friends" vanished with the East India Company.

New India House. In the early half of the eighteenth century a new India House was built in Leadenhall Street. It was here that the Directors grew into merchant princes, and administered the affairs of provinces, until they built up our Anglo-Indian empire. Here too began the later conflict between the Company and the House of

Commons. George III. was bent on coercing parliament and removing his ministers at will. But during the coalition ministry of Lord North and Charles James Fox, there was a battle royal between parliament and the crown.

Fox's India Bill.

In 1783 Fox introduced his bill for abolishing the Court of Directors, and transferring their power and patronage to seven commissioners nominated in the bill. An agitation arose which threw the whole kingdom into a ferment. The King claimed the right of governing all countries conquered by his subjects. Accordingly he claimed the right of nominating the seven commissioners, and thus getting all the power and patronage of the Court of Directors into his own hands. But the House of Commons would not trust the King. Whigs and Tories saw that their liberties would be endangered by such additions to the royal prerogative, and they passed Fox's bill by large majorities.

Hostility of George III.

King George was furious. His only hope was that the obnoxious bill would be thrown out by the Lords. He caused a message to be conveyed to every peer, that his Majesty would withdraw his friendship from any one who voted for the bill. Accordingly the bill was thrown out by the Lords. Fox and Lord North were ignominiously dismissed, and William Pitt the younger became prime minister.

Pitt's India Bill.

Pitt's India Bill of 1784 was a marvel of statesmanship. The Court of Directors was left in the full exercise of all patronage as regards first appointments in England to the ranks of the Indian civil services, or to cadetships in the armies of the three Presidencies. All promotions in India were left to the local governments and to the Governor-General in

CHAP. III. Council. Parliament exercised a constitutional control over the whole administration of the Anglo-Indian empire; and the patronage, whether in England or in India, was wisely kept out of the hands of either ministers or the crown.

Abolition of monopoly. Under the charter act of 1813 the trade of the Company with India was thrown open to the British nation, but the Company still retained its monopoly of trade with China. The Company, however, suffered little by the loss of its monopoly as regards India. It was an old-established firm of two centuries standing. Its settlements and shipping were all in full swing, and it continued for twenty years longer to carry on a splendid business, which suffered but little by the rivalry of private interlopers. Meanwhile, as already seen, it had become the paramount power in India by its successful wars against Nepal and Burma, the extinction of the Peishwa, the humiliation of Sindia and Holkar, and the extermination of the predatory system.

End of Company's trade. Under the charter act of 1833 all trading on the part of the East India Company, whether with India or with China, was brought to a close. The East India Docks were emptied of the Company's shipping, and the trade of Europe in the Eastern seas was thrown open to the whole world.

Licensing system. Another radical change was also effected. Ever since the first establishment of the Company's settlements in India, no British born subject, not in the service of the Company, had been permitted by law to reside in India without having previously procured a license from the Court of Directors. This license system was brought to a close in 1833, and any British born subject might take up his residence in India, and trade or travel wherever he pleased. CHAP. III.

Constitutional changes.

The constitution of the British government in India was remodelled. The Governor-General of Bengal was created Governor-General of India with increased control over Madras and Bombay. The Council of India, which hitherto consisted of the Governor General as President, two Bengal civilians, and occasionally the commander-in-chief of the Bengal army, was increased by the addition of a law member. Mr., afterwards Lord, Macaulay was appointed to the new post. His labours will be noticed hereafter in dealing with the constitutional changes of 1853.

Centralisation.

Henceforth all legislative authority and financial control were centred in the government of India; and the governments of Madras and Bombay were stripped of all power to enact laws, and prohibited from creating any new office or making any grant of money, without the consent of the Governor-General of India in Council, or the sanction of the Court of Directors.

Stagnation at Madras and Bombay.

The charter of 1833 was not an unmixed good. It stopped all progress in Madras and Bombay by bringing those Presidencies too closely under the control of Bengal. For twenty years they had no representatives in the Council at Calcutta. They had framed their own systems of land revenue. They were relieved of the cares of trade, which had been a worry to Governors and Governors-General from the days of the Marquis of Wellesley to those of Lord William Bentinck. But after the year 1833 they were more or less paralysed by the loss of all discretion and responsibility in matters

CHAP. III. of legislation and expenditure. Great events were about to agitate Northern India, but for twenty years Madras and Bombay were without a history, and the work of administration was as lifeless and monotonous as the working of a machine.

Popular administration of Bentinck.

Lord William Bentinck left India in 1835. His administration had been eminently popular with all classes of the community; and his memory is preserved to this day as that of a just and able ruler, who paid due regard to the rights and claims of Asiatics as well as of Europeans.

Sir Charles Metcalfe, 1835—6: coming collisions with Asiatic powers.

Sir Charles Metcalfe, the Bengal civilian, who was sent on a mission to Runjeet Singh in 1808, and since then had filled some of the most responsible posts in the Anglo-Indian empire, acted as Governor-General between the departure of Lord William Bentinck in 1835 and the arrival of Lord Auckland in 1836. A new era was beginning to dawn upon India. Great Britain was about to appear, not only as mistress of an Anglo-Indian empire, but as an Asiatic power coming more or less into collision with four other Asiatic powers—Persia, Russia, Afghanistan and China.

CHAPTER IV.

FOURTH PERIOD: RISE TO ASIATIC POWER.

1836—56.

§ 1. Russian advance checked by Nadir Shah, 1722–38. § 2. First Cabul war under Lord Auckland, 1838-42. § 3. Lord Ellenborough, 1842–44: return from Cabul and conquest of Sind. § 4. War in Gwalior: reduction of Sindia's army. § 5. Lord Hardinge, 1845–48: Sikh rule in the Punjab. § 6. First Sikh war: Moodki, Ferozshahar, Aliwal, and Sobraon. § 7. Lord Dalhousie, 1848–56: Second Sikh war: Chillianwalla and Goojerat: annexation of the Punjab. § 8. British rule: patriarchal government. § 9. Second Burmese war, 1852: annexation of Pegu. § 10. Lord Dalhousie as an administrator: no roads in India. § 11. Trunk road, trunk railway, telegraphs, Ganges canal. § 12. Annexations of Nagpore, Satara, Jhansi, and Oudh. § 13. India Bill of 1853: new competitive Civil Service. § 14. New Legislative Council: Lord Macaulay and the Penal Code. § 15. Departure of Lord Dalhousie, 1856. § 16. Lord Canning, 1856-62: expedition to the Persian Gulf. § 17. Mogul family at Delhi. § 18. Condition of Oudh.

Lord Auckland, 1836–42: jealousy of Russia.

LORD AUCKLAND landed in Bengal at a grave political crisis. Great Britain was growing jealous of Russia as regards India, and tact and common sense were required, not to promote a war, but to prevent one. Jealousy of Russia was a new sensation. Great Britain had been indignant at the partition of Poland, but the two nations had become reconciled during the wars against France and Napoleon. Later on Russia began to extend her empire, and to menace Turkey on one side and Persia on the other; and at last it dawned on the people of the British Isles that unless there was a

CHAP. IV. speedy understanding between British and Russian diplomatists, the Cossack and the sepoy would cross swords on the banks of the Oxus.

Central Asia: Afghanistan and Turkistan.

§ 1. Central Asia is a new world which has been slowly opening up to European eyes. It includes the vast territories of Afghanistan and Turkistan, which intervene between British India, Persia, Russia, and China. It is a region of desert and mountain, ruined gardens and dried-up springs—the relics of empires which flourished in the days of the so-called Nimrod and Sennacherib, and the later days of the fire-worshippers, but were brought to rack and ruin by the Tartars and Turkomans in the armies of Chenghiz Khan and Timur.

Cradle of India.

The whole of this region, and, indeed, the whole of Central and Northern Asia, has been the cradle of the people of India from the remotest antiquity. Hindus and Mohammedans are all immigrants from beyond the Indus. The Dravidian races, the pre-Aryan people, brought their devil worship and noisy orgies from Northern Asia into Hindustan. Eventually they were driven to Southern India by the Aryan people, who brought the Vedic gods and hymns, the sacred hôma and the ministration of Rishis, from Persia and Media into Northern India. The Rajputs, the Greeks, and the Indo-Scythians of Hindustan, were all strangers from the north-west. The Turks and Afghans, who invaded India during the Crusades, and the Moguls, who established their empire in the days of the Tudors, were all sojourners from the same remote region. Thus Russia is only following the old instinct of Dravidians and Aryans, as she advances southward from the steppes towards Persia and India. She expands on land just as Great Britain expands on the sea. CHAP. IV.

The marches of Tartar, Turk, Afghan, and Mogul belong to a distant period. The march of Russia began in the first quarter of the eighteenth century. Peter the Great had been humiliated by Turkey on the banks of the Pruth, and looked to Persia for compensation. Persia was on the brink of ruin. In 1722 the Afghans had advanced to Ispahan; and the Czar and the Sultan prepared to divide her remaining territory. Turkey took the western provinces, whilst Russia occupied the provinces along the south of the Caspian. The Caspian was a base for an advance on India, and had Peter lived he would have found his way to India. The road was easy *viâ* Meshed to Herat, and the Mogul empire would have fallen into his hands like an over-ripe plum. The British at Calcutta were a little hive of traders, who would have been helpless to resist a Russian invasion. Most probably they would have preferred Russia to the Mogul, and would have sent a deputation to the Russian camp to pray for the protection of the Czar.

Russian advance to Persia, 1722.

But Peter the Great died in 1727, and Nadir Shah, the last of the "world stormers," stepped in and snatched Persia from Russia. Nadir Shah was a Turk of the noble tribe of Afshar; a brigand in his youth, but destined to be as great a general as Cyrus or Napoleon. In 1727, the very year that Peter the Great died, Nadir Shah joined the dethroned Shah of Persia, drove the Afghans back to their own territories, and conquered Khorassan as far as Herat. Eventually he imprisoned the Shah, and usurped the throne of Persia. He compelled Turkey to retire from the

Checkmated by Nadir Shah, 1727.

CHAP. IV. western provinces, and Russia to retire from the provinces on the Caspian.

Persian invasion of India, 1738–39.

In 1738 Nadir Shah captured Candahar, invaded the Punjab, and entered Delhi in triumph. His battalions of Persians and Turkomans, trained and disciplined under picked officers, were irresistible against Afghans and Moguls. He did not want to conquer India, but only to plunder it. He carried off the treasures of Delhi, the spoil of Hindustan, and the peacock of jewels which had blazed for a hundred years over the throne of the Great Mogul. Thus, within twelve years of the death of Peter the Great, the parade of jewels, which might have adorned the Kremlin, became the prize of Nadir Shah.

Nadir Shah and his Persian officers.

Nadir Shah was the last of the line of Asiatic warriors that began with Sargon and Cyrus, and culminated in Chenghiz Khan and Timur. He was tall, powerful, and loud-voiced, with an eye of lightning, and an expression that alternately terrified and charmed. He stood out head and shoulders above his Persian officers, arrayed in a plain cloak lined with black lambskin from Bokhara, a crimson turban, a richly-mounted dagger in his belt, and a huge battle-axe of steel in his hand. He was ever at work from morn till night, inspecting troops, administering justice, dictating letters, or transacting business by word of mouth. His fare was of the plainest—boiled rice, with a little meat, bread, cheese, radishes, and parched peas—whilst his drink was butter-milk or water. His officers were Asiatic dandies, clad in rich pelisses trimmed with furs, smart vests with gold and silver lace, crimson hats with four peaks, or arrayed in coats of mail with steel helmets and sharp pikes. They scorned the frugal fare which satisfied their

Turkish master. They delighted in Persian dishes, such as pillaws stuffed with plums and raisins, savoury stews, dainty bits of meat known as kabobs, together with grape jelly, and confections; and they revelled in wine and strong waters, to the horror of all strict Mohammedans.

CHAP. IV.

Russian advance: war declared, 1838.

§ 2. A century passed away. Nadir Shah was forgotten, and Russia was again menacing Persia and dabbling in the Caspian. In 1837 Persia was besieging Herat under the pretence that it had formed part of the empire of Nadir Shah; but Russia was in the background putting forth Persian claims as a cat's-paw for seizing Herat. Great Britain, however, was resolved that neither Persia nor Russia should take Herat from the Afghans, to whom it had properly belonged ever since the death of Nadir Shah. In October, 1838, Lord Auckland declared war to compel Persia to retire from Herat. It was also determined to dethrone Dost Mohammed Khan, the ruler of Afghanistan, because he had been carrying on a suspicious intercourse with Russia, and to set up Shah Shuja in his room, because he had been dethroned many years previously by Dost Mohammed Khan, and was therefore the rightful ruler of Afghanistan. Moreover Shah Shuja had been living many years in British territory under British protection, and was therefore likely to prove a more faithful ally against Russia than Dost Mohammed Khan.

Political mistakes.

The declaration of war was a mistake. Persia had already taken the alarm, and raised the siege of Herat. Dost Mohammed Khan may have been a usurper, but he had been accepted. by the Afghan people as their

CHAP. IV. ruler, and he was a man of undoubted capacity. If he had been properly treated in 1836-37 he might have become as useful an ally to the British government as he proved himself to be twenty years later. Shah Shuja, on the other hand, whom the British wished to set up in his room, was a weak and worthless prince, and it was doubtful at the time whether the Afghan people would accept him as their ruler, especially if he were forced upon them by the British government.

First Afghan war, 1838-42

Thus began the first Cabul war. The British army was shut out from the Punjab by Runjeet Singh, and compelled to take a circuitous route through Sind. A bridge of boats was constructed to carry the army over the Indus at Sukkur; but in those days Sind was a foreign territory, and no reliance could be placed on its rulers. Indeed, had the British met with a defeat in Afghanistan, the Amirs, or rulers of Sind, would possibly have destroyed the bridge, and cut off their return to India.

British advance to Cabul, 1839.

In February, 1839, the British army crossed the river Indus, and advanced along the Bolan Pass to Quetta, and thence to Candahar. Major Rawlinson remained at Candahar as minister and envoy of Shah Shuja, supported by a force under the command of General Nott. The main army, under Sir John Keane, advanced northward, captured the important fortress of Ghazni, and conducted Shah Shuja to Cabul, whilst Dost Mohammed Khan fled away northward to Bokhara. Shah Shuja was placed on the throne of Afghanistan, under the guidance of Sir William Macnaghten, the minister and envoy at Cabul, protected by the British army under

Keane, who was subsequently created Baron Keane of Ghazni.[1] CHAP. IV.

British successes, 1840.

The year 1840 brought unexpected good fortune. Runjeet Singh died in 1839, and his successor opened the Punjab to the march of British troops. Russia sent a counter expedition from Orenburg towards Khiva, but it was stopped by snows and want of water, and compelled to return. Shah Shuja, however, was only maintained on the throne at Cabul by British arms and gold. The Afghans cared nothing for him. So long as they received subsidies from the British authorities they remained loyal, but there was no enthusiasm. The hill tribes, who occupied the passes into the Punjab, were equally loyal so long as they received pay, but otherwise might turn against the British at any time, and cut off their return to India. The shopkeepers and bazaar dealers at Cabul were satisfied, for they reaped a golden harvest from their British customers. Towards the close of 1840 Dost Mohammed Khan returned to Cabul and surrendered to Sir William Macnaghten. This was a stroke of luck which for a brief space threw the destinies of Central Asia into the hands of British rulers. The Dost was sent to Calcutta as a prisoner but treated as a guest, and often played at chess at Government House. Meanwhile British officers and officials fancied they were perfectly safe, and were joined by their wives and families, who gladly exchanged the depressing temperature of India for the cool climate of Cabul.

In 1841 the prospect was less charming. The

[1] The capture of Ghazni was mainly due to the cool intrepidity of the late Sir Henry Durand, then a lieutenant in the Bengal Engineers.

CHAP. IV. subsidies were cut down and there was general discontent. The Afghans were sick of Shah Shuja and weary of British occupation, and there was a secret longing for a return to the old life of riot and rapine. The wild hill tribes, who were supposed to guard the passes leading to the Punjab, were still more disaffected; but these matters were kept secret, and Sir William Macnaghten and the other officials kept up a show of confidence, whilst difficulties and dangers were hedging around them more and more closely from day to day.

Afghan disaffection, 1841.

British army in danger.

At the same time the position of the British army was unsatisfactory. It should have held the great fortress of Bala Hissar, which commanded the whole city of Cabul, and could have put down any disturbance with the utmost ease. But Shah Shuja was jealous of the presence of British soldiers, and they were lodged in a cantonment three miles from the city, with no defence beyond a low mud wall which horsemen could gallop over. Lord Keane returned to India, and was succeeded in the command by General Elphinstone, who was too old for the post. Still there was no show of apprehension. Sir William Macnaghten lived with his family in a house close to the cantonment. He was appointed Governor of Bombay, and was to have been succeeded by Sir Alexander Burnes as minister and envoy. Burnes lived in a house within the precincts of the city, and thought himself as safe in Cabul as in Calcutta.

Threatening outlook.

As the year 1841 wore away, disappointments and anxieties began to tell on Sir William Macnaghten. Shah Shuja was a useless burden, like the old man of the sea on the shoulders of Sinbad. The hill tribes had closed the passes between Cabul and Jellalabad, and in October Sir Robert Sale was sent with a brigade to re-open communications. Sale fought his way to Jellalabad, and there entrenched his troops and waited for reinforcements. CHAP. IV.

On the 2nd November there was an outbreak in the city of Cabul. Burnes barricaded his house, but was soon environed by an angry mob of Afghans. He sent an urgent message to the British cantonment for a battalion of infantry, and two field-pieces, which at that early hour could have penetrated the city and effected his deliverance. But the danger was underrated, and no force was sent lest it should offend Shah Shuja. That same afternoon the gateway of the house was burnt down by the mob, and Burnes and twenty-three others were brutally murdered. Outbreak and murder.

By this time the outbreak had culminated in an insurrection. The population of the villages round about had joined the rioters, and thousands of Afghans were hurrying into the city of Cabul in the hope of plunder. Later in the afternoon two battalions of British infantry tried to cut a way through the narrow streets and crowded bazaars, but found the task beyond their power, and were compelled to return to the British cantonment. Akbar Khan, the eldest son of Dost Mohammed, appeared at the head of the insurrection; whilst Shah Shuja was shut up in the Bala Hissar, helplessly waiting for the British to suppress the rebellion, and deliver him from the fury of his subjects. Afghan revolt.

Sir William Macnaghten and General Elphinstone were paralysed by the dangers and anxieties of their Murder of Macnaghten.

CHAP. IV. position. Provisions were running short in the British cantonment; supplies were withheld by the people of Cabul; and soldiers and sepoys were becoming demoralised. At last it was decided to retreat to Jellalabad—the half-way house between Cabul and Peshawar; and negotiations were opened with Akbar Khan for the supply of provisions and carriage. The greed of the Afghans was insatiable. Akbar Khan demanded vast sums as ransom, and the surrender of British officers as hostages for the payment. On the 23rd December, 1841, there was a final meeting between Sir William Macnaghten and the Afghan chiefs, and the British minister and envoy was suddenly attacked and murdered by Akbar Khan.

British disaster in the Khyber, 1842.

Notwithstanding the murder, negotiations were re-opened. In January, 1842, the British forces began to retreat from Cabul, followed by Akbar Khan and a large army of Afghans. More money was demanded, and more hostages were surrendered, including British ladies and children. Then followed treacheries and massacres. The British army, numbering four thousand troops and twelve thousand camp-followers, entered the Khyber Pass beneath a heavy fall of snow. The hill tribes crowned the precipitous heights on either side, and poured a murderous fire on the retreating masses, whilst the soldiers of Akbar Khan joined in the horrible work of murder and plunder. The whole of the surviving force perished in the Khyber Pass with the exception of a surgeon named Brydon, who escaped on a pony to Jellalabad, and lived to tell the tale for more than thirty years afterwards.

One British officer appears to have kept his head

amidst all these bewildering disasters. This was Captain Eldred Pottinger, a man who knew how to lead Asiatics, and how to control them. He was inside Herat throughout the siege, and by sheer pluck and fertility of resources kept the enemy at bay until the siege was raised. He was one of the hostages made over to Akbar Khan, and was sent with the others to a fortress in the northern mountains. There he bribed the Afghan commandant with a written promise of a future ransom. He hoisted the British flag over the fortress, took possession of the surrounding country, collected the revenue, called in supplies, and kept up the spirits of ladies and children amidst the general depression and humiliation. Eventually the prisoners were delivered from their enemies and restored to their families and friends; but Eldred Pottinger died and was forgotten.

Eldred Pottinger.

§ 3. Before the tidings of disaster reached England, Lord Ellenborough was appointed Governor-General of India, in succession to Lord Auckland. In February, 1842, he touched at Madras, and heard of the destruction of the British army in the Khyber Pass. Meanwhile an avenging army, under the command of General Pollock, was marching to the relief of Sale, who was closely besieged at Jellalabad by an Afghan army under Akbar Khan. The British garrison at Jellalabad had defended the place with the utmost resolution, and before the arrival of General Pollock, Akbar Khan had been compelled to raise the siege.

Lord Ellenborough, 1842–44.

Up to this time nothing was known of General Nott at Candahar. The fact was that he and Major

Candahar.

CHAP. IV. Rawlinson were holding out against overwhelming odds, as Elphinstone and Macnaghten ought to have done at Cabul. History teaches that such a surrender as that of Macnaghten to Akbar Khan too often means "massacre." It meant "massacre" at Patna, in the days of Mir Kasim, and during the sepoy mutiny of 1857 it bore the same meaning at Jhansi and Cawnpore.

Close of the Afghan war, 1842. General Pollock advanced westward from Jellalabad, whilst General Nott advanced northward from Candahar. Both armies met at Cabul. Shah Shuja had been murdered, and Akbar Khan had fled away to the northward. All the British hostages, including the ladies and children, reached Cabul in safety. Dost Mohammed Khan was set free at Calcutta, and returned to Cabul and recovered his throne. Thus the first Cabul war was brought to a close, and for some years the Afghans were ignored.

Outside troubles. The disasters of 1841-42 led to disturbances in Asiatic states outside British territory. The Amirs of Sind were tempted to violate their treaty obligations. In 1843 they were defeated by Sir Charles Napier in the battles of Meanee and Hyderabad, and their territories were eventually incorporated with the Bombay Presidency. There was also some excitement in Nipal and Burma; but British prestige was restored by the victories of Pollock, Nott, and Napier, and the disorders soon died away. Meanwhile, the British government was drawn into a war with China; but relations with China have not as yet been brought to bear upon British rule in India.

Gwalior affairs, 1843. § 4. In 1843 Lord Ellenborough interfered in the affairs of Gwalior. The ruling prince, who was known by the hereditary name of Sindia, had died without leaving any son, real or adopted. He had been a weak and incapable ruler, and had permitted the army of Gwalior to grow too powerful for the state, and to swallow up two-thirds of the public revenue. CHAP. IV.

Overgrown army, 1843.

The disbandment of the army was necessary, not only for the well-being of Gwalior, but for the security of the British government. It nnmbered 40,000 men and 200 guns. Meanwhile, the Sikh army in the Punjab had grown more dangerous. It consisted of some 60,000 men, well provided with artillery, who had been drilled and trained by French officers. It was no longer under the control of a strong ruler like Runjeet Singh, and at any moment might cross the Sutlej into British territory. Under such circumstances a junction of the Sikh army with the army of Gwalior would have raised a terrible storm in Hindustan.

Revolt, 1843.

The death of Sindia rendered some action necessary. He had left a widow who was only twelve years of age. This girl, however, was permitted to adopt a small boy of eight, and a minister was appointed, under the sanction of Lord Ellenborough, to conduct the administration of Gwalior during the minority. Shortly afterwards the girl dismissed the minister from his post, and he was fool enough to accept the dismissal. The girl then appointed a minister of her own, and won over the army by large distributions of money, in open defiance of the paramount power. The consequence was that disturbances broke out in Gwalior, and many persons were killed.

Settlement, 1843.

Lord Ellenborough proceeded to Agra, and ordered the British army to advance to Gwalior under Sir Hugh Gough. Two battles were fought on the same

CHAP. IV. day, the 29th of December, 1843, one body of the Gwalior army being defeated at Maharajpore, and another at Punniar. Lord Ellenborough then carried out the necessary reforms. The army of Gwalior was reduced from 40,000 men to 9,000, and the number of guns from 200 to thirty-two. A subsidiary force was created of sepoys, trained and commanded by British officers, which was afterwards known as the Gwalior Contingent. The government was taken out of the hands of the girl-widow, and entrusted to a council of regency, consisting of six nobles of Gwalior, who acted under the advice of the British Resident until the adopted prince attained his majority.

Lord Ellenborough re-called, 1844.

In June, 1844, Lord Ellenborough was recalled by the Court of Directors. It was urged that he was too fond of war, but it was whispered that he had given mortal offence by promoting military officers to posts previously occupied by civilians. The question raised some controversy at the time, as the recall was opposed by Sir Robert Peel and the Duke of Wellington; but it has long ceased to be of importance, and may be dropped into oblivion.

Sir Henry Hardinge, 1845-48.

§ 5. Sir Henry Hardinge succeeded Lord Ellenborough as Governor-General. At this period the Punjab was a political volcano, and the Sikh army was a menace to Hindustan.

Rise of the Sikhs, 1400-1500.

The Sikhs were religious fanatics, dating back to the fifteenth century. Their founder was a prophet, or Guru, named Nanuk Guru, who was at once priest and king. The object of the Guru was to reconcile the Hindu religion with the Mohammedan by teaching that there was but one God, one Supreme Spirit, and that the Vishnu of Hinduism and the Allah of

Islam were one and the same deity. The church of Nanuk was a platform of comprehension. A brotherhood was formed, known as Sikhs, and all its members were declared to be equal in the eyes of God and His Guru, whatever might be their individual caste, wealth, or position.

Sikh religion.

The Sikh religion was in reality a revival of a Buddhism recognising deity. Nanuk Guru bears a striking resemblance to Gotama Buddha. He was born in 1460 of the royal race of Kshatriyas, the modern Rajputs, or "sons of Rajas." He taught that goodness in thought and deed was especially pleasing to God. He denounced the distinctions of caste, and preached universal charity and toleration. He was followed by a line of nine Gurus, who taught the same doctrines and formed an apostolic succession, inspired by God, and worshipped as incarnations or avatars of deity. The city of Amritsar, the "pool of immortality," became the sacred city of the Sikhs, and every year formed a centre of Sikh gatherings like those of the Hebrews at Jerusalem and those of Mohammedans at Mecca.

Persecutions of Aurangzeb.

The new faith was eagerly accepted by Hindus, especially those of the lower castes, but Mohammedans stood aloof from the heresy. The stern Aurangzeb, who reigned as Great Mogul from the days of Oliver Cromwell to those of Queen Anne, persecuted the Sikhs with relentless ferocity, and the ninth Guru was beheaded in the imperial palace of Delhi in the presence of Aurangzeb and his courtiers.

Guru Govind: the Khalsa.

Under Guru Govind, the tenth and last of the old Sikh pontiffs, the Sikhs were transformed by persecution from a brotherhood of saints into an army of warriors. Guru Govind stands out as the real founder

CHAP. IV. of the Sikh Khalsa or "saved ones." He set apart five faithful disciples, namely, a Brahman, a Rajput, and three Sudras, to form a Khalsa, and to be a model for all other Khalsas. He consecrated them by sprinkling holy water; he gave to each the name of Singh, or "lion warrior," but he gave to the whole five collectively the name of Khalsa; and he solemnly promised that wherever a Khalsa was gathered together, he, their Guru, would be in the midst of them.

Army of the Khalsa. Henceforth the Sikhs were known as the "Army of God and the Khalsa." The constitution was changed. Guru Govind was taken prisoner by the Moguls and executed, and his successors lost their spiritual prestige. The Sikhs were divided into twelve misls or clans, each having its own chief or Sirdar; but the Sirdars changed with the times. Some took the field at the head of their sons and vassals, zealous only for God and the Khalsa. Others were mere freebooters, who led bodies of irregular horse to devastate and plunder. Others again formed a brotherhood of fanatics known as Akalis, who called themselves soldiers of God, and were distinguished by steel bracelets and dark-blue dresses and turbans.

Runjeet Singh, 1800-39. Out of these discordant elements Runjeet Singh created his famous army of the Khalsa. By consummate tact he stirred up the old enthusiasm of the Sikh soldiery, whilst employing French officers to drill and command them. He added Cashmere and Peshawar to his dominions, and was known as the "Lion of Lahore." His depravity is indescribable; his court at Lahore was a sink of iniquity, like the cities of the plain; but, knowing the real source of his power, he gloried in the title of "Commander-in-Chief of the Army of God and the Khalsa." When he died, in 1839, four queens and seven slaves were buried alive with his remains.

Hopeless anarchy.

Between 1839 and 1845 the Punjab was sinking into hopeless anarchy. There was a deadly conflict between Sikhs and Rajputs. Plots and murders followed in rapid succession. Princes, ministers, and generals were carried off in turns by assassination or massacre. Meanwhile the treasures of Runjeet Singh were squandered in wild debauchery, or lavished on the army. There was a British envoy at Lahore, but he could do nothing. On one important occasion he reported that every minister of state had been drunk for several days. On another occasion he entered the council-hall unexpectedly, and found the prime minister figuring in the guise of a dancing-girl amidst the applause of his colleagues. An infant, named Dhuleep Singh, said to be the son of Runjeet Singh, was the nominal sovereign; but the queen-mother, a woman of low origin, and her minister and paramour, were the rulers of the country.

Army supreme.

By this time the army of the Khalsa were masters of the state—the prætorian guards of the Punjab. It was dangerous to the Sikh government, and was only kept quiet by money and concessions. It demanded more pay, and got it. The French officers fled for their lives. The Sikh officers were compelled to obey certain little Khalsas, which by this time had come to be elected by the soldiery in every corps, and were supposed to be animated by the invisible but presiding spirit of Guru Govind. The army was bent on sacking the capital and slaughtering all who stood in their way, whilst the Akalis, the

CHAP. IV. fanatical soldiers of God, were burning to purge the court at Lahore of its iniquities.

Non-intervention. The Sikh rulers implored the British government to protect them against the army of the Khalsa; but non-intervention was still the ruling policy, and the British government refused to interfere. Meanwhile the dangers of Sikh invasion had been minimised by the reduction of the army of Gwalior, and the British government underrated the strength of the Sikh army. Amidst the general lull the crash came. The ministers were afraid of a reign of terror at Lahore, and sent the army of the Khalsa across the river Sutlej to plunder the cities of Hindustan.

Sikh invasion, November, 1845. § 6. The British government was taken utterly by surprise. There was no warning whatever, and the enemy was estimated to number 100,000 men with 150 large guns. Ferozpore, the frontier station of the British army on the north-west, was held by a British force of 10,000 men. The Sikhs might have overwhelmed Ferozpore, and marched on to Delhi and Agra before the main army could have taken the field. Fortunately for the British the Sikh generals were cowards and traitors, thinking of nothing but themselves. The British force at Ferozpore moved out and offered them battle, but they shrank from a collision. They divided the Sikh army into two bodies: one stopped to watch Ferozpore, whilst the other entrenched a camp a few miles off at Ferozshahar.

Moodki, December. Sir Henry Hardinge and Sir Hugh Gough were soon moving to the frontier with a British army. On the 18th of December a battle was fought at Moodki. The Sikh general fled at the outset, but the

Sikh soldiers opened fire with a rapidity and precision which for a while staggered the British. At last the British gained a victory, but it was not decisive. CHAP. IV.

Two days after Moodki, the British attacked the Sikh force at Ferozshahar. They met with a resistance which they never expected. The Sikhs were again deserted by their general, but fought with the reckless bravery of zealots; and Sir Hugh Gough charged up to the muzzles of their guns with cold steel before he could carry their batteries. Night came on, and the firing ceased. During the darkness there was an uproar in the enemy's camp, and it turned out that the Sikh soldiers were plundering their own treasury—the military chest which their general had left behind in his hasty flight from the field. Next morning the battle was renewed, but the Sikhs had lost their enthusiasm, and were soon in full retreat to the Sutlej. Ferozshahar.

Early in 1846 the Sikh army recrossed the Sutlej by a bridge of boats. Sir Harry Smith defeated one force at Aliwal, but the main army of the Khalsa was strongly entrenched at Sobraon. In February Hardinge and Gough advanced to storm the entrenchment. Then followed the hardest and bloodiest battle which the British had hitherto fought in India. The Sikhs fought with the desperation of despair, but were slowly beaten back by the fiery resolution of the British. At last they retreated to the Sutlej, and thousands were drowned in the river. Their general had fled on the morning of the battle, and had broken down the bridge to prevent their return to the Punjab. Aliwal and Sobraon, 1846.

Thus ended the first Sikh war. The British army

CHAP. IV.

Mixed government, Sikh and British.

marched in triumph to Lahore, and Sir Henry Hardinge, now Lord Hardinge, began to settle the future government of the Punjab. He was unwilling to annex the country, for the British nation was already jealous of the territorial possessions of the East India Company. He dared not withdraw the British army lest the army of the Khalsa should spring again into life and sweep away the Sikh *régime.* He tried a compromise. He recognised the infant, the queen-mother and her minister, as *de facto* rulers of the Punjab. He reduced the army of the Khalsa to a third of its former strength. He annexed the frontier province on the north, known as the Julinder Doab, and he demanded a subsidy of a million and a-half sterling towards the expenses of the war.

Sale of Cashmere.

The money was not to be had. Out of twelve millions sterling that were found in the Lahore treasury after the death of Runjeet Singh, only half a million remained. The difficulty was overcome by the Viceroy of Cashmere, a Rajput named Golab Singh, who held the province in subordination to the Sikh government. He offered one million sterling, provided the British government recognised him as Maharaja of Cashmere, independent of Lahore. The bargain was struck, and Cashmere was sold to Golab Singh.

Council of Regency.

Still it was impossible for the British to withdraw from the Punjab without bringing on a second war. Before the end of 1846 the queen-mother was found to be utterly unfit to rule, whilst her minister was stirring up the people of Cashmere to revolt against the Maharaja. The minister was removed from his post. Eight of the leading Sirdars at Lahore were formed into a council of regency, under the direction of Sir Henry Lawrence, the British Resident at Lahore; and it was determined that a small British force should remain in the Punjab until the infant Dhuleep Singh attained his majority. CHAP. IV.

§7. Two years passed away. In 1848 Lord Hardinge was succeeded by Lord Dalhousie, and returned to England accompanied by Sir Henry Lawrence. Sir Frederic Currie, a Bengal civilian, was Resident at Lahore, and the Punjab was to all appearance quiet. About this time the Sikh governor of Multan, named Mulraj, quarrelled with the council of regency at Lahore, and resigned his post in disgust. Two Englishmen, Mr. Vans Agnew and a Lieutenant Anderson, were sent to Multan with a Sikh escort to take overcharge. Lord Dalhousie, 1848–56.

Multan is situated on the river Chenab, about 200 miles to the south-west of Lahore. The two Englishmen reached the place in April, and took up their quarters at a mosque in the suburbs. Mulraj paid them a visit, and there was some disagreement about the accounts, but the two Englishmen went over the fortress with Mulraj, and all three left the place together on horseback. At that moment the two Englishmen were felled from their horses. Mulraj galloped away into the country, and the two Englishmen were carried away to the mosque and brutally murdered. Mulraj returned to the fortress, and issued a proclamation calling on the people of all religions to revolt against British supremacy. Revolt at Multan, April, 1848: murder of two Englishmen.

The Sikh and British authorities at Lahore treated the outbreak as an isolated rebellion. Lieutenant Herbert Edwardes, a rising officer, marched an Revolt of Shere Singh.

CHAP. IV. irregular force against Multan; but though he defeated the rebels, he could not capture the fortress. A Sikh noble, named Shere Singh, marched from Lahore to co-operate with Edwardes, and a British force under General Whish was also sent in a like direction. It turned out, however, that Shere Singh was negotiating with the rebels inside the fortress, whilst swearing fidelity to the British authorities outside. When the British guns had opened fire, and the capture of the fortress was a mere question of hours, Shere Singh suddenly beat the drum of the Khalsa, proclaimed a religious war against the British, and started for the north with the whole of his men as fast as their long Sikh legs could carry them. Whish saw that pursuit was hopeless, and could only entrench his troops and wait for reinforcements whilst keeping watch on Multan.

Army of the Khalsa

The hot weather was coming on, British advance was delayed, and the British authorities at Lahore were discovering that a second Sikh war was inevitable. The queen-mother was organising a general confederacy against the British government, but her intrigues were found out in time, and she was sent to Benares to repent at leisure. Rebel chiefs were plotting in all directions to get rid of the British government, and bring back the old days of anarchy and plunder. Later in the year many villages were found empty. The able-bodied men had gone off to join rebel chiefs, and fight once more for God and the Khalsa; and no one remained behind but the halt and the lame, the women and the children.

Afghans occupy Peshawar.

To crown all, Dost Mohammed, Khan of Cabul, had joined the rebel Sikhs. As a Mohammedan he must have hated the Sikhs and their religion, especially as Runjeet Singh had wrested the important valley of Peshawar from Afghan dominion. But he saw his opportunity to recover Peshawar. He overran the valley and captured the fortress of Attock; and he determined that whatever might happen, he would hold Peshawar for the future against Sikh or Englishman.

Gough's advance, 1848.

In November, 1848, the British army, under Lord Gough, entered the "land of the five rivers." On the 13th of January he approached the army of Shere Singh, which was strongly entrenched at Chillianwalla on the left bank of the Jhelum—the Hydaspes of the Greeks—and probably not far from the spot where Alexander routed the Rajput army of Porus. The Sikh army was hidden from view by a dense jungle. Lord Gough ordered a reconnoitre; he proposed to give his army a night's rest, and to begin the battle next morning.

Chillianwalla, 13th January, 1849.

Shere Singh upset this arrangement. He did not care to fight the British army after a night's rest, and after his position had been reconnoitred. He stirred up the Irish blood of Lord Gough by opening a fire on the British camp. The impetuous general returned the fire, and ordered an advance. For a brief interval nothing was to be heard but the roar of artillery, whilst the battle was hidden from view by smoke and jungle. Presently the British guns were silenced by the advance of infantry, and soon afterwards the sharp rattle of musketry told that the conflict had begun. But the battle of Chillianwalla was disastrous. The Sikh artillery continued to roar after the British artillery was silenced. A brigade of British infantry was beaten back. A cavalry brigade was repulsed with a loss of guns. At last, the ringing cheer of

CHAP. IV. British infantry told that the day was gained, but it was dearly purchased with the loss of 2,400 officers and men. The Sikhs were driven from their position, but they entrenched themselves still more strongly on better ground only three miles off. Had there been a forward movement on the following morning, the doubtful success of the 13th of January might have been converted into a decisive victory.

Fall of Multan, 22nd January.

On the 22nd of January Mulraj surrendered the fortress of Multan to General Whish. This enabled Whish to bring his forces to the help of Lord Gough. Later on Shere Singh began a march to Lahore, but was stopped by Gough and Whish at Goojerat on the right bank of the Chenab.

Goojerat, 21st February.

The battle of Goojerat was fought on the 21st of February, 1849. It was known as "the battle of the guns," for there was no premature advance of infantry or cavalry, as at Chillianwalla. For two hours and a-half the Sikh army was pounded with British shot and shell, and then, and not till then, a charge of bayonets and a rush of cavalry completed the destruction of the army of the Khalsa. The victory at Goojerat saved the reputation of Lord Gough. Sir Charles Napier had been sent out to supersede him as commander-in-chief, on account of the losses at Chillianwalla; but before Napier could reach India the war was over, and Chillianwalla was condoned, although it could not be forgotten. The Punjab was once more prostrate at the feet of the British, and the Afghans were driven out of Peshawar.

Annexation of the Punjab, 1849.

The mixed government of Sikhs and British had failed in the Punjab, under Sir Henry Lawrence and Sir Frederic Currie, as it had failed in Bengal nearly a century before under Clive and his successors.

Lord Dalhousie decided, and to all appearance rightly, that annexation was the only chance of salvation for the Punjab. So the weak and helpless relics of the family of Runjeet Singh were pensioned off by the conquerors, and his kingdom was incorporated with the British empire, and formed into a province under British rule.

British rule in the Punjab.

§ 8. The administration of the Punjab was, in the first instance, placed under a Board of three members. But the Board did not work smoothly, and Lord Dalhousie objected to Boards, and preferred fixing responsibilities on individuals. Accordingly Mr. John Lawrence, a younger brother of Sir Henry Lawrence, was appointed sole ruler of the Punjab under the title of chief commissioner. It will be seen hereafter that John Lawrence was destined to leave his mark in history; to become Governor-General of India, and finally to take his seat in the House of Lords. The Punjab was delivered from the grinding exactions of Sikh officials, and brought under the just and impartial rule of British officers. Within the space of less than a decade, the kingdom of Runjeet Singh, which had been distracted by wars and disorders worse than those of England under the Heptarchy, was brought under the civilised and European administration of the nineteenth century.

Non-Regulation.

The Punjab was parcelled out into divisions and districts, like the Bengal and North-West Provinces. It was not, however, brought under the "Regulations," which had the force of laws in Bengal, Madras, Bombay, and the North-West Provinces. For some years it was known as a non-Regulation province; in other words, British administration in the Punjab was

CHAP. IV. carried on according to the spirit of the Regulations, and on the same lines as the administration of the North-West Provinces, but a large margin of latitude and discretion was allowed to the chief commissioner, and he was empowered to issue his own instructions and orders, which might sometimes be out of harmony with the Regulations.

Patriarchal government. The result was that a so-called patriarchal rule prevailed in the Punjab, which was admirably adapted to the transition state of the "land of five rivers." British officers laboured to govern the country, and to administer justice amongst a mixed population of Sikhs, Mohammedans, and Hindus, according to local circumstances and usages, rather than according to the strict letter of the law which had prevailed for generations in Regulation provinces.

District officers. Under the non-Regulation system the duties of magistrate, collector, and civil and sessions judge were discharged by a single officer, who was known as the deputy-commissioner. The deputy-commissioner was thus not only the head of the civil administration of his district, but the magistrate and judge. Below him were certain grades of assistant commissioners, whose duties were of a similarly comprehensive character. Half of these grades were taken from the ranks of the Indian civil service, and the other half from British officers in the Indian army. Below them were grades of uncovenanted officers, European and Asiatic, known as extra assistant commissioners, who corresponded more or less with the class of deputy-collectors created by Lord William Bentinck.

Commissioners. The commissioners of divisions controlled the administration of the districts under their charge after the manner of commissioners in Bengal, Bombay, and the North-West Provinces. They also heard appeals from the courts of deputy-commissioners. Another officer, known as the "financial commissioner," controlled the expenditure of the entire province, in subordination to the chief commissioner. CHAP. IV.

Judicial commissioner: Punjab code.

There was no Supreme Court, and no Sudder Court, in the Punjab. In those patriarchal days a single officer, known as the "judicial commissioner," controlled all the law courts in the province, and was the last court of appeal. Meanwhile a code of laws was drawn up, under the directions of the chief commissioner, by his secretary, Mr. (now Sir Richard) Temple. Since then Sir Richard Temple has filled high positions in India, which were only second in importance to those occupied by his illustrious master.

Land settlement: village system.

The land settlement in the Punjab was carried out on the same lines as that in the North-West Provinces. Proprietary rights of village communities, joint or otherwise, were recognised as far as possible. The village system was perhaps as perfect in the Punjab as in any other part of India, but for years the rights of village proprietors had been ignored or stamped out under Sikh rule. The revenue collectors of Runjeet Singh cared nothing for proprietary right, nor indeed for any law or usage which debarred them from exacting as much revenue as possible from the cultivators of the land.

North-West Provinces.

Meanwhile the land settlement of the North-West Provinces, which had been modified by Lord William Bentinck, was brought to a close under the supervision of Mr. Thomason, the Lieutenant-Governor. It was based on the principle of recognising, defining,

CHAP. IV. and recording all existing rights of proprietors of every kind and sort, from those of hereditary chiefs and landlords, down to village proprietors, joint or otherwise. The settlement included a full record of the rights of all proprietors in every village. Every field was measured and mapped; every house was entered on a list. All shares in the land, and all joint and separate liabilities for revenue, were registered. The customs of the village were recorded, and formed a manual of village law. Finally, details of all lawsuits under the settlement officers were preserved, and formed a history of the village settlement. This system was carried out in the Punjab and other new provinces of British India. In Bengal, however, it is stopped by the zemindari system; whilst in Madras village rights are equal under the ryotwari system.

Second Burmese war, 1852.

§ 9. In 1852 a second Burmese war was forced upon Lord Dalhousie. A treaty of commerce and friendship had been concluded with the king of Burma at the end of the first war, but of late years it had been grossly violated. Burmese officials had condemned British sea captains to fine and imprisonment on false charges, and British merchants residing at Rangoon were preparing to abandon their property and leave Burmese territory unless they were protected by their own government.

Arrogant officials.

Commodore Lambert was sent to Rangoon to investigate complaints. He was treated by the Burmese officials with such insolence and arrogance that negotiations were impossible. Eventually he seized a Burmese ship by way of reprisal, but engaged to restore it on receipt of something like 1,000*l*. as nominal compensation for British sufferers. In reply the Burmese fired on the commodore's steamer, and the firing was promptly returned. From that moment war was inevitable. CHAP. IV.

A British expedition under General Godwin reached Rangoon. The Shway Dagohn pagoda, the great cathedral of Buddhism in Burma, was taken by storm; and then all fighting was over. The court of Ava was powerless and paralysed. It could not resist British forces, and simply left the British authorities to do as they pleased. Upper Burma was abandoned to the king, and the rich valley of Pegu, and port of Rangoon, were added to the British empire; and eventually the three divisions of Pegu, Arakan, and Tenasserim were formed into the province of British Burma. Annexation of Pegu.

The annexation of the Punjab and Burma are the crowning events of the nineteenth century. Lord Wellesley had delivered India from Tippu, and established the paramount power of the East India Company over the Mogul viceroys and the Mahratta princes. Lord Hastings had converted Nipal into a staunch ally, and stamped out the predatory powers of Central India. Lord Dalhousie annexed the empire of Runjeet Singh, excepting Cashmere, and the empire of the Alompras, excepting Upper Burma, and thus laid down frontiers which remained unchanged for an entire generation.[1] New frontiers of British Empire.

[1] As these pages are passing through the press Upper Burma has been annexed to the British empire. In 1870 the author was sent by the British government on a semi-political mission to Mandalay and Bhamo. In those days the reigning king respected British supremacy, and British representatives were maintained at the capital and the frontier. These political ties were subsequently loosened, and annexation became a state

CHAP. IV.

Lord Dalhousie as an administrator. Progressive policy.

§ 10. But Lord Dalhousie left his mark in history as an administrator rather than as a conqueror. Having annexed the Punjab and Pegu, he threw his whole soul into the administration. The Punjab was soon traversed with roads like a Roman province, and one magnificent and difficult road was completed from Lahore to Peshawar. Rangoon was cleared of malarious jungle, and planned out in streets and roads like a European city. The working of British administration in the new provinces has been most successful. Lord Dalhouise not only delivered the population from oppression and violence, but introduced order, liberty, and law, such as prevails in no Oriental country outside the British pale from the Atlantic Ocean to the Chinese Seas. Lord Dalhousie may have petted the Punjab and Pegu at the expense of Madras and Bombay, but he was never unmindful of the interests of the Anglo-Indian empire. He is the first Governor-General who laboured for the benefit of India in the interests of the British nation, as well as in those of the East India Company.

Public works of the East India Company.

Public works in India before the advent of Lord Dalhousie had chiefly consisted of military and civil buildings, such as barracks, arsenals, jails, and hospitals. The Company, however, was the landlord of India, and the bulk of the people were its tenants; it had therefore sought to improve the condition of its tenants after the manner of land-

necessity. Like most of the Buddhist kings of Burma, Theebaw was a professed water drinker, but much given to strong liquors, in which state he committed the most revolting cruelties. Similar horrors are related of the old kings of Burma in the author's *Short History of India, Afghanistan, Nepal, and Burma*, chap. xv.

lords. It encouraged the cultivation of tea, coffee, and cotton. It restored choked-up channels, which had been dug by Mohammedan Sultans of former days for watering their palaces, gardens, and hunting grounds; and it converted them into canals for irrigating a large acreage in the North-West Provinces. Such was the origin of the Western and Eastern Jumna canals, which were constructed in the days of Lord William Bentinck and Lord Auckland. Each canal received the water from the upper stream on the slope of the Himalayas, and irrigated the high lands which were above the level of the lower stream. Above all, the Company sanctioned the Ganges canal which was purely a British undertaking, constructed for navigation as well as for irrigation.

Northern India: old caravan routes.

But India was without roads. Rough caravan routes traversed Northern India in the seventeenth century, and European travellers landing at Surat could find their way to Ajmere, Agra, and Delhi. From Delhi again there was a caravan route through the Punjab and Afghanistan to Persia and Turkistan. But in the eighteenth century all were closed. Rajput rebels and outlaws stopped all travelling between Surat and Agra; the Jhat brigands of Bhurtpore stopped it between Bengal and Delhi; and Sihks and Afghans cut off all trade with Persia and Turkistan.

Water-ways.

In Northern India the ordinary route from Calcutta to the north-west was by water. The rivers Jumna and Ganges flow from the Himalayas in a south-easterly direction until they meet at Allahabad in the centre of Hindustan. The Jumna flows past Delhi and Agra; the Ganges flows past Cawnpore; and

CHAP. IV. after meeting at Allahabad, the two rivers flow in one united stream past Benares, Patna, Monghyr, and Calcutta, until they reach the Bay of Bengal. But travelling up country against the stream was always tedious, and a journey which formerly occupied months by water, now only occupies the same number of days by rail.

Deccan: no traffic. In the Deccan the routes were much worse. There was no traffic between Bombay and the Mahratta country until 1831, when Sir John Malcolm opened a cart-road through the western Ghats, and thus broke through the mountain wall which cut off Bombay from the interior. In the Nizam's country there were no roads except a rough route between Hyderabad and the seaport at Masulipatam, which was cursed by every British Resident from the days of Clive and Verelst down to very modern times.

Southern India: palanquins. In Southern India there were neither caravan routes nor waterways of any moment. Hindu Rajas never opened out the country like the Mohammedans of Northern India. Hindu infantry and light Mahratta horsemen required no roads; and Rajas and other Hindu grandees were carried in palanquins. Europeans travelled in palanquins down to the present generation, and were in no fear of robbers. Ladies and children were borne along through jungles and over rivers; leopards and tigers were kept off at night by lighted torches; and the sure feet of the half-naked coolies carried travellers safely over rocky heights and troubled waters.

Macadamised roads. Mr. Thomason, who was Lieutenant-Governor of the North-West Provinces from 1843 to 1853, was the first Bengal administrator who constructed macadamised roads. His object was to connect the large cities under his jurisdiction, but the work once begun soon advanced apace. A trunk road was commenced between Calcutta and Delhi, and in 1850 mail carts ran for the first time between the two capitals of Northern India. The annexation of the Punjab gave a further impetus to road-making, and Calcutta and Delhi were soon brought into communication with Lahore and Peshawar. CHAP. IV.

Proposed railways.

Meanwhile railways had created a furor. Promoters in the British Isles were anxious to construct railways in India at the expense of the East India Company, but the idea did not recommend itself to the men who had the largest experience of India. There was a natural reluctance to accept schemes by which speculators might profit at the Company's expense, whilst the gain to the people of India would be doubtful. It was currently believed, by men who had spent the best part of their lives in the country, that Hindus would never travel by railway; that they would trudge on foot, and carry their families and goods in carts and cars, as they had done in the days of Porus and Megasthenes.

Lord Dalhousie, a new type of Indian statesmen.

§11. Lord Dalhousie was the type of British administrators of the modern school. He had served two years' apprenticeship in Great Britain as President of the Board of Trade under Sir Robert Peel, and he was especially familiar with the construction of British roads and railways. In India he opened the great trunk road from Calcutta to Delhi, and post carriages, known as "dak gharies," soon superseded the old river "budgerows." Other metalled roads were begun in Madras and Bombay. Still one thing was wanting. Calcutta was united to all the great

CHAP. IV. capitals of Northern India—Allahabad, Agra, and Delhi—but Bombay and Madras were as far off as ever from both Northern India and each other.

Trunk railway lines. Railways would remedy the evil, and Lord Dalhousie was bent on introducing them. He planned a trunk system which in the present day unites the three Presidencies, and connects them with the north-west frontier. He induced railway companies to undertake the construction, by giving a government guarantee of five per cent. interest per annum on the outlay; and before he left India three experimental lines were already in progress, namely, one from Calcutta, a second from Bombay, and a third from Madras. Such was the origin of the three great railways of India, namely, the "East Indian," which runs through Northern India; the "Great Indian Peninsula," which runs through the Deccan; and the "Madras railway," which runs through Southern India.

Telegraph system, 1853–55. Between 1853 and 1855 the telegraph system was constructed, which electrified Europeans and awakened the Asiatics from the torpor of ages. Madras and Bombay could talk with all the great cities of Northern India, and Rangoon was placed in telegraphic communication with Lahore and Peshawar. Unfortunately there was only one line of wires from Allahabad to Delhi, and when the wires were cut by the sepoy mutineers of 1857, communication was cut off. This incident, however, belongs to the *régime* of Lord Dalhousie's successor.

Ganges canal, 1854. In 1854 the Ganges canal, the greatest work of irrigation ever accomplished, was completed by Sir Proby Cautley and opened by Lord Dalhousie. The British nation has never realised this grand undertaking of the old East India Company. It receives the water on the lower slope of the Himalayas, and runs along the Doab, or high lands between the Jumna and Ganges, throwing out distributaries at intervals. About eighty miles to the south-east of Delhi it separates into two branches, one flowing into the Ganges at Cawnpore, and the other flowing into the Jumna near Etawah. The whole length of the canal and branches for navigation is 614 miles; the length of the distributaries for irrigation is 3,111 miles. CHAP. IV.

Annexation policy.

§ 12. Lord Dalhousie was so convinced of the superiority of British administration, that he considered every opportunity should be taken for bringing the territories of feudatory princes under British rule. Hitherto it had been the policy of the East India Company to perpetuate the dynasties of its feudatories. If a feudatory prince was without a son, he was advised by the British Resident to adopt one. But Hindu princes shrink from the idea of adopting a son. It is often as difficult to persuade a Raja to adopt as it used to be to persuade Englishmen to make wills. He puts it off with some vague intention of marrying another wife, which he is permitted to do under Hindu law when the first wife is barren. Accordingly Hindu princes often die without leaving any son whatever, real or adopted. Under such circumstances the widow was permitted to adopt a boy, and the East India Company permitted this boy to succeed to the principality.

Question of adoption.

Adoption, however, is purely a religious ceremonial. It is the outcome of the religious belief of the Hindus that when a man dies his soul goes to a sort of

CHAP. IV. purgatory until his sins are washed away; and that during this interval it is the duty of a son, real or adopted, to offer cakes and water to refresh the soul in question. The East India Company accepted the adoption as giving a claim to the principality, because it settled the succession when a natural heir was wanting. Lord Dalhousie decided that the adoption gave no claim to the principality, but only to the personal property of the deceased feudatory, because he was anxious to bring the territory under British administration.

Satara and Nagpore. The Court of Directors refused to accept the views of Lord Dalhousie in the case of "protected allies," such as Sindia, Holkar, and the princes of Rajputana. But they accepted his views as regards "dependent principalities," such as Satara and Nagpore, which had been created, or artificially resuscitated, by the Marquis of Hastings, and in which the Hindu rulers had turned out very badly. Accordingly, Nagpore and Satara became British territory, and were brought under British administration.

Jhansi in Bundelkund. A chiefship in Bundelkund, known as Jhansi, was also annexed to the British empire. The chiefs and princes of Bundelkund were situated far away to the south of the river Jumna. They were cut off by hills and jungles from the civilising influences of British rule, and retained much of the lawlessness and anarchy of the eighteenth century. The chief of Jhansi died without leaving any heir, real or adopted. The widow was allowed to adopt a son for the offering of cakes and water, but not allowed to adopt a successor to the principality, and the territory accordingly lapsed to the British government, and was brought under British administration. The widow was very angry.

She had expected to rule Jhansi as queen regent; but a Hindu lady brought up in the seclusion of a zenana cannot always be trusted with the irresponsible powers of a despot. She yielded to her fate, but it will be seen hereafter that she bottled up her wrath and waited for revenge.

Obsolete controversy.

Since Lord Dalhousie's time the controversy as regards adoption has become obsolete. The right of adopting a son, who should not only offer cakes and water to the soul of the deceased, but succeed him in the government of the principality, has been distinctly recognised by the British government. Meanwhile the aspect of the question has entirely changed. In the days of Lord Dalhousie few, if any, of the Indian feudatories of the British government showed any signs of progress. In the present day the heirs to principalities are taught in schools and colleges, and are learning something of India and the great world around them by the help of railways and telegraphs. It is therefore to be hoped that a day may yet dawn when British systems of administration may be worked in every feudatory state in India by trained Asiatic officials.

Exceptional annexation of Oudh.

Last of all, Lord Dalhousie annexed the Mohammedan kingdom of Oudh to the British empire. This was an exceptional measure, having nothing whatever to do with the Hindu usage of adoption. The Nawab of Oudh had assumed the title of "king," but had degenerated under British protection into an Oriental ruler of the worst possible type. His kingdom was parcelled out amongst a landed aristocracy, known as talukdars, who were half landlords and half revenue collectors, like the zemindars of Bengal. Every talukdar of position had a fortress of his own, with

CHAP. IV. a garrison and guns. He collected rents from the ryots, but paid little or no revenue to the king's officers, unless compelled by force of arms. The king lived secluded in his palaces at Lucknow, surrounded by greedy and corrupt officials, immersed in Oriental pleasures, ignorant of what was going on outside his capital, yet maintaining a rabble army, which was either in mutiny for want of pay, or plundering the villages for bare necessaries. A British Resident was appointed to Lucknow, but he could only interfere by way of advice, remonstrance, or warning. A British force was stationed in Oudh, under the direction of the Resident, but only for the maintenance of the public peace, and not for interference in the administration. Deposition of the king would have done no manner of good, for there was not a prince of the family capable of governing the country in his room. It was thus impossible to maintain the dynasty without sacrificing the interests of ten millions of population whom the British government was bound to protect. At last, in 1856, the territory of Oudh was annexed to the British empire, and brought under British administration.

India Bill of 1853: new Civil Service.

§ 13. In 1853 the last charter of the East India Company, which had been granted in 1833 for a term of twenty years, was brought to a close. Parliament refused to renew the charter, but declined as yet to abolish the Company, and meanwhile carried out some constitutional changes. It placed the Indian civil service on a national basis, by abolishing the system of nomination by the Court of Directors, and introducing the system of competitive examinations, which was eventually thrown open to all British subjects—Asiatic as well as European. CHAP. IV.

New Legislative Council.

In like manner Parliament broadened the supreme government of India by creating a new legislative council. The Governor-General in Council continued to exercise supreme control over the executive. At the same time this executive council was formed into a legislative council by the addition of representative members; namely, the chief justice and one puisne judge of the Supreme Court at Calcutta, and one representative member from each of the four presidencies, namely, Madras, Bombay, Bengal, and the North-West Provinces.

Constitutional germ.

§ 14. The legislative council was opened in 1854. It was the first germ of representative government in India. Lord Dalhousie introduced parliamentary forms, and the debates were conducted with a spirit which recommended them to the attention of the Indian public, official and non-official, Asiatic and European. The Governor-General and executive council exercised a veto on the introduction of bills. But four Indian civilians represented the governments of four presidencies, and the judges of the Supreme Court represented, more or less, the interests of the public outside official circles. Moreover, although the Asiatic populations had no voice in the debates, they were enabled to express their objections in the form of petitions, which were duly considered by the committees of the council on the several bills. In a word, the legislative council of India, imperfect as it may have been, was an advance in the development of constitutional

CHAP. IV. government of India, and will accordingly be brought under review in the concluding chapter.

Macaulay and the Penal Code. The new legislative council brought to light Lord Macaulay's draft of a Penal Code, which had been shelved for nearly twenty years. The delay, however, had not been without its advantages. Mr. (now Sir Barnes) Peacock, took charge of the bill under which the Code became law, and subjected its clauses to a careful revision. Moreover, the representative civilians from the four presidencies, and two judges of the Supreme Court at Calcutta, had opportunities for discussing any or every clause from local and imperial points of view, which could scarcely fail to adapt the Penal Code to all parts of British India.

Characteristics of the Code. The Penal Code had evidently been drafted in Lord Macaulay's best style. It was eminently clear and concise, free from redundancies and repetitions, and singularly happy in the definitions of offences and law terms. It embodies illustrations, as well as explanations, of every conceivable offence known to criminal law. Consequently, no educated individual, Asiatic or European, who refers to the Penal Code, can possibly make any mistake as regards the criminal law in British India. It did not, however, take effect until 1860. Meanwhile events transpired which opened up an entirely new era in the progress of Great Britain as an Asiatic power.

Lord Dalhousie leaves India, 1856. § 15. In 1856 Lord Dalhousie left India for ever. He had alarmed Anglo-Indians of the old school by his energetic promotion of moral and material progress without regard to the ignorance or prejudices of the Asiatic populations; but besides his grander measures, he carried out a thousand and one smaller reforms which to this day are felt and appreciated by Asiatics as well as by Europeans. It was Lord Dalhousie who introduced cheap postage; who caused Calcutta to be lit with gas; who purified the south-west breezes of fever and malaria by clearing the jungles of the Sunderbunds; who sat by the cradle of the new legislative council of 1854, and thus nourished the earliest germ of representative government which British rule had planted in India. In a word, Lord Dalhousie prepared the way for that great measure which will be told in a future chapter, namely, the transfer of the government of India from the East India Company to the British Crown. CHAP. IV.

§ 16. Lord Canning succeeded Lord Dalhousie in 1856. To all outward appearance there was no cause for alarm in any part of India. Persia had again laid siege to Herat, as she had done in 1837; but the British government had come to an understanding with old Dost Mohammed of Cabul, and had given him money and arms. A mission was sent to Candahar under Major (now Sir Peter) Lumsden. A British expedition was sent to the Persian Gulf under Sir James Outram, and captured Bushire. Eventually Persia withdrew her pretensions as regards Herat, and peace was concluded in March, 1857. Lord Canning, 1856–62. War with Persia, 1856–7.

Meanwhile the status of the so-called king of Delhi, the relic of the Great Mogul, was under consideration. For more than half a century the family had lived in a palace at Delhi on a yearly pension from the British government. There was much marrying and giving in marriage, and the Status of the "king" at Delhi.

CHAP. IV.

Proposed removal from Delhi.

palace was a hive of princes and princesses without any apparent occupation save that of petitioning for increased pensions. Lord Ellenborough contemplated removing the family from Delhi, but the measure was postponed. At last Lord Dalhousie took action. The so-called king was very old, and could not live many years. Lord Dalhousie recognised a grandson as successor to the pageant throne, on the condition that when the old king died, the whole family should clear out of Delhi and take up their abode in a royal residence some miles off, known as the Kutub.

Palace intrigues.

This design was frustrated. The old king had married a young wife, and she had a son, and she determined that her son should be king. The grandson, who had been recognised by Lord Dalhousie, died suddenly; it was said that she had poisoned him. Lord Canning ignored her son, and recognised a brother of the dead prince as heir to the title, on the same conditions. Henceforth the queen, like the princess of Jhansi, bottled up her wrath and waited for revenge.

Land settlement in Oudh.

Lord Canning, however, was somewhat uneasy about Oudh. A British administration had been introduced under a chief commissioner, with commissioners of divisions and deputy commissioners of districts, but nothing was done to reconcile the talukdars in the provinces to the change of rule. On the contrary, a land settlement was introduced corresponding to that which had been effected in the North-West Provinces. But half a century had elapsed since the acquisition of the North-West Provinces. Meanwhile the talukdars of Oudh had ceased to be mere middle men, and had grown into landed proprietors; whilst the rights of village proprietors, individual or joint, had been ignored or stamped out by the new landlords.

Disaffection of talukdars.

The early British administrators settled the revenue direct with the villagers, and told the talukdars that their claims to proprietorship, if they had any, would be considered hereafter, or might be settled in the law courts. Under such cool treatment the talukdars of Oudh might well be disaffected towards their new British rulers. Rightly or wrongly, by long possession, or by recent usurpation, they had become *de facto* landlords, and under the new system they saw their estates transferred to their tenants. Early in 1857, however, Sir Henry Lawrence was appointed chief commissioner of Oudh, and he was expected to reconcile all parties.

Imagined wrongs of Oudh villagers.

Strange to say, the villagers of Oudh, who had profited so much by the new land settlement, had a secret grievance of their own which no one seems to have suspected. They held their lands on better terms than their fathers or grandfathers, but many families had lost position in the eyes of their neighbours. For generations Oudh had been the chief recruiting ground for the Asiatic soldiery of the Bengal army; and under Mohammedan rule every sepoy was the great man of his family, and indeed the patron of his native village. If any villager had a grievance, he applied to the sepoy, and the sepoy applied to his British officer, and his petition was forwarded to the British Resident at Lucknow; and the Mohammedan court was too anxious to please the Resident to make any difficulty about redressing wrongs so strongly supported, whatever might have been the abstract merits of the case. When, however, the king was replaced by a chief

CHAP. IV. commissioner, the sepoy was referred to a British courts for justice, and was no better off than his neighbours. This loss of privilege and prestige rankled in the heart of sepoys from Oudh, and they began to look upon annexation as a wrong done to themselves, although they had not, and could not have, any sympathies for the deposed king.

Coming catastrophe. Such was the state of affairs in India when the storm of 1857 was about to burst upon Hindustan, which was to shake British power in Northern India to its very foundations, and sweep away the East India Company for ever. The outbreak was hardly felt in the older presidencies of Bengal, Madras, or Bombay, nor in the Punjab or Pegu, nor in Nagpore or Satara, the provinces recently annexed without conquest, nor, with few exceptions, in the feudatory states under British suzerainty. The main fury of the storm was spent on Oudh and the North-West Provinces; and the significance of this localisation will appear in the after history.

CHAPTER V.

SEPOY REVOLT: BENGAL, DELHI, PUNJAB.

1857.

§ 1. European soldiers and Asiatic sepoys. § 2. Three British armies in India: Bengal, Bombay, and Madras. § 3. Sepoy army of Bengal: Brahmans and Rajputs. § 4. Enfield cartridges: general horror of pork: Hindu worship of the cow. § 5. Agitation of the sepoys at Barrackpore. § 6. First mutiny against the cartridges: Berhampore. § 7. Second mutiny: Barrackpore. § 8. Oudh: mutiny at Lucknow: suppressed. § 9. Mutiny and massacre at Meerut. § 10. Mohammedan revolt and massacre at Delhi: general excitement. § 11. British advance from the Punjab to Delhi. § 12. Siege of Delhi by Europeans, Sikhs, and Ghorkas. § 13. Punjab and John Lawrence: antagonism between Sikhs and Mohammedans. § 14. Sepoy plots at Lahore and Mian Mir: quashed. § 15. Peshawar and frontier mountain tribes. § 16. Execution of sepoy mutineers at Peshawar. § 17. Brigadier John Nicholson: worshipped by a Sikh brotherhood. § 18. Proposed withdrawal from Peshawar. § 19. Mutiny at Sealkote: wholesale executions. § 20. Siege and storm of Delhi, September 1857: peace in the North-West.

CHAP. V.

Military rule in India.

It is a common saying that "India is held by the sword;" but the phrase is misleading, and in one direction it is absolutely untrue. The British army is not maintained to rivet a foreign yoke on the subject populations. Its main duty has been to keep the peace between rival princes, to put down fighting between antagonistic religions, and to protect India against foreign aggression.

Paucity of European troops.

§ 1. The small number of European troops in 1857 proves that India was free. In the Bengal provinces, which cover a larger area than Great Britain and

Ireland, and a denser population, there were scarcely any European troops. A single regiment sufficed to garrison Calcutta; and of this regiment one wing was quartered in Fort William within the city, whilst the other wing was quartered in Dumdum arsenal, seven miles off. With this exception, there were no European troops within 400 miles of Calcutta. One European regiment was quartered at Dinapore, to the westward of Patna, and another at Rangoon, in the newly-acquired province of Pegu. There was also a European regiment at Lucknow in Oudh, and two European regiments at Meerut in the North-West Provinces, about forty miles from Delhi, and a thousand miles from Calcutta. But the bulk of the European regiments in India were quartered in the Punjab, the frontier province on the north-west. This frontier is the only vulnerable side of India. It faces Afghanistan; but it also faces a possible combination of European and Asiatic powers, which may some day menace the British empire in India.

Sepoys or Asiatics.

The army of the East India Company was mainly composed of native soldiers, known as sepoys. The term "native," however, is equivocal, and sepoys are best called Asiatics, to distinguish them from British soldiers, who are known in India as Europeans. They were formed into regiments corresponding to European battalions, and were drilled and commanded by European officers corresponding to regimental officers in Her Majesty's army. Each regiment had also an Asiatic staff of sepoy officers, known as naiks, havildars, jemadars, and subahdars—corresponding to corporals, sergeants, lieutenants, and captains. Such regiments were known as "regulars."

In 1857 the regular army of the East India

Company comprised in round numbers about 200,000 Asiatics, commanded by 4,000 European officers, and about 45,000 British-born soldiers. But the European regiments were not all taken from Her Majesty's service. The East India Company had enlisted nine European regiments for exclusive service in India, who were known as Fusiliers and Locals. Moreover, in addition to the regular sepoys, there were battalions known as irregulars, because they had fewer regimental European officers. They were raised specially for service in particular provinces, and also for service in the contingent and subsidiary forces maintained by feudatory states under existing treaties.

Army strength.

The sepoy army had been the pride and glory of the East India Company for more than a hundred years. It won its first laurels in the old wars against the French in Southern India; and from the battle of Plassy in 1757, to the dawn of 1857, it had shared the triumph of the British army in building up the Anglo-Indian empire. For perfection of discipline, and fidelity to their European officers, the sepoys might for many years have been favourably compared with the soldiers of any continental army. Hindus and Mohammedans fought side by side with Europeans, and one and all were bound together by that brotherhood in arms, which grows up between soldiers of all races and climes who have been under fire together in the same campaign.

Tried fidelity.

On the parade-ground and on the battle-field all differences of race, caste, and religion were for the moment forgotten. Together, sepoys and soldiers fought, not only against the French, but against Nawabs and Sultans who were Mohammedans, and

No religious distinctions.

CHAP. V. against Mahrattas and Rajas who were Hindus. Together, they had crossed the Indus and the Sutlej to fight against Afghans and Sikhs; climbed the shelves and precipices of the Himalayas to punish the aggressions of the Ghorkas of Nipal; and ascended the waters of the Irrawaddy to chastise the arrogance of Burmese kings. When the sepoys were called out by the British magistrate to repress riots between Hindus and Mohammedans, they put their religion into their pockets and fired with the utmost impartiality on both parties, although in their hearts they must have sympathised with one side or the other. But the pride of the sepoy, whether Hindu or Mohammedan, was to be "faithful to his salt"—in other words, to be loyal to the master from whom he drew his pay.

Sepoy ways.

But sepoys have ways of their own which Europeans cannot always understand, unless they have served with them shoulder to shoulder, and listened patiently and considerately to the outpourings of their grievances. A sepoy is proud of his corps, jealous for its reputation, and respectful to his officers. Hindus of the higher castes, such as Brahmans and Rajputs, and Mohammedans of noble and ancient families, are alike amenable to British discipline. But sepoys can be stung to insubordination by insult or injustice, like soldiers of other races. Sepoys have been known to sacrifice caste prejudices to help European officers in time of need, but they resented needless interference or looks of scorn with the sullen pride of Orientals. At Vellore, in 1806, the Madras sepoys were driven to mutiny by the contemptuous orders of the military authorities as regards caste marks and turbans, and above all by the jeers of the

Mysore princes, who taunted them with becoming Christians. Yet during the first Cabul war and other distant campaigns, sepoys often forgot their caste in cases of emergency, and cheerfully obeyed orders which they would have resented in their own country, or in the presence of inconvenient witnesses. CHAP. V.

Mutiny at loss of batta.

Injustice again, real or imagined, is as intolerable to sepoys as it is to children. More than once a regiment has been deprived of batta, or field allowances, under circumstances which kindled a burning sense of wrong. This batta is given during service in foreign territory, but is withdrawn after the return of the sepoys to British territory. Thus, sepoys who had borne the brunt of the wars in Sind and the Punjab, were suddenly deprived of batta when those countries became British provinces, and naturally rebelled against what must have appeared to them a crying injustice. The sepoy complained that he had helped to conquer Sind for the East India Company, and was then punished by the loss of batta. The paymaster pointed to the regulations, but the result was disaffection amounting to mutiny.

Disbandment.

Under such circumstances there was no alternative but disbandment. There can be no pardon for mutineers, yet capital punishment, or even a long term of imprisonment, would be needlessly severe in dealing with ignorant sepoys. As it was, their doom was terrible in the eyes of their fellows. In a moment they were deprived of all hope of pension, which secured to every sepoy, a life provision in his native village when age or infirmity compelled him to retire from the army.

CHAP. V.

Three armies: Bengal, or Northern India.

§ 2. The Company's regular forces in India were formed into three distinct armies, namely, those of Bengal, Madras, and Bombay, and each army had its own commander-in-chief. The armies of Madras and Bombay were mostly recruited in their respective presidencies; but the people of Bengal are not a fighting race, and the Bengal army was mostly recruited from the warlike populations of Oudh and the North-West Provinces. Again the Bengal army was not kept within the limits of the Bengal presidency, but was distributed over the whole of Northern India as far as the north-west frontier. It was consequently larger than the two other armies put together. It garrisoned Bengal, the North-West Provinces, and the newly-acquired provinces of Oudh and the Punjab; whilst it overlooked, more or less, the Asiatic states to the south and west of the Jumna, including the principalities and chiefships of Rajputana, the territories of Sindia and Holkar, and the smaller domains of a host of minor feudatories.

Bombay in the Deccan; Madras in the South.

The Bombay army garrisoned the Western Deccan and Sind, and the Madras army garrisoned Southern India and Pegu; but neither of these armies played any prominent part in the great sepoy revolt of 1857-58. Some disaffection was shown in the Bombay army which was nearest to the Bengal sepoys, and caught something of the contagion. The Madras army was for the most part still further south; and only one regiment caught the infection, and was promptly disbanded.

Hindus in Bengal army.

§ 3. The sepoy army of Bengal was mainly composed of Hindus. Taking the average strength of every regiment at 1,000 sepoys, there would be 800

Hindus and 200 Mohammedans; and the antagonism between the two religions was supposed to secure an additional safeguard against mutiny or disaffection. CHAP. V.

High castes: Brahmans and Rajputs.

High caste was the main characteristic of the Hindu sepoys in the Bengal army. Of the 800 Hindus in every regiment, about 400 were Brahmans, the sacred caste of India, who claim to be gods, and are supposed to be endowed with supernatural powers. Next to the Brahmans were about 200 Rajputs, the royal caste of India, who claim to be "sons of Rajas," and are soldiers by birth as well as calling. The remaining 200 Hindus were men of low caste, who were regarded as inferior beings. The Brahmans were powerful over all, and were worshipped by the Rajputs as well as by the low castes.

Discipline and caste.

Pride of caste was thus the moving spirit of the Bengal army. This, however, was not perceptible on the parade ground or field of battle, except in the lofty mien, haughty bearing, and splendid physique of the men. The Bengal sepoys were taller on the average than any European armies, excepting perhaps the Russian guard.[1] On duty the Brahman and Rajput obeyed the word of command when given by a low caste sepoy officer. Off duty, the low caste sepoy officer prostrated himself in token of worship before the Brahman soldier under his command.

Growing insubordination of the Bengal sepoys.

But pride of caste had its disadvantages, and for years the Bengal sepoys had displayed a laxity of discipline, and a spirit of insubordination towards their European officers, which had been unknown

[1] *English and India*, by M. E. de Valbezen, late Consul-General at Calcutta, Minister Plenipotentiary.

CHAP. V. in the older days. They had been pampered and humoured to an extent which diminished their efficiency, and many officers of experience lamented the change. But any report to that effect was naturally offensive to the higher military authorities; and those who were most alive to the growing evil found that it was best for their own interests to keep their opinion to themselves.

Calcutta, Dumdum, Barrackpore, Berhampore.

It has been seen that Calcutta was garrisoned by a single regiment of Europeans, one wing being quartered in Fort William and the other in the arsenal at Dumdum, about seven miles off. Nine miles north of Dumdum, and sixteen miles north of Calcutta, is the pleasant station of Barrackpore, where the Governor-General has a park and country mansion, and where four sepoy regiments were cantoned with their European officers, but without European troops. About 100 miles still further north is the station of Berhampore, hard by the old capital of Murshedabad; and here a regiment of sepoy infantry was posted, with half a regiment of sepoy cavalry and a battery of sepoy artillery.

Sepoy huts and lines.

A sepoy regiment in the Bengal army was cantoned in ten rows of huts, a company of 100 sepoys in each row. The arms and ammunition of each company were kept in a circular magazine in the front of each line. The European officers, with or without wives and families, lived round about in one-storied houses with thatched roofs, known as bungalows. The European officers rarely visited the sepoy lines during the heat of the day, but two European sergeants were appointed to each regiment to lodge close to the lines and report all that was going on.

Enfield rifle: musketry schools at Dumdum, Meerut, and Sealkote

§ 4. In 1856 the Russian war was over, and the Enfield rifle, which had been used with such success in the Crimea, was introduced into India. Accordingly three musketry schools were established in Northern India for teaching the sepoys of the Bengal army the use of the new rifle. One school was established at Dumdum for the instruction of the sepoys in the Bengal presidency; another at Meerut, forty miles from Delhi, for those in the North-Western Provinces; and the third at Sealkote for those in the Punjab. Under this arrangement, detachments from the different regiments were to be sent from time to time to one or other of these schools until the whole Bengal army was familiar with the use of the Enfield. It will be seen hereafter that the three most dangerous mutinies in India grew out of these musketry schools.

Greased cartridges.

In those days every sepoy and soldier had been accustomed for generations to bite off the end of his paper cartridge before loading his musket. Accordingly a supply of cartridges for the new rifle was received from England, and forwarded to each of the three schools, and further supplies of the same pattern were manufactured in the arsenal at Dumdum by low-caste workmen known as Lascars. Suddenly it leaked out that the new cartridges were greased with the fat of cows, or with the fat of pigs. Thus every Hindu sepoy who bit the cartridge would lose his caste and religion as if he had eaten beef; whilst every Mohammedan sepoy would be polluted by contact with pork, and not only lose his religion, but be barred out for ever from the heaven of celestial houris.

A Lascar employed in Dumdum arsenal met a

CHAP. V. Brahman sepoy going to Barrackpore, and asked him for a drink of water out of his brass lotah. This was an unusual request, intended to vex and annoy the Brahman. A thirsty low-caste Hindu might ask a high-caste man to pour water into his mouth, but would not offend the Brahman by the bare suggestion of drinking out of his lotah. The Brahman turned away in disgust at the idea of low-caste lips polluting his drinking-cup. The Lascar retorted that the Brahman would soon be as impure as himself, for he would bite the new cartridges which had been smeared with the fat of cows and pigs, and would lose caste altogether.

Discovery at Dumdum.

Horror of Hindus and Mohammedans.

The Brahman was thunderstruck at this taunt. Europeans who have never visited India can scarcely realise the horrors that must have seized on his Brahmanised imagination. Suet and lard are such familiar ingredients in European cookery, that no one in the British Isles could have been surprised at their being used for greasing Enfield cartridges. But to Europeans that have lived in India, the bare fact that cartridges should have been greased with suet or lard, to be bitten by Hindu or Mohammedan sepoys, seems a mad freak of fortune which is altogether incomprehensible. In the fierce antagonism between the two religions, Hindus have thrown dead pigs into Mohammedan mosques, and Mohammedans have thrown slaughtered cows into Hindu temples ; but the British government stood on neutral ground. It had always professed to hold an even balance between the two religionists, and any attempt to destroy the caste of Hindus, or the religion of Mohammedans, was altogether foreign to the ideas of Asiatics or Europeans.

Pigs unclean.

It is easy to understand why both Hindus and Mohammedans regard swine as unclean. The Jews have had the same horror of pigs and pork from time immemorial. To this day, both Hindus and Mohammedans shudder, or affect to shudder, at the idea of Europeans cleaning their teeth with brushes made of bristles; and none but those of enlarged experiences, who have been Europeanised out of their religious prejudices, or smitten with a passion for European luxuries, would venture to eat a slice of ham.

Cow worship.

The cow is not more to Mohammedans than it is to Europeans, but the Hindus worship it as a deity. Gratitude for the milk and butter which she gives to the family has swelled into affection and adoration, which have invested a common-place animal with attributes that are at once mystic and divine. The cow is the living representative to the Hindu of all that is beautiful and spiritual in women, and of all that is mysterious in the sex. The cow is the incarnation of the earth, the mother of all things, the goddess of good fortune, the living manifestation of Lakshmi; she who was created by the gods, who descended from the heaven of Indra and churned the ocean, until the bright goddess rose out of the waves, like a Hindu Aphrodite, to become the wife of the supreme spirit, Vishnu. To kill a cow is a sacrilegious crime, like killing a Brahman, a woman, or a Raja. To taste the flesh of a cow is as revolting to the Hindu imagination as tasting the flesh of a mother.

Eating beef a mortal sin.

Eating or tasting beef through the most distant medium is a mortal sin in the eyes of Hindus. Under Hindu rule, when the caste system was enforced by village communities, the vile sinner was driven from

CHAP. V. his wife, family, kinsfolk, and village by the ban of Brahmanical excommunication. In the days of Mohammedan persecutions, thousands of Hindus were compelled to swallow shreds of beef by tyrants of the stamp of Tippu Sultan of Mysore, in order to force them to become Mohammedans. There was no way of escape. They had no alternative but to accept Islam, marry a Mohammedan wife, and enter a new life and career with a new home and surroundings.[1]

Excitement at Barrackpore.

§ 5. The ball set rolling from the arsenal at Dumdum soon assumed monstrous dimensions in the cantonment at Barrackpore. The sepoys blindly accepted the conclusion that Her Majesty the Queen and Lord Canning had arranged a secret scheme for converting them all to Christianity. The greased cartridges, they decided, must have been manufactured expressly to destroy their religion; to compel them to become Christians, and to eat beef and drink beer until they became as strong as Europeans, and were able to conquer Persia, Russia, and China. Wild fictions, the outcome of

[1] During the first Cabul war of 1839–42, Hindu sepoys were taken prisoners by the Afghans, and subjected to a similar process in order to convert them to Islam. But times had changed since the establishment of British supremacy. Money would expiate any spiritual crime, or purchase any pardon or privilege from the Brahmans. When the prisoners returned to India they received back pay from the British government for the whole term of their captivity. Accordingly, after a long series of abstruse calculations, the Brahmans discovered that this back pay would exactly meet the cost of expiation. But the sepoys refused the bait. They preferred keeping the back pay in their pockets, and remaining within the fold of Islam. What became of their Hindu wives and families is a mystery to this day.

Oriental imaginations which would not have imposed upon a European child, were greedily accepted and talked over as matters of fact, by the ignorant and credulous sepoys. India, it was said, was being bound in iron fetters by railway lines and telegraph wires; and now the poor sepoy was to be cut off from his countrymen and co-religionists, and to become the helpless vassal of his European masters, like the genii who are slaves to magicians and sorcerers.

Fruitless explanations.

These ridiculous stories soon reached the ears of the European officers. General Hearsey, who commanded the Calcutta division, assembled the sepoys on the parade ground at Barrackpore, and reminded them that the British government had never meddled with their religion or caste, and had heavily punished any European officer who had attempted to do so. But his words were thrown away; the brains of the sepoys were too heated, and their convictions too deeply rooted, to be explained away. For months they had been discussing the expedition sent from Bombay to the Persian Gulf to defeat the designs of Russia on Herat; and now there was to be a war with China. The general might say what he pleased, but the British government had obviously manufactured the greased cartridges to destroy the caste of the poor sepoys, to make them eat beef and drink beer until they were strong enough to conquer the world.

Secret incendiarism.

The sepoys at Barrackpore were bewildered and terrified. They were too afraid to speak, and began to set houses on fire. The suspicious telegraph office, the magic house at Barrackpore, was burnt down. Other buildings followed. The agitation was reported

CHAP. V. to the military authorities at Calcutta. The composition of the cartridge was explained to the sepoys. The drill was changed, and the sepoys were no longer required to bite the cartridge. But nothing would stop the panic. The sepoys argued with severe logic that if the cartridges had not been greased with the objectionable fat there would have been no occasion to change the drill. Eventually the issue of the greased cartridges was stopped altogether, but the sepoys were as suspicious as ever. As yet, however, there was no open mutiny at Barrackpore. Discipline was maintained with the usual strictness, and the word of command was obeyed without demur. Barrackpore was too near Calcutta, too near the stronghold of British supremacy which had controlled Bengal for a hundred years, for the sepoy as yet to dream of open mutiny.

Contagion at Berhampore.

§ 6. Matters were at this pass when a small guard of sepoys was sent on duty from Barrackpore to Berhampore, a hundred miles to the northward. Here, it will be remembered, was a regiment of sepoy infantry, half a regiment of sepoy cavalry, and a battery of sepoy artillery. The new arrivals from Barrackpore were duly feasted by their comrades of the sepoy infantry, and the whole story of the greased cartridges was told with all the latest embellishments of fiction.

Cartridges refused.

The next day, the 25th of February 1857, a parade for exercise with blank ammunition was ordered for the following morning. Blank cartridges were issued to the infantry of the same pattern that had been used for generations, but the sepoys refused to accept them. Colonel Mitchell was in command of the station, and threatened the men with court martial. Accordingly the sepoys took the cartridges in gloomy silence and returned to their lines. CHAP. V.

Mutiny.

In the middle of the night the regiment rose as one man; it was the 19th Native Infantry of the Bengal army. Every company seized arms and ammunition from its magazine, and then the whole regiment rushed out of the lines and shouted defiance. Colonel Mitchell had no European force to suppress the outbreak; nothing but half a regiment of sepoy cavalry and the sepoy battery, and it was extremely doubtful whether the men would fire on the mutineers. However he ordered out the cavalry and battery, and advanced with his European officers towards the infantry lines by the light of torches. As he approached there was a halt and a pause. Tanks of water were in the way, and horses and guns might have been lost in the darkness.

Hesitation.

Neither side wished to take action. The mutineers shrank, as yet, from firing on their European officers. The sepoys, under Colonel Mitchell, might have refused to fire. The whole cantonment might have joined in the mutiny, and the civil stations in the country round about would have been in sore peril. So there was a parley. The colonel pointed out to the mutineers the absurdity of their fears and the enormity of their offence, and conjured them to give up their arms and return to their lines. The mutineers, on their part, were not prepared to push matters to extremities. Their excitement had cooled down as they saw their European officers advancing with the Asiatic cavalry and artillery, whilst the lurid scenery was lit up by flaming torches. Accordingly it was arranged that they should return to their lines, and that the force advancing against them should return to their own quarters.

Alarm at Calcutta. The news of this unexpected outbreak at Berhampore naturally alarmed Lord Canning. He had much sympathy for the deluded and infatuated sepoys, but the mutiny could not be ignored. It was absolutely necessary to disband the regiment, but there was no European force to carry out the measure. Unless European soldiers were present, the sepoys might have resisted disbandment, and other sepoy regiments might have joined the mutineers. No soldiers could be spared from the European regiment which was quartered at Fort William and Dumdum. Accordingly steamers were sent to Burma to bring away the European regiment quartered at Rangoon.

Sepoy terrors. § 7. On the 20th March the European regiment from Rangoon entered the Hughly river. The 19th Native Infantry was marched from Berhampore to Barrackpore, knowing that it was to be disbanded. At Barrackpore the sepoys were in a ferment. They felt that they were to be coerced by the European soldiers. It was not forgotten that some thirty years before, a sepoy regiment at Barrackpore had refused to go to Burma unless paid double batta, and had been scattered by a volley of grape, and its number erased from the army list. Accordingly the sepoys at Barrackpore had good reason to fear that they might be mowed down by the artillery unless they accepted the greased cartridges.

Mungal Pandy. Of the four sepoy regiments at Barrackpore, the 34th Native Infantry had the greatest cause for alarm. It was the 34th that furnished the sepoy guard which played so much mischief at Berhampore; and the sepoys of the 34th openly expressed their sympathy with those of the 19th. About the end of March it was reported to Lieutenant Baugh, the Adjutant of the 34th, that the sepoys in his regiment were much excited, and that one of them, named Mungal Pandy, was marching through the lines with a loaded musket, calling on the sepoys to rise against their officers, and swearing to fire at the first European that appeared on the scene.

Assault on Lieut. Baugh.

Lieutenant Baugh at once put on his uniform, mounted his horse, and rode off to the parade ground with a pair of loaded pistols in his holsters. There was the quarter-guard of the regiment, consisting of twenty sepoys under the command of an Asiatic lieutenant, known as a jemadar. In front of the quarter-guard was the gun which fired the salutes at sunrise and noon. Mungal Pandy saw Baugh riding up, and got behind the gun, and deliberately fired at him. The horse was wounded and the rider was brought to the ground. Baugh, however, disengaged himself, snatched a pistol, and advanced on Mungal Pandy before the latter could reload his musket. Baugh fired and missed. At that moment Mungal Pandy rushed at him and cut him down with a sword.

Outbreak and suppression.

The European serjeant-major of the regiment had followed Baugh at a distance, and shouted to the quarter-guard to help their officer. But the sepoys sympathised with Mungal Pandy, and the jemadar forbade them to stir. The serjeant-major came up breathless, and attempted to seize Mungal Pandy, but he too was struck down. On this the jemadar advanced with his twenty sepoys, and began to strike Baugh and the serjeant-major with the butt

CHAP. V. ends of their muskets. At this moment a Mohammedan orderly, who had followed Baugh from his house, ran up and arrested Mungal Pandy just as he had reloaded his musket. He was followed by General Hearsey and other officers. The general drew a pistol from his belt and rode up to the quarter-guard, ordered the men to return to their post, and threatened to shoot with his own hands the first sepoy who disobeyed orders. By this bold action the regiment was overawed, and the storm cloud passed away just as it was about to burst upon the station.

Disbandment of 19th Native infantry.

Two days afterwards there was a solemn parade at Barrackpore. All the European force available was assembled on the ground, including the regiment from Rangoon and a wing and two batteries from Dumdum. The 19th Native Infantry was marched into Barrackpore, repentant and ashamed. They had petitioned for forgiveness, but there was no pardon for mutiny. The orders of Lord Canning were read aloud, setting forth their crime, exposing the absurdity of their fears, and ordering the disbandment. The men laid down their arms and marched away. The 19th Native Infantry had ceased to be.

Hesitation.

For some weeks the 34th Native Infantry was not disbanded. Mungal Pandy and the jemadar were tried, convicted, and hanged, but the plague of mutiny was not stayed. Not a sepoy would point out the men of the quarter-guard who assaulted the European officers. April, however, passed away, and nothing was done.

Disaffection in Oudh.

§ 8. Meanwhile there were unpleasant reports from Oudh. Sir Henry Lawrence, the new chief commissioner, was anxious to redress the wrongs of the Oudh talukdars, but was vexed by the mutinous spirit of the sepoys. He had a single regiment of Europeans and two batteries of European artillery. He had to deal with four sepoy regiments of the Bengal army—three of infantry, and one of cavalry. Worst of all, he had to deal with irregular regiments of sepoys, who had been in the service of the king of Oudh, but had been taken over by the East India Company. They retained their Asiatic officers, but were drilled and commanded by a limited number of European officers, and hence were termed irregulars. These Oudh irregulars sympathised with the regular Bengal sepoys, and were beginning to manifest a hostile spirit by refusing to accept the cartridges.

Sir Henry Lawrence Chief Commissioner.

In 1857 the province of Oudh was separated from the North-West Provinces by the river Ganges and the town of Cawnpore. The capital was at Lucknow, in the centre or heart of Oudh, about fifty-five miles to the north-east of Cawnpore. Sir Henry Lawrence, the chief commissioner, lived in a large mansion at Lucknow, which was known as the Residency. The city of Lucknow extends four miles along the right bank of the river Goomti, and all the principal buildings, including the royal palaces and gardens, and the Residency, are situated between the city and the river. On the opposite bank were the British cantonments; and two bridges over the river connected the city and Residency on the one bank with the cantonments on the opposite shore.

Mutiny at Lucknow.

On the afternoon of the 3rd of May a startling event occurred in the cantonments. Four sepoys of an irregular regiment entered the bungalow of the European adjutant. They were armed to the teeth, and they told him to prepare for death. They had come to kill him, they said, not because they disliked him, but because he was a European and a Feringhi. The adjutant was unarmed. He promptly replied that it was of no use to kill him, for that the mutiny would be suppressed, they would be hanged, and another adjutant would be appointed in his stead. The would-be murderers were struck by his words, and left the house without doing him any injury.

Suppression by Lawrence.

The news reached Sir Henry Lawrence in the evening, and he resolved to act at once. He crossed the river and called out the European forces and the four regiments of regular sepoys, and then advanced against the mutineers, whose lines were seven miles off. The rebels were taken by surprise; they could do nothing. They were ordered to form in front of their lines, and they obeyed. They saw cavalry and infantry, soldiers and sepoys, on either side, and a battery of eight guns in front. They were ordered to lay down their arms, and they did so. The port-fires of the artillery were lighted. The mutineers were seized with a panic, and cried out, "Do not fire!" They then rushed madly away. The ring-leaders and most of their followers were arrested that night by the Bengal sepoys, and were confined pending trial. It will be seen hereafter that within a single month, the very sepoy regiments that arrested the mutinous irregulars rose against their European officers. Meanwhile, however, the quick action of Sir Henry Lawrence prevented any premature explosion, and gave him the month to prepare against the possible contingency.

Next day the outbreak and suppression of the mutiny were telegraphed to Lord Canning at Calcutta.

Disbandment of 34th Native infantry.

He was delighted with the promptitude and prudence of Sir Henry Lawrence. He saw the necessity for taking some decided action at Barrackpore. The European officers of the 34th Native Infantry reported that the sepoys were disaffected, and that they themselves had lost all confidence in the men. Accordingly Lord Canning determined to disband the regiment. On the 6th of May, at early morning, the Europeans were once again drawn up on the parade ground. The 34th Native Infantry was disbanded as the 19th had been five weeks before, but, unlike the sepoys of the 19th, they showed no signs of contrition. Still, it was hoped that the disbandment of the 34th would put an end to the mutiny.

Sepoys and Europeans at Meerut.

§ 9. So far the agitation was the work of the greased cartridges in Dumdum arsenal. But there was a second school of musketry at Meerut in the North-West Provinces, a thousand miles from Calcutta and only forty miles from Delhi. The military cantonment at Meerut covered an area of five miles, and was the largest in India. At one end were the lines of three sepoy regiments, two of infantry and one of cavalry, whilst the bungalows of the European officers were scattered about. At the other end of the cantonment were the European barracks, in which a European force was quartered strong enough to have routed four times the number of sepoys. There was a regiment of Dragoon Guards, known as the Carabineers; a battalion of the 60th Rifles; two troops of horse artillery, and a light field battery. The European barracks were thus at a long distance from the sepoy cantonments, and the interval was occupied by shops, houses, and gardens.

CHAP. V.

Disaffection.

At Meerut there was to all appearance literally nothing to fear from the sepoys. The Europeans were all-powerful. Yet at Meerut the agitation against the greased cartridges was as uncontrollable as elsewhere. General Hewitt commanded the station, and he and the colonels of the sepoy regiments expostulated with the men on the absurdity of imagining that the British government had the slightest desire to interfere with their caste or religion. But their remonstrances were thrown away. Buildings were burnt down; the sepoys left off saluting their officers; and it was whispered that they had resolved never more to touch a single cartridge.

The test.

At last General Hewitt determined to bring the sepoys to the test in the presence of the European force, and, if necessary, to stop the contagion by condign punishment. The regiment of sepoy cavalry was selected. A parade of ninety men of the several squadrons was ordered for the morning of the 6th of May. The old cartridges were issued, the same which had been used for generations, but eighty-five men stood out and refused to handle them. The delinquents were arrested and tried by a court martial of sepoy officers. They were all convicted of mutiny; eighty were sentenced to imprisonment with hard labour for ten years, and the remaining five to a like imprisonment for six years. All were recommended to the mercy of General Hewitt, but the recommendation was ignored, and it was determined to carry out the sentence at once in accordance with orders received by telegram from Lord Canning.

Parade for punishment.

The mutineers were placed under a strong European guard, consisting of two companies of the 60th Rifles, and twenty-five men of the Carabineers. The parade for punishment was held at daybreak on Saturday the 9th of May. The three regiments of sepoys were drawn up to behold the disgrace of the delinquents; and the men of the sepoy cavalry also were brought out to look on the degradation of their comrades. The sepoys on parade must have felt their hearts burning within them, but they were powerless to save. The Carabineers and Rifles were on the ground, and were ordered to load and be ready. The batteries of artillery were in position, and received the same orders. The slightest movement of disaffection or revolt would have been followed by a terrible slaughter. Not a sepoy stirred from the ranks. The prisoners were brought on the ground, stripped of their uniforms and accoutrements, and put in irons. They were utterly broken in spirit. They put up their hands and cried for mercy, and were then led away, cursing their comrades for not coming to their rescue.

Folly and mischief.

Then followed an act of inconceivable folly. The eighty-five sepoys who had been kept for three days under a strong guard of European soldiers, were made over to the civil authorities, and lodged in the civil jail, only two miles from the sepoy cantonments, under the charge of Asiatic warders. The consequence was that the sepoys brooded over the fate of their comrades, and secretly determined on rescuing them from the jail, and murdering their European officers.

Sunday morning.

Strange to say, not an idea of danger seems to have crossed the minds of the British authorities at Meerut. The Europeans went to church on Sunday morning, lounged through the heat and languor of the day, and prepared for church in the evening. Meanwhile

CHAP. V. there had been agitation and excitement in the sepoy lines, but nothing to excite alarm. The native women of the bazaar taunted the sepoys of the cavalry with not having rescued their comrades, and that was all.

Mutiny and massacre. Suddenly, about five o'clock on that Sunday afternoon, the sepoys seized their arms and ammunition, and rushed out of their lines, with loud shouts and discharges of musketry. A detachment of sepoy cavalry galloped off to the jail, and liberated not only their eighty-five comrades, but all the other prisoners, 1,500 in number. The whole body then returned to the cantonment and joined the sepoys, who were burning down bungalows, and murdering every European they met, regardless of sex and age. Ladies riding in carriages, and officers driving in their buggies, who had left their homes without a suspicion of evil, were assaulted and fired at as they drove along. In a word, within a brief space of time the sepoy cantonments, and the roads round about, were a scene of riot, bloodshed, and outrage, which are beyond description. At last, fearing that the European soldiers would soon fall upon them, the whole mass of sepoys, the cavalry in front and the infantry straggling behind, rushed off to Delhi. The movement was only natural. Delhi was the only walled city in the North-West Provinces in which they could find a refuge. No European troops were quartered within the city or the suburbs; and a vast magazine of arms and ammunition was seated in the heart of the city, mostly in charge of Asiatics, who would doubtless open the gates at the first demand for surrender.

For a long time nothing was known at the European

barracks of the mutiny and murder that was going on in the sepoy cantonment. When the news arrived of the outbreak, there was much delay and confusion. The Rifles were paraded for church, and time was lost in serving out arms and cartridges. The Dragoons were put through a roll-call, and then lost their way amongst the houses and gardens between the European barracks and the sepoy lines. When the lines were reached, the sepoys had gone off to Delhi, and darkness was setting in. Had the Dragoons galloped after the sepoys, the mutiny might have been crushed, and there would have been no revolt at Delhi. Inaction.

But the military authorities at Meerut were unequal to the crisis. Nothing was thought of but the safety of the station. The Rifles and Dragoons were kept at Meerut to guard the treasury and barracks, whilst the sepoy mutineers were pushing on to Delhi to set up the old king—a Mohammedan prince, in whom the Hindu sepoys had no interest or concern. Messages, however, were sent to Brigadier Graves, who commanded the Delhi station, to tell him what had taken place at Meerut, but no Europeans whatever were sent to help him in the terrible extremity which awaited him. Heedlessness.

§ 10. All night the sepoy mutineers were running to Delhi; anxious only to escape from the vengeance of the Europeans. When and where they first began to cherish wild hopes of restoring the Mohammedan *régime*, and setting up the last representative of the Great Mogul, as the sovereign and Padishah of Hindustan, is a mystery to this day. One thing only is certain; the Hindu sepoys, who composed four-fifths of the mass of mutineers, could have had no Escape to Delhi.

CHAP. V. sympathy in the revolt of the Mohammedans, beyond providing for their own immediate safety against the wrath of the Europeans.

Mohammedan rule at Delhi.

Delhi, however, had been the capital of the Mohammedans of India when the Caliphs were still reigning at Bagdad; and Mohammedan Sultans and Padishahs had ruled Hindustan for centuries before the rise of British power. In 1857 the relics of Mohammedan dominion were still lingering at Delhi under the shadow of British supremacy. The last representative of the once famous Great Mogul was still living in the imperial palace at Delhi, a pensioner of the British government, but bearing the empty title of "king." The ruins in the neighbourhood of Delhi are monuments of the triumphs of Islam and the Koran, raised by warriors from Cabul and Bokhara, who were reverenced as Ghazis—as destroyers of idols and idolaters. Indeed, the pilgrim who still wanders amongst the palaces, mosques, mausoleums, towers, domes, archways, terraces, and gardens of Delhi, and the country round, may yet recall the days when the Hindus were a conquered people, and the Mohammedans were their oppressors and persecutors.

Sepoy garrison at Delhi.

In May, 1857, British power at Delhi was represented by three regiments of sepoy infantry, and a sepoy battery of artillery, under the command of Brigadier Graves. There were no European troops at Delhi, except the regimental officers and serjeants attached to each corps, and nine Europeans who had charge of the British magazine in the heart of the city, with a host of Asiatic subordinates. None of the sepoys had as yet shown any sign of disaffection, but it will appear hereafter that they had all caught the contagion of mutiny, but kept their secret until the moment for action arrived. CHAP. V.

Cantonment on the Ridge

The sepoy regiments were cantoned on a rising ground, known as the Ridge, which was situated about a mile to the north of Delhi, and overlooked the whole city. The bungalows of the European officers were scattered about the vicinity. At the furthest end of the Ridge was a strong position, known as Flagstaff Tower. Further away to the left, the river Jumna skirted the eastern side of Delhi; and the mutineers from Meerut were expected to enter the city in this direction by a bridge.

Mutineers expected.

Brigadier Graves had but a short warning. The mutineers would certainly travel all night, and would probably arrive early on the Monday morning. It was useless to cut away the bridge, as the hot weather was at its height, and the stream was easily fordable. Everything depended on the loyalty of the sepoys at Delhi. So long as they remained staunch, the brigadier might hope to defend the city and cantonment against the mutineers from Meerut. If, however, the sepoys at Delhi joined the rebels, there was nothing to be done but to await the European reinforcements which might be expected from Meerut. Meanwhile, the brigadier sent circulars to all non-military residents to take refuge in Flagstaff Tower.

Preparations for battle.

The three regiments of sepoy infantry, and the battery of sepoy artillery, were ordered out. The guns were loaded, and every preparation made for the coming battle. The brigadier addressed the men in stirring language. Now was the time, he said, for the sepoys at Delhi to show their loyalty to the Company. The sepoys responded with loud cheers. One regiment in particular eagerly demanded to be led against

CHAP. V. the mutineers; and the brigadier marched them out to fight the rebels, leaving the two other regiments on the Ridge.

Treachery. Presently the cavalry from Meerut were seen galloping towards the city. After them at no great distance was a large mass of rebel infantry, with their bayonets gleaming in the sun, and their red coats soiled by the dust of the night march. Neither horse nor foot showed the slightest hesitation. As the cavalry approached the brigadier ordered his men to fire. The rattle of musketry followed, but not a single trooper fell from his horse. The faithful sepoys had fired in the air.

Firing in the air. Then followed a pause. The European officers held on in sheer desperation; they hoped to be reinforced by British soldiers from Meerut. The sepoys hesitated for a while, lest they should be cut to pieces by the Europeans, whom they too expected to arrive. Could the Europeans have appeared in time, Delhi might have been saved in spite of the suspicious firing in the air.

Treachery. Useless firing was a treachery that was new to sepoy regiments commanded by British officers, but it was common enough in Asiatic armies commanded by their own generals or princes. Mogul history abounds in stories of Asiatic officers corrupted by gold, and ordering their troops to fire on an enemy without bullet or ball. Such treachery was scarcely possible under European officers, and consequently the rebel sepoys loaded their muskets with cartridges, and then fired into the air.

Rebels in the palace. It was soon evident that the king was making common cause with the rebels, for the sepoys from Meerut were pouring through the palace to join their comrades in the city. No Europeans arrived from Meerut, and the Delhi sepoys began to fraternise with the rebels.

British refuge.

Brigadier Graves rallied a few of his men who still remained faithful, and escaped to Flagstaff Tower. Here he found a large number of European ladies and children, and all the gentlemen who had been able to reach the place of refuge. A company of sepoys, and two guns served by sepoy gunners, still guarded the Tower, and had they remained faithful might have kept off the enemy. But the force on the Ridge was rapidly melting away. The hearts of all the sepoys were with the rebels. All were burning to join the scoundrels in the city in the work of plunder and destruction; and those who were posted at the Tower only waited for an opportunity to move off in the same direction.

Massacre of Europeans.

Meanwhile the old "king of Delhi" had connived at the slaughter of Europeans. Mr. Frazer, the commissioner of the Delhi division, and Captain Douglas, who commanded the palace guards, were cut down within the royal precincts. Mr. Jennings, the chaplain, and some ladies and children, numbering altogether about fifty souls, had taken refuge within the palace walls, in the hope of being protected by the royal pensioner against the mutinous sepoys. Had the ladies and children been admitted into the inner apartments, they would have been safe. But there was a rush of rebel sepoys into the presence of the old king to make their salams and hail him as their Padishah; and they loudly demanded the death of every European. The old king could not or would not interfere, and told the sepoys that he made the prisoners over to them, to do with them as they

CHAP. V. pleased. The unhappy victims were shut up in a dark room with coarse and scanty food. They were offered their lives on the condition that they became Mohammedans, and entered the service of the king as menials or slaves. One and all refused, and one and all were eventually butchered in the palace of Aurangzeb.

Flagstaff Tower.

The Europeans in Flagstaff Tower were in sore peril. Ladies were terrified and anxious for absent husbands, whilst children were clamouring for milk and food. The men were distracted by the suddenness of the danger, and the stories of murder and outrage that came from the city. All eyes were strained in the direction of Meerut. Every one longed for the arrival of European soldiers to relieve them from the agony of suspense, and quash the fearful rebellion that was surging up in Delhi.

Explosion of the magazine.

Later on in the afternoon, the great magazine in the heart of Delhi was seen from the Ridge to explode in a cloud of smoke and flame. It was in charge of Lieutenant Willoughby of the Bengal artillery, but he had only eight Europeans with him ; the guards and workmen were all Asiatics. Arms were served out to every one; loaded guns were pointed to the gateways; and a train of gunpowder was laid to the chief magazine. A vast host of rebels pressed round the enclosure, and demanded the surrender of the magazine in the name of the king. Admittance was refused, but the rebels brought ladders to the walls, or climbed to the roofs of neighbouring buildings, and poured a hot fire on the inmates of the magazine. Most of the workmen joined the rebels. Those who still remained staunch threw away their rifles, and seemed bereft of their senses. At last Lieutenant Willoughby ordered Sergeant Scully to fire the train.

In a moment there was a great upheaval. Hundreds of rebels were blown into the air; but unfortunately the greater part of the stores fell into the enemy's hands. Willoughby and three others got away out of the city—scorched, bruised, and insensible; but Willoughby was murdered a few days afterwards in a neighbouring village. Scully was wounded by the explosion, and killed by the rebels; he and his four companions were seen no more.

Flight from Flagstaff Tower.

By this time all hope of rescue had died out from the fugitives in Flagstaff Tower. It was feared that the rebels would return to the Ridge to complete the work of slaughter. All fled the best way they could—men, ladies, and children; some in carriages, others on horseback, and many on foot. Even at this distance of time, it is terrible to think of their sufferings. Many were slaughtered by the rebels, but some found refuge in the houses of Hindu villagers, who treated them with kindness and hospitality at the risk of their own lives.

Last telegram.

Before the day was over the clerk at the telegraph office on the Ridge sent his last telegram. "The mutineers from Meerut are masters of Delhi; several Europeans have been murdered; the office must be closed." Shortly afterwards the rebel sepoys swarmed out of the city to complete the work of destruction on the Ridge, and the poor telegraph clerk was cut to pieces and heard of no more.

Sudden alarm.

Within a few moments the fatal news reached every capital in India:—Lahore in the Punjab; Agra and Allahabad in the North-West Provinces; Lucknow in Oudh; Benares, Patna, and Calcutta in Bengal; Bombay in the Deccan; Madras in the remote south. From Calcutta and Bombay the

CHAP. V. revolt of Delhi sent a thrill through the whole British empire. Men familiar with India, her history, and her people, could not believe the news. It was the heaviest blow to British prestige in India since the tragedy of the Black Hole in Calcutta. A century of European civilisation had been swamped by a mutiny of Asiatic sepoys against greased cartridges. Delhi was lost; the Mogul *régime* was restored; the North-West Provinces were slipping away from the British empire.

Reviving hopes. The public mind was greatly agitated by the disaster. Many could not realise the fact that Delhi had revolted; that the old king had been proclained Padishah of Hindustan. Others rushed to the opposite conclusion and thought that India was lost. In India European hearts were kindled with a burning desire for the recovery of the revolted city. It was hoped that Delhi would be retaken in a few days, and the contagion of mutiny brought to a close by the destruction of the mutineers. Indeed it was obvious to the British authorities that the European forces at Meerut might have crushed the rebellion at the outset, had a Clive, a Gillespie, or an Ochterlony been in command. Sir Henry Lawrence had suppressed a still more dangerous outbreak at Lucknow with a disaffected city in his rear, and the revolt at Delhi ought to be suppressed at once in a like manner.

General Anson at Simla. § 11. General Anson, the commander-in-chief of the Bengal army, was at Simla in the Himalayas, nealy 200 miles to the north of Delhi. He was an officer of good repute, but of no Indian experience, and was chiefly known as the Major A., who had written a treatise on whist. He received a telegram from Lord Canning to make short work of Delhi, and other telegrams to the same effect from Mr. John Lawrence, the chief commissioner of the Punjab. General Anson began to assemble a force at Umballa, and he despatched a regiment of Ghorkas to the Sutlej to escort a siege-train from the Punjab over the river. He was anxious to fortify Umballa, about sixty miles from Simla on the road to Delhi. He ordered three European regiments on the Himalayas to march at once to Umballa. John Lawrence, however, was dead against any delay. He wanted to recover Delhi, not to entrench Umballa; and he promptly telegraphed that "clubs were trumps, not spades." Meanwhile the sudden change from the cool hills to the hot plains brought on cholera amongst the Europeans. The vanguard of the European force left Umballa on the 19th of May, but eight days afterwards General Anson died of cholera.

Demand for European soldiers.

Meanwhile Lord Canning had telegraphed to Bombay for the European troops that were returning from the Persian expedition, and to Madras, Ceylon, Burma, and Singapore for every European soldier that could be spared. His object was to form a European column at Calcutta, and to push it up the valley of the Ganges with all speed to Allahabad, to crush any incipient mutiny on the way, and to penetrate and suppress the growing disaffection in Oudh and the North-West Provinces. It was out of the question that a column from Calcutta could reach Delhi, and he looked to Mr. John Lawrence, the chief commissioner of the Punjab on the other side of Delhi, to send all the Europeans and artillery he could spare to join General Anson.

CHAP. V.

General Barnard. Sir Henry Barnard succeeded Anson as commander-in-chief. He pushed on the force to Alipore, within ten miles of Delhi. On the 7th of June he was joined by the European brigade from Meerut, and prepared to advance against Delhi.

Rebel position. By this time the Delhi rebels were prepared to await an attack in the open. They had taken up a strong position to the right of the great trunk road leading to the city, and had utilised its natural advantages with remarkable skill. One body of rebels was posted in a vast caravanserai; a square enclosed by walls, with towers at the four corners. The walls were loop-holed for musketry, and the towers were occupied by sharp-shooters. In front of the caravanserai they had a battery of artillery and a howitzer, raised on an elevation and defended by earthworks, faggots and gabions. The main force, however, was posted in a neighbouring village, where the houses and gardens furnished an excellent cover for infantry. This position was defended by seven regiments of sepoy infantry, two of sepoy cavalry, and a strong battery of sepoy artillery. To those regular forces were added the artillerymen of the palace at Delhi, and volunteers of all kinds, attracted by hatred of the Feringhi, enthusiasm for Islam, and thirst for blood and plunder.

Battle of the Serai. The battle of Serai was fought on the 9th of June. At sunrise Sir Henry Barnard advanced with two regiments of European infantry and two guns. He could not silence the fire of the rebel battery, and it was carried with the bayonet by a regiment of European infantry. Meanwhile the other regiment drove the rebels away out of the village. The combined British force stormed the caravanserai and gave no quarter.

At this juncture Brigadier Hope Grant appeared with three squadrons of cavalry and two guns, and utterly routed the rebel army and pursued it to the suburbs of Delhi.

Return to the Ridge.

That same afternoon the British returned as conquerors to the old cantonment on the Ridge. Within a month of the revolt, they had avenged the massacre at Delhi, and restored the prestige of British sovereignty.

Sepoy vagaries.

The battle of Serai revealed strange inconsistencies. The rebel sepoys, who had shot down their officers, and were in open revolt against British rule, were as proud as before of their exploits under British colours. The Company's medals were found on the red coats of the dead rebels, officers as well as men. Stranger still, pouches full of the very greased cartridges that brought on the mutiny were picked up on the ground occupied by the rebel army.

Mischievous delay.

The month's delay however had done considerable mischief. The plague of mutiny had broken out at other stations, and the rebel garrison at Delhi had been reinforced by large bodies of mutinous sepoys. The details were nearly all alike—sudden outbreaks, shooting at officers, setting fire to bungalows, and plundering the treasury. The mutineers, however, did not in all cases rush off to Delhi. Some crept sadly to their own homes, and buried the silver rupees they had brought away, or joined the bands of outlaws and brigands that began to ravage the surrounding country. Meanwhile the European officers of nearly every sepoy regiment, whilst ready to believe that other regiments would revolt, were prepared to stake their lives on the fidelity of their own men, and opposed any attempt to disarm them.

CHAP. V.

Rebellion in the North-West Provinces.

In due course the disaffection of the sepoy army began to stir up certain classes of the civil population. The Bengal provinces were free from this taint, excepting perhaps at Patna where the Mohammedans are very strong. Indeed in Bengal proper the Hindu villagers often arrested rebel sepoys of their own free will, and made them over to the British authorities. In the Madras and Bombay presidencies there were no signs of discontent. But in Oudh, as already described, and in the North-West Provinces between Delhi and Allahabad, there was a growing disaffection. Rebellion was preached by Mohammedan fanatics yearning for the restoration of Islam as the dominant religion. Dispossessed talukdars, who thought themselves, rightly or wrongly to have been unjustly dealt with in the settlement of the land revenue, took a part in the disturbances. In a word all the turbulent and ill-conditioned elements of the population in the north-west,—all "who were discontented or in debt,"—readily joined in the insurrection; possibly to revenge some fancied injury, but mostly from that love of riot and plunder which had been universal in Hindustan under Mahratta supremacy. At the same time a spirit of hostility to Europeans was manifested, which was without precedent in the history of British rule in India. Towards the end of June, Mr. John Colvin, the Lieutenant-Governor of the North-West Provinces, with all the European residents in the neighbourhood were closely besieged by mutineers and rebels in the fortress of Agra.

Siege of Delhi: perils of British.

§ 12. The British force reached the Ridge on the evening of the battle. It then numbered 4,000 troops, half Europeans and the other half Sikhs and Ghorkas.

The city might have been taken by surprise at an earlier date, but the month's delay had elated the sepoys, and given them time to look to their defences. The British troops were encamped behind the Ridge, and were thus protected from the fire of the rebels. They were, however, the besieged rather than the besiegers. They were threatened on all sides, except the rear, by mutineers and rebels. The rear, however, was open to the Punjab, and all reinforcements and supplies were brought up from the Punjab. For weeks, and indeed for months, the British force could only hope to hold their position until reinforcements could arrive from Lahore or Calcutta. The city of Delhi was strongly fortified with walls and bastions loaded with cannon, and environed by a broad, deep ditch, filled from the river Jumna, which rendered it as impregnable as Babylon of old. It was impossible to storm such fortifications without a strong army of British soldiers and an adequate siege train, all of which were anxiously expected from the Punjab.

Strength of the rebels.

Meanwhile the rebels inside the walls of Delhi were being constantly reinforced by fresh bodies of mutineers. They were in possession of the arms, ammunition, and other stores, which had been collected in the British magazine for more than a generation. They were in receipt of daily supplies of provisions from the neighbouring villages, and it was impossible to cut off the convoys. A force of 4,000 men could scarcely be expected to environ a city seven miles in circumference, or even to approach within cannon shot of the walls.

§ 13. Bengal was completely separated from Delhi

CHAP. V. by the disaffection which flooded the North-West Provinces. All hope of crushing the rebels at Delhi rested on the Punjab; and John Lawrence sent Europeans and Sikhs, siege guns and supplies of all kinds, as fast as they were available to the British force behind the Ridge. In June the "Punjab Guides" reached the Ridge, one of the best regiments in the Indian army. It belonged to the Punjab Frontier Force, which was recruited from the mountain tribes between the Punjab and Afghanistan, and trained and commanded by British officers.

Punjab and John Lawrence.

Sikh hatred of Mohammedans.

In 1857 the Sikhs had learnt to respect their European rulers, who maintained order and law. They had no sympathy for the Mohammedans, nor for the king of Delhi. On the contrary, they remembered the murder of their Gurus and saints by Aurangzeb and his successors, and were burning to be revenged on Delhi and the Mogul. During the reign of Runjeet Singh they had outraged the Mohammedans of the Punjab by polluting their mosques and profaning the tombs of their holy men. Accordingly the Sikh warriors of the Khalsa, the very men who had fought against British supremacy at Chillianwalla and Goojerat, were now anxious to join the Europeans in putting down the revolt at Delhi and sacking the capital of Islam in India.

Mutinous spirit of sepoy garrisons.

John Lawrence had thus nothing to fear from the Sikhs. Nor had he anything to fear from the Mohammedans, for they were only anxious for protection against the Sikhs. The Hindus of the Punjab cared for no one but themselves; most of them were traders and money-lenders whose interests were bound up in the maintenance of British rule. The terror of the Punjab lay in the sepoy regiments of the Bengal army that garrisoned the country. The sepoys in the Punjab had no real ground for alarm at the greased cartridges; the issue had been stopped at the school of musketry at Sealkote, on the Cashmere frontier. But the contagion was as virulent as ever. They were maddened by the conviction that the British government was bent on destroying their religion and caste; and when they heard of the outbreak at Meerut and revolt at Delhi, they were bent on mutiny and massacre.

Lahore and Mian Mir.

Lahore, the capital of the Punjab, is situated in the heart of the province, about half-way between Delhi and Peshawar. The fortress at Lahore was held by a battalion of Bengal sepoys, which was relieved once every fortnight—that is, on the 1st and 15th of every month. There was also a European guard within the fortress of about a hundred British soldiers. Six miles from Lahore was the cantonment of Mian Mir, where three regiments of Bengal sepoys were quartered, together with one regiment of Europeans, and two batteries of European artillery.

Sepoy plots.

§ 14. News of the revolt at Delhi reached Lahore on the 12th of May. Without a moment's delay, a secret plot was formed between the sepoys in the fortress at Lahore and those in the cantonment at Mian Mir for the slaughter of Europeans. On the 15th May, when the sepoy battalion in the fortress was to be relieved by another sepoy battalion, the two were to join together, murder their own officers and then overwhelm the European guard. A signal was thereupon to be given to the cantonment at Mian Mir, on which the sepoy regiments were to

CHAP. V. break out in mutiny, murder their officers, and environ and overwhelm the regiment of Europeans.

Defeated. Fortunately the plot was betrayed by a Brahman to the British authorities, and the scheme was defeated. On the morning of the 15th of May, the sepoy regiments in the cantonment at Mian Mir were drawn up on parade as usual. Suddenly, they were ordered with a loud voice to lay down their arms. Before them was a thin line of European infantry which presently fell back, and revealed the mouths of twelve guns pointed at the sepoys with lighted fires. The European infantry began to load their rifles behind the artillery, and the sepoys could hear the clicking of locks and ramrods. The would-be rebels saw that the game was up. They threw away their muskets and sabres in sheer terror. More than 3,000 Asiatic sepoys, who were preparing to murder their officers, had surrendered their arms to less than 600 Europeans. The plot in the fortress at Lahore was crushed in a like fashion. The European guards had been strongly reinforced by a detachment from the regiment at the cantonment at Mian Mir; and the two sepoy battalions were disarmed before they could unite for the slaughter of Europeans.

Chamberlain's flying column. Later on it was found that all the Bengal sepoys in the Punjab were more or less tainted. Measures were taken to avert or counteract the evil. Suspected regiments were removed to localities where the Sikhs were most hostile to the Bengal army. A flying column of Europeans, Sikhs and others, was organised to act against threatened points and overawe intending mutineers by rapid movement and vigorous action. In the first instance it was commanded by

Brigadier Neville Chamberlain, who rose to be one of the most distinguished officers of the time. Later on, the column was commanded by Brigadier John Nicholson, the hero of the day, who, as will be seen hereafter, was cut off in the very zenith of his fame.

Peshawar valley.

§ 15. The valley of Peshawar was another cause of anxiety. It lies in the north-west corner of the Punjab beyond the river Indus, and faces the Khyber Pass. It is the key to India, the route by which Alexander the Great and the early Mohammedan conquerors invaded the Punjab.

Frontier tribes.

Ever since the British conquest, the Peshawar valley had been harassed by the same mountain tribes that had worried the Macedonians, the Mohammedans, and the Sikhs under Runjeet Singh. Tribes living within the circle of British outposts could be compelled to live in peace; but tribes living beyond the border, and outside British influence, were turbulent, murderous and predatory. Occasionally they assassinated a British officer, or gave an asylum to criminals, or committed raids on British territory or on tribes living under British protection, and not unfrequently stole horses and other property from the British cantonment. All this while they were strictly forbidden to cross the border into British territory; and any tribesman who dared to disobey this law, was liable to arrest and imprisonment until the elders of his tribe made their submission and paid a fine.

Peshawar canton-ment.

The valley of Peshawar was held by 9,000 Bengal sepoys and about 3,000 Europeans. Here, as at Lahore, there was a perpetual fear of mutiny and murder. A secret enemy was dwelling in the

CHAP. V. British camp that was capable of any amount of secresy and treachery. Accordingly the cantonment was declared in a state of siege. The Europeans took up strong positions, and some of the Bengal regiments were disarmed.

Mutiny and murder.

§ 16. Towards the end of May a sepoy regiment rose against its officers. The colonel had staked his life on the fidelity of his men, and they had not been disarmed; and owing to this infatuated belief in the fidelity of the sepoys, the rebels had been able to set out for Delhi with their arms and ammunition. The colonel was in the ranks to the last, labouring to keep the men to their colours; but his efforts were vain, and he retired broken-hearted and shot himself. The rebels, however, were pursued and scattered, by the flying column under Neville Chamberlain, and 120 were taken prisoners and brought back to Peshawar.

Executions at Peshawar.

The prisoners were tried for mutiny and were all condemned to death. But John Lawrence recoiled from such wholesale executions. He did not want to exact vengeance on the mutineers, but to terrify other regiments from following their example. Forty of the worst were sentenced to death, but the remaining eighty were imprisoned for periods varying from three to seven years. The condemned forty were blown from guns at Peshawar on the 10th of June.

Volunteering of Sikhs and tribes.

The disarmament of the sepoy regiments, and the executions at Peshawar, convinced the populations of the Punjab that the British were masters. There may have been some of the old Sikh soldiers of the Khalsa, who were still yearning for the expulsion of the British from the land of the five rivers; but even in their case the old hostility was forgotten in the feverish longing to be revenged on Delhi for the persecution and slaughter of their saints. Possibly they were still more eager to plunder the palaces and bazaars of Delhi. The mountain tribes outside the British frontier, who professed to be Mohammedans, were as enthusiastic as the Sikhs to share in the sack of Delhi. They implored pardon for all past offences, paid up all fines, and volunteered to help the British to capture the revolted city. CHAP. V.

John Lawrence sent the Punjab Guides to Delhi, and raised nineteen or twenty regiments of Sikhs and others. But he could not spare more Europeans. Mutiny threatened him on all sides. At Julinder three Bengal regiments murdered their officers, broke open prisons, and ran off to Delhi before the flying column under Neville Chamberlain could overtake them. Sore peril.

§ 17. At this crisis Neville Chamberlain was sent to join the British force on the Ridge, and John Nicholson took the command of the flying column. He disarmed several sepoy regiments without firing a shot, but had no mercy for rebels. He was a fine type of the zealous and single-minded European officers of the old East India Company's army; a hero who was reverenced by Asiatic soldiery for his dash and valour, and worshipped by his men as one of the demigods of India. Indeed in one case the worship of Nicholson was literal. A religious fraternity of Sikhs took the name of "Nicholsons"; or as they pronounced it "Nikkal Scynes." They wore salmon-coloured garments John Nicholson, the sainted warrior.

CHAP. V. and black felt hats as a distinctive garb, and they sang hymns with a chorus of "Guru Nikkal Scyne." In 1854 a deputation of these worshippers waited on Nicholson, threw themselves at his feet and chanted his praises. He remonstrated, but they persisted, and he ordered his native servants to whip the nonsense out of them. The devotees, however, gloried in being flogged, and declared that it was a just punishment for their sins. Nicholson was obliged to run away from his worshippers. It will be seen hereafter that he fell in the storming of Delhi. When the news of his death reached the fraternity, two of them committed suicide, whilst the third embraced Christianity out of respect for the memory of his "Guru."

Proposed withdrawal from Peshawar.

18. John Lawrence was hedged round with dangers. European regiments were urgently demanded for the siege of Delhi, and he could not spare a man. He was compelled to keep 3,000 Europeans for the defence of the valley of Peshawar, and he had only 2,000 Europeans left to garrison the rest of the Punjab. In this dilemma he proposed to abandon Peshawar and make it over to Dost Mohammed Khan of Cabul. He argued that if the force locked up in Peshawar could be sent against Delhi, the city might be captured in a week, and the revolt brought to a close. Subsequent events strengthened this impression. On the 23rd of June, the centenary of the battle of Plassy, the besieging force at Delhi was nearly overpowered by the rebels. Several sepoy regiments had mutinied in Rohilcund, to the north-west of Oudh, and joined the rebels at Delhi. The Gwalior contingent, a subsidiary force

officered by Europeans, and maintained in Sindia's territory, had broken out in mutiny. Altogether John Lawrence was convinced that Delhi must be captured at all hazards, and that it was absolutely necessary to retire from Peshawar.

Opposition.

But the military authorities at Peshawar, including General Sidney Cotton and Colonel Herbert Edwardes, vehemently opposed the measure. They were unanimously agreed that the loss of Peshawar would entail such a loss of prestige as to turn Sikhs and Afghans against the British government. They urged that relief might be already at hand; that five or six European regiments might be advancing from Bengal to Delhi, and that four or five times that number might be on the high seas from England.

Negatived by Lord Canning.

The burning question was referred to Calcutta for the decision of Lord Canning. The reply was a long time coming, but it settled the matter at once. "Hold on Peshawar to the last!" John Lawrence was overruled.

Mutiny at Sealkote.

§ 19. In this extremity John Lawrence determined to disarm every Bengal sepoy in the Punjab, and then to send every European soldier and gun to Delhi that could be spared. Nicholson hurried on the disarming, when news arrived that the sepoy brigade at Sealkote, on the Cashmere frontier, had broken out in revolt, murdered their officers, and then gone off to Delhi. Nicholson hurried after the brigade, overtook it on the banks of the Ravi, and almost annihilated it. Nearly every rebel was slain, or drowned in the river, or surrendered by the villagers to the British authorities.

CHAP. V.

Terrible execution. There was one more tragedy in the Punjab which cannot be ignored. A sepoy regiment mutinied after it was disarmed, and tried to escape to Delhi. It was pursued by a British magistrate with a detachment of irregular horse. About 280 escaped to an island in a river, and being without arms and without food, they were compelled to surrender. The magistrate, however, could not possibly dispose of 280 rebels. He could not imprison them, and it was dangerous to let them loose. In this terrible emergency he saw no alternative but to have them shot in gangs. It was a measure which can only be justified by the law of self-defence and state necessity. The magistrate left the scene pale and trembling.[1]

Siege of Delhi. § 20. Towards the end of June the hot season passed away. The rains began; military operations before Delhi became possible in the daytime. Sir Henry Barnard died on the 5th of July, and was succeeded by General Archduke Wilson. On the 14th of July an attack on the British outposts was repulsed by General Chamberlain. Towards the middle of August, John Nicholson arrived from the Punjab with his flying column. On the 4th of September a heavy siege train arrived from the Punjab, and fifty large guns were placed in position.

Captured, September 1857. From the 8th to the 12th of September, four batteries poured a constant storm of shot and shell on the doomed city. On the 13th the breaches were

[1] This last fact was vouched by an English civil servant who was living at the time with the late Mr. Cooper, the magistrate in question. Unfortunately Mr. Cooper subsequently published a description of the execution in a tone of levity which was generally condemned.

practicable. At three o'clock on the following morning, three assaulting columns were formed in the trenches, whilst a fourth was kept in reserve. The Cashmere gate was blown open by gunpowder; one column pushed through the gateway, whilst the others escaladed the breaches. The advancing columns were exposed to a ceaseless fire from houses, mosques, and other buildings, and John Nicholson received a mortal wound. Then followed six days of desperate street fighting. On the 20th of September the British flag waved in triumph over the old capital of Hindustan and the palace of the Great Mogul.[1]

Peace in the north-west.

Immediately after the fall of Delhi, a column was sent down the grand trunk road, to relieve the fortress at Agra, and to open up communications between Delhi and Allahabad. Within a few short months peace and order were restored to the North-West Provinces, and the brigandage and anarchy which for a brief interval revived the memory of the old Mahratta days, disappeared, it is hoped for ever, from Hindustan.[2]

[1] Eventually the king and his family were sent to Rangoon, where he died in 1862.

[2] Mr. John Colvin, a distinguished Bengal civilian and Lieutenant-Governor of the North-West Provinces, who was shut up in the fortress at Agra, died during the siege. Many old Anglo-Indians still remember his career with interest. He was private secretary to Lord Auckland during the first Cabul war. His son, Sir Auckland Colvin of the Bengal Civil Service, is now Financial Minister to the Government of India under Lord Dufferin.

CHAPTER VI.

SEPOY REVOLT: NORTH WEST, CAWNPORE, LUCKNOW.

1857–58.

§ 1. Bengal and Lord Canning: General Neill's advance from Calcutta. § 2. Sacred city of Benares: Hindu population overawed. § 3. Fortress at Allahabad: treachery and massacre. § 4. Cawnpore: extreme peril. § 5. Story of Nana Sahib. § 6. European refuge in the barracks. § 7. Nana Sahib at Cawnpore: aspirations after Hindu sovereignty: delusion of General Wheeler. § 8. Mutiny and treachery: barracks beleaguered by Nana Sahib. § 9. First massacre at Cawnpore: massacre at Jhansi. § 10. Advance of General Havelock. § 11. Second massacre of women and children: the well. § 12. Lucknow and Sir Henry Lawrence: May and June. § 13. Siege of British Residency at Lucknow: July to September: death of Sir Henry Lawrence. § 14. Havelock's advance and retreat. § 15. Advance of Havelock and Outram. § 16. Relief of Lucknow. § 17. Sir Colin Campbell's advance: deliverance of the garrison. § 18. Mutiny of the Gwalior contingent: defeated. § 19. End of the mutiny and rebellion: causes.

CHAP. VI.

Surprises.

THE progress of events in Northern India, from the revolt at Delhi in May to the capture of the city in September, was a mystery to every Anglo-Indian. Many had foreseen that the Bengal army was in an evil way; that Bengal sepoys had been pandered until the discipline of the army had become dangerously loosened. But no one foresaw mutiny, murder, and massacre. Every fresh budget of news was consequently a surprise which baffled the oldest civilian and the most experienced general. There was much angry controversy, and much bitter recrimination; but such obsolete quarrelling may well be dropped into oblivion. The lessons which the mutiny teaches are best gathered from a plain narrative of events, not by conjectures as to plots and conspiracies which may have had no better origin than those of Oates and Bedloe. CHAP. VI.

British soldiers.

§ 1. Whilst Mr. John Lawrence was sending Europeans and Sikhs from the Punjab to reinforce the besiegers on the Ridge at Delhi, Lord Canning was sending similar reinforcements from Bengal to Allahabad, to relieve the beleaguered garrisons at Cawnpore and Lucknow, and to crush the growing disaffection in Oudh. Immediately after the revolt at Delhi, Lord Canning had sent telegrams and steamers to Madras and Bombay, to Ceylon, Burma, and Singapore, to send to Calcutta every European soldier that could be spared. Every local government responded to the call, and Lord Elgin, who was at Singapore pushing on a war with China, sent two British regiments, that were coming round the Cape, to the help of Lord Canning. It was a noble sacrifice. Lord Elgin's heart was in the Chinese war, but he felt as a Briton, that the suppression of a sepoy revolt in India was of far more pressing importance to the British empire than hostilities against China.

Allahabad and Cawnpore

During the latter part of May, European soldiers were landed at Calcutta, and sent in batches to Allahabad. At that time Lord Canning was most anxious to relieve Sir Henry Lawrence at Lucknow. The railway had been completed for a hundred miles from Calcutta. Accordingly the soldiers were sent by railway from Calcutta, then by boats up the river Ganges to Allahabad, at the junction of the Ganges and Jumna, about half way between Calcutta and Delhi. From Allahabad they were sent a hundred

CHAP. VI. and twenty miles still further up the Ganges to the town of Cawnpore, where the river formed a line of frontier between the North-West Provinces and Oudh. It will be seen hereafter that only a few Europeans reached Cawnpore, and that none of those sent up from Calcutta ever reached Lucknow.

Neill's advance. The British reinforcements were commanded by Colonel Neill, a Madras officer who had served in the Crimean war, and was distinguished by force of will. On one occasion the station-master at Calcutta proposed sending away a railway train without the soldiers, because the latter were delayed. To his utter surprise he was arrested by Neill, and kept under a guard until every soldier had taken his seat. The incident is trivial, but it tells the character of Neill.

Delay at Benares. § 2. Colonel Neill did not reach Allahabad for some days. He was detained at Benares from the 4th to the 9th of June. This city, the Jerusalem of the Brahmans, is situated on the river Ganges, about 420 miles above Calcutta and eighty miles below Allahabad. It had a population of 300,000, mostly Hindus. The cantonment is two or three miles from the city, and was occupied by a regiment of Bengal infantry, one of irregular cavalry, and a Sikh regiment. There was no European force whatever to keep the city and cantonment in check beyond thirty British gunners, but this number would have been ample had there been no scare about greased cartridges. No danger was to be apprehended from the civil population of Benares. The sepoy regiments in the cantonment were the only cause for alarm.

Yet the Hindu population of Benares had always

Turbulence of the people.

been bigoted and turbulent. During the persecuting reign of the Mogul Aurangzeb, in the seventeenth century, the Hindus of the sacred city were kept down by brute force, and compelled to pay the poll-tax levied on infidels, whilst Mohammedan mosques were built on the ruins of Hindu temples. Under the tolerant rule of the British, the Hindus had been more contented, but there had been occasional fights between Hindus and Mohammedans, especially at festival times. Moreover, the Hindus at Benares were under the thumb of the Brahmans, and were more bigoted and exacting under British rule than they had dared to be under Mohammedan domination. A British magistrate, however, had generally kept the peace in Benares with the help of Asiatic police, but occasionally he found it necessary to call out a detachment of sepoys.

Hostility of the Brahmans: stamped out by Gubbins.

For many years the Brahmans at Benares utterly refused to have the sacred city lighted or drained. They declared that lighting and drainage were contrary to the Hindu religion, and the arguments of the British magistrate to the contrary were a sheer waste of words. At last, in 1851, the British magistrate, a Mr. Frederic Gubbins, carried out these municipal reforms in the teeth of a Hindu mob. Then followed a commotion at Benares precisely similar to that which occurred at Madras in the seventeenth century, when the British rulers endeavoured to reform the sanitary condition of their city. The traders and bazaar dealers shut up their shops, and refused to supply the cantonment with grain. Mr. Gubbins was pelted and fired at, and fled for his life. He called out a detachment of sepoys, arrested the ringleaders of the riot, and

CHAP. VI. lodged them in the jail. From that moment Mr. Gubbins was lord of Benares. He rode through the city and ordered all the shops to be opened, and there was no one to say him nay.

British and Mogul rule. All this was of course very wrong. The Supreme Court at Calcutta, with its bench of British judges, trained to respect the liberties of British subjects, would have been aghast at such proceedings. But from the days of Warren Hastings to those of Lord Canning, the Supreme Courts at Calcutta, Madras, and Bombay were prevented by the Act of Parliament passed in 1781 from interfering in any way with the administration of the Company's servants outside the limits of the Presidency capitals. It might, however, be added that the action of the British magistrate, arbitrary and high-handed as it must appear to British readers, was mild and merciful in comparison with Mogul severities. Under an imperious ruler like Aurangzeb, trains of armed elephants were driven through the masses in the streets, and trampled down all that came in their way, until the crowd broke up and fled in terror at the carnage.

Brave civilians. Right or wrong, the action of Mr. Gubbins in 1851 was remembered by the people of Benares in 1857. Mr. Gubbins was by this time judge at Benares, and a Mr. Lind was magistrate and collector. The Bengal sepoys in the cantonment were disaffected, but there was no sign of insurrection in the city. The British residents were in alarm, and it was proposed to remove to the fortress of Chunar, on the other side of the river Ganges, which was occupied by invalided British soldiers. But Gubbins and Lind refused to desert their posts and abandon Benares. Accordingly the other British residents resolved to stay likewise; and it was arranged that in the event of a mutiny of the sepoys, they should all take refuge on the roof of the treasury, about two miles from the cantonment, which was guarded by Sikh soldiers. CHAP. VI.

Mutiny at Benares: disasters.

Colonel Neill arrived at Benares on the 4th of June. A detachment of Europeans had been obtained from Her Majesty's 10th Foot, which was posted at Dinapore, and preparations were being made for disarming the Bengal sepoys. Neill joined in the work, but there were untoward incidents. The Europeans were drawn out and the three guns were loaded. The Bengal sepoys were ordered to lay down their arms, and some obeyed. Suddenly, however, the whole regiment of sepoys took alarm and fired at the Europeans. The gunners opened fire on the mutineers. The irregular cavalry joined in the outbreak. The British officer in command of the Sikh regiment was shot dead. The Sikhs were seized with panic and fired on the Europeans. The gunners then discharged a volley of grape at the Sikhs; and sepoys, irregular horse, and Sikhs fled in hot haste from the cantonment, and dispersed in all directions over the surrounding country.

Loyalty of Sikhs and Hindus.

This disaster might have sealed the fate of the Europeans at the treasury. When the Sikh regiment at the cantonment was scattered by a discharge of grape, the Sikh guards at the treasury might have revenged the slaughter by firing at the Europeans on the roof. Fortunately Mr. Gubbins was there, and so too was an old Sikh general, who had fought against the British in the Sikh wars, and was residing at Benares under surveillance, but had become reconciled to British supremacy. Both

CHAP. VI. Gubbins and the Sikh exile pointed out to the guards, that cannonading the Sikhs at the cantonment must have been unpremeditated, and was probably a misunderstanding or an accident. Had it been otherwise, the Europeans at the treasury would never have placed themselves under the protection of Sikh guards. This explanation satisfied the Sikh guards, and the station was saved. It should be added that British authority was nobly supported by the Raja of Benares and another Hindu gentleman of high rank and influence.

Allahabad: strategic importance.

§ 3. Colonel Neill spent some days in driving the mutineers from the neighbourhood of Benares, and then went on to Allahabad. On his arrival he found the city in a state of insurrection and uproar, whilst the Europeans were shut up in the fortress, and besieged by mutineers and rebels. The city of Allahabad was situated, as already described, at the junction of the Ganges and Jumna, in the centre of Northern India, and about half-way between Calcutta and Delhi. It is the strongest fortress between Calcutta and Agra. It commands the whole river communication between Bengal, Oudh, and the North-West Provinces. It also commanded the old trunk road between Calcutta and Delhi. In the treasury there was £200,000 in silver. Yet, when the mutinies broke out in May, the station and fortress were garrisoned entirely by Asiatics, namely, one Bengal regiment, half a Sikh regiment, and a battery of sepoy artillery. There were no European soldiers whatever at Allahabad, except the British officers in command of the sepoys.

The colonel and officers of the Bengal sepoys had

Misplaced confidence.

the most perfect confidence in their men. They had always encouraged the sepoys in their sports, and contributed toward the expenses. It was rumoured in the newspapers that the sepoy regiment was disaffected, but the colonel published an unqualified denial, and declared that the rumour was false and malicious. The British residents at Allahabad were, however, by no means satisfied with this denial. They were alarmed at the reports which reached them of mutiny and murder elsewhere, and after the revolt at Delhi, they complained that they were not sufficiently protected. But no European soldiers were available, not even to garrison the important fortress. Accordingly the British authorities tried to allay the public fears by ordering up sixty-five European invalids from Chunar. Thus the European garrison of the great fortress at Allahabad, which commanded all communications between Bengal and the North-West, consisted for a while of sixty-five invalids. Eventually 100 European non-combatants formed themselves into a volunteer company, and helped to garrison the place. Meanwhile, every batch of European soldiers that arrived from Bengal was at once sent 120 miles further up the river Ganges to the city of Cawnpore, the frontier station towards Oudh.

Treachery.

Allahabad was tranquil. In spite of the outbreak at Meerut, the revolt at Delhi, and the reports of mutinies at other stations, all fear of danger seemed to have passed away. On the 1st of June, the suspected Bengal regiment volunteered to join the besieging force at Delhi. This movement was at once accepted as a certain proof of the loyalty and fidelity of the sepoys. The thanks of Lord Canning were sent by

CHAP. VI. telegraph to the officers and men, and news arrived at the same time that the sepoys had mutinied at Benares, and were in full march to Allahabad *en route* for Delhi.

Expected mutineers from Benares. Preparations were at once made for repulsing the rebels. The fortress was garrisoned by sixty-five European invalids, 100 European volunteers, 600 Sikhs, and 100 sepoys of the faithful Bengal regiment. The guns of the fortress were pointed to the Benares road. The only entrance to Allahabad in that direction was by a bridge over the Jumna. Accordingly two guns and two companies of the Bengal sepoys were ordered down to the bridge to open fire upon the mutineers from Benares.

Asiatic craft. On the 6th of June every European at Allahabad was expecting the mutineers from Benares. In the afternoon the thanks of Lord Canning were publicly read on the parade ground to the remaining companies of the Bengal sepoys. The men cheered like Europeans, and when the regiment fell out, the British officers shook hands with the sepoys. The mess dinner in the evening was attended by every British officer at the station who was not on duty elsewhere. At the mess table nothing was to be heard but rejoicings and congratulations. The Bengal regiment at Allahabad had proved its loyalty, and received the thanks of the Governor General. Eight young ensigns, mere boys, who had just arrived from England, were present at this memorable dinner.

Mutiny and massacre. Suddenly an alarm was sounded. No alarm was felt, however, because every one thought that the rebels from Benares had reached the bridge. The officers buckled on their swords, mounted their horses, and rode down to their lines to call out the men. On reaching the parade ground they were received by a volley of musketry from their own sepoys, the men with whom they had shaken hands that very afternoon. The colonel managed to escape to the fortress, but most of the officers were shot dead. At the same time the sepoy guards at the mess house fell on the young ensigns who had been left behind. The boys fought desperately for their lives, but were overpowered by numbers and brutally murdered.

Jumna bridge.

By this time the sepoys at the bridge heard the firing in the cantonment, and at once broke out in mutiny, and turned against their officers. The British officers were taken by surprise and could do nothing. Some were shot dead, but most of them plunged into the river Jumna, and escaped by swimming to the fortress.

Fortress at Allahabad.

All this while the Fort at Allahabad was in imminent danger. There were 200 Europeans within the walls, but many were invalids, and nearly all the others were volunteers. They had to deal with 400 doubtful Sikhs and 100 Bengal sepoys. They heard the sound of firing, and thought that the rebels had arrived from Benares; but the blazing bungalows in the cantonment soon told a very different story. The Bengal sepoys were promptly disarmed and turned out of the fortress. The Sikhs were left to do as they pleased. They soon began to plunder the European stores, which private merchants had deposited in the Fort for safety; and they sold the liquors to the European soldiers for small sums, so that drunkenness soon added to the general terror and confusion. The result was most lamentable. When British soldiers can buy excellent wines and spirits at a few pence

CHAP. VI. a bottle, they soon become drunk and incapable; and such was the state of affairs inside the fortress of Allahabad after the mutiny of the 6th of June.

Devilry. Meanwhile the horrible devilry outside the fortress was as murderous and destructive as at Meerut. The whole station was mad with excitement and riot. Houses were plundered and burnt. Women and children were tortured and butchered. The jail was broken open and every prisoner released. The sepoys plundered the treasury and divided the money amongst themselves, and then dispersed to their several homes to place the silver in a place of safety. But many suffered from their own folly. They were pursued by the very miscreants who had been let out of the jail, and many were savagely murdered and stripped of their ill-gotten treasures.

Neill restores order. Three days afterwards Colonel Neill reached Allahabad with a detachment of Europeans from Benares. He recovered the bridge, entered the fortress, took over the command of the station, and soon put an end to the drunkenness and disorder. He could not punish the Sikhs, for they were the only Asiatic soldiery who were likely to prove faithful, whilst the Bengal regiments were breaking out in mutiny on all sides. Accordingly he stopped the drunkenness of the European soldiers by buying up all the remaining liquors from the Sikhs, and making them over to his commissariat officers. He then turned the Sikhs out of the Fort, and encamped them without the walls but within range of the guns.

Cawnpore advance stopped. § 4. On the 30th of June Colonel Neill left Allahabad for Cawnpore with 400 Europeans, a regiment of Sikhs, and two squadrons of sepoy cavalry on whom he could not depend. Three days afterwards he received a terrible message from Sir Henry Lawrence at Lucknow. The sepoys had mutinied at Cawnpore. A Mahratta Brahman, named Nana Sahib, had taken possession of the town and cantonment with a large army of Mahratta soldiers and rebel sepoys. The Europeans at Cawnpore had been closely besieged by the enemy, but their fate was unknown. Neill, however, was ordered not to advance unless he had two complete regiments of Europeans under his command. Neill was therefore compelled to return to Allahabad, and to halt there for the arrival of more Europeans from Bengal.

Story of Cawnpore.

The story of Cawnpore is the most heart-rending episode in the annals of British India. In the earlier years of the century it had been the most important military station in Northern India. It was from Cawnpore that Lord Lake had started westward on his famous campaign against Sindia and the French sepoy battalions, which ended in the capture of Delhi and the deliverance of the Mogul from the Mahrattas. But the old glory had departed from Cawnpore. For years the British government had been concentrating its European strength at Meerut, Lahore, and Peshawar. Cawnpore was stripped of all European soldiers, and nothing remained of the British regiments that had once been quartered there, but some half-ruined barracks and a hospital.

General Wheeler.

In 1857 four regiments of sepoys were cantoned at Cawnpore, namely, three of infantry and one of light cavalry. But there was a large trading community of Europeans and the mixed race known as Eurasians. Moreover, there was a considerable number of ladies and children, families of the British officers of the

CHAP. VI. European regiment quartered at Lucknow. The station at Cawnpore was commanded by General Sir Hugh Wheeler, an old sepoy officer, who had served under Lord Lake, and was present during the Afghan and Sikh wars. He had been fifty-four years in India, and could thus look back upon a military career which began in 1803. He was familiar with sepoy ideas, feelings and aspirations. Yet not even General Wheeler, with his long experiences, was able to provide against such an unprecedented disaster as a mutiny of the Bengal army against greased cartridges.

Sore peril. Cawnpore is seated on the southern bank of the Ganges. It overlooks Oudh on the east and the North-West Provinces on the south and west. It is the vertex of an angle, fifty-five miles south-west from Lucknow, and 120 miles north-west from Allahabad. The European residents had been greatly alarmed at the revolt at Delhi, for both the town and the cantonment were absolutely at the mercy of the sepoys.

Barracks and hospital. Sir Hugh Wheeler had anxiously watched the flood of mutiny which was closing around him from the North-West Provinces, from Oudh, and from Bengal. He was anxious to provide for the safety of the Europeans without alarming the sepoys. Accordingly he repaired the old barracks and hospital as a refuge for the Europeans, entrenched them as well as he could, and stored up provisions for a siege. At the same time he ordered the British officers to show confidence in the sepoys by sleeping at the lines, and to spare no pains to keep the men staunch to their colours.

§ 5. About six miles to the northward of Cawnpore was a castellated palace, at a place known as

Ex-Peishwa at Bithoor.

Bithoor. Here the ex-Peishwa of the Mahrattas had been permitted to reside after his surrender to Sir John Malcolm, in 1818. He was harmless, and like all Brahmans was resigned to his fate. He lived like a king who had retired from business with an ample fortune, and he indulged in every sensual pleasure which money could command. He died in 1853, leaving no son, real or adopted.

Nana Sahib.

A boy was brought up in his household who was known as Nana Sahib. He also was a Mahratta Brahman, the son of a dependant of the ex-Peishwa; he was a favourite of the exiled prince and was treated as one of the family. Accordingly, when the ex-Peishwa died in 1853, Nana Sahib boldly asserted that he was an adopted son. The widow of the ex-Peishwa denied the fact, and asserted her own claims to the property. The truth has long ceased to be a matter of any consequence. Nana Sahib and the widow appear to have come to some secret understanding. He was permitted to inherit the castellated palace and grounds at Bithoor, as well as the money savings which amounted to about half a million sterling, and had been invested in government paper. He also provided for the widow in the palace of Bithoor.

Preposterous claims.

Nana Sahib had thus obtained all that he could possibly have claimed had he been adopted according to all the forms of Brahmanical law. But he laid claim to a continuation of the pension of £80,000 a year, which had been granted to the ex-Peishwa at the instance of Sir John Malcolm; and Lord Dalhousie refused to take his pretensions into consideration. Nana Sahib invented lies, which were plausible only to those who were not

CHAP. VI. familiar with the real circumstances. He declared that the ex-Peishwa had surrendered his dominions on the understanding that the pension should be granted to him and to his heirs for ever. But this falsehood was contradicted by history, and no one gave it the slightest credence except the enemies of the East India Company, or the opponents of Lord Dalhousie's policy.

Pertinacity. Nana Sahib was a genuine Mahratta, and would have persisted in forcing his claims from time to time upon the British government if he had lived for a hundred years. He was polite and smooth-tongued, flattering every European of influence that came in his way, and ever boasting of his loyalty to the British government. He professed to take the utmost pleasure in the society of Europeans, and was noted for his entertainments at Bithoor, to which he invited all the European society at Cawnpore. He affected to live in state like a Hindu Raja; he kept six guns for firing salutes, and entertained a large number of Mahratta troops and followers. But he never forgot his claim to the pension. He constantly harped upon the so-called injustice that deprived him of it; and he employed agents both in India and Great Britain to urge the British government to treat the pension as perpetual and hereditary.

Cunning. When the Bengal sepoys began to express horror at the greased cartridges, Nana Sahib denounced their folly in supposing that the British government had planned the destruction of their religion. When the news arrived of the outbreak at Meerut, he persuaded the civil officials at Cawnpore to send their wives and other ladies to Bithoor until the storm had blown over. He boasted that he could protect them against any number of sepoys, and arrangements were actually made for securing the ladies at Bithoor in the event of a mutiny. Later on, when the revolt at Delhi had become common talk, the Nana proposed to organise a body of 1,500 Mahrattas to take the sepoys by surprise, and put them all to the sword, should they show the slightest symptom of mutiny.

Anxieties of the Europeans.

By this time the anxiety of the Europeans at Cawnpore was becoming intolerable. The ladies especially suffered severely. On any night a signal might be given, and a mob of armed sepoys might be rushing about like madmen, burning down bungalows and murdering the women and children in their beds. All were yearning for the recapture of Delhi. Indeed, every European in India felt that the plague of sepoy mutiny would never be stayed until Delhi was once again in the hands of the British government.

Expected mutiny, 21st May

§ 6. On the 21st of May, Sir Hugh Wheeler received a distinct warning that the sepoys were about to mutiny. He sent to all the European residents at Cawnpore to repair towards evening to the empty barracks. He despatched an express to Lucknow to beg Sir Henry Lawrence to spare him two or three companies of the European regiment. He was alarmed for the safety of the treasury, which was seven miles from the barracks under the charge of sepoy guards. He attempted to remove the treasure to the barracks, but the sepoys refused to part with it, declaring that they could guard it where it was. Sir Hugh Wheeler was obliged to yield, for he had no means at hand to coerce the sepoys; but he accepted the offer of Nana Sahib to place a

CHAP. VI. body of his Mahratta soldiers on guard at the treasury. That very night 200 Mahratta soldiers, armed with matchlocks and accompanied by two guns, were moved from Bithoor and quartered at the treasury. The arrangements seem to have been made for the convenience of the sepoys, rather than for the security of the Europeans. The jail was close to the treasury, with its criminal inmates; so too was the magazine which contained the military stores. All three buildings were near the river Ganges on the road to Delhi.

Horrible suspense. The confusion and terror which prevailed that night may be imagined. Ladies and children were hurried from their homes, and huddled together in the old hospital building. Guns were drawn up on each side. The children were hushed off to sleep, but the ladies were too terrified to close their eyes. Next morning eighty-four European soldiers arrived from Lucknow and cheered the inmates of the hospital and barracks. But during the week that followed, the suspense was almost beyond endurance. One lady lost her reason, and all suffered from trials, privations, exposure and alarms which cannot be described. Daily and hourly they expected an insurrection of Asiatics who knew not how to pity or how to spare. Some wished that the storm would burst upon them and put an end to the harrowing anxiety that was eating into their souls. Amidst all these dangers the British officers still slept at the sepoy lines.

Hope. On the 31st of May, after a horrible night, the first instalment of European reinforcements arrived from Bengal. Others appeared during the two following days, and brought the joyful news that they were the forerunners of several regiments; that European troops were pouring into Calcutta from Madras, Burma and Ceylon, and were being hurried up by river steamers, bullock trains and country carriages. Sir Hugh Wheeler was so confident of being very shortly more than a match for the sepoys, that with a chivalrous regard for the safety of Sir Henry Lawrence, he sent a portion of his Europeans back to Lucknow.

Sickening delay.

Then followed the delays at Benares and Allahabad; the stoppage of reinforcements; the hope deferred that maketh the heart sick. To crown all, the Indian sun was burning fiercely on the barracks, and the hot winds of June were blowing through the rooms. Many Europeans were carried off by sickness, and their fate was almost to be envied, for life itself was becoming intolerable. Had the Europeans been all men, they might have cut their way to Agra, and forced a passage down the river to Allahabad. But Sir Hugh Wheeler had 300 women and children on his hands, and it was impossible to carry them away in the face of sepoys and rebels. No other alternative was thought of for a moment. No European could dream at such a crisis of leaving women and children to the tender mercies of sepoys.

Nana Sahib at Cawnpore.

§7. All this while there were no suspicions of treachery as regards Nana Sahib; yet in reality the Mahratta Brahman was moving about like an evil spirit in disguise. To show his loyalty and attachment to the British, he left his palace at Bithoor, and took up his quarters at a house within the civil station at Cawnpore. His real purpose was to excite the sepoys to revolt, but to prevent them from rushing off to Delhi, and rallying round a Mohammedan sovereign. He was not a Mohammedan, but a Hindu; besides that, he was a representative of Hindu sovereigns, the extinct Mahratta Peishwas, who, according to his own views, were the rightful rulers of India. In his secret heart he fondly dreamed of upsetting British supremacy, and restoring the old days of Mahratta anarchy, when the Brahman Peishwa ruled at Poona as the head of the Mahratta confederacy, whilst his lieutenants, Sindia and Holkar, plundered Hindustan in his name.

Blindness of the Europeans.

A more dangerous character than Nana Sahib never entered a British cantonment in India. The civil officials and the army officers were alike deceived. No one believed in his truth or honesty, but they imagined that he was looking after his own interest with that pertinacity which characterises Mahrattas. In other words, that he was rendering ostentatious services in the hope of being rewarded with the life pension of the deceased Peishwa.

Unpopularity of Nana Sahib.

But Nana Sahib encountered overwhelming difficulties from the outset. Like all Mahratta Brahmans he had the highest opinion of his caste and claims. Indeed his assumption was unbounded. But the Brahmans and Rajputs of Oudh and the North-West Provinces, who formed the bulk of the sepoy army of Bengal, were by no means inclined to accept a Mahratta sovereign, unless they were highly paid for their allegiance. They were prepared to make him their tool, and to tender him sham reverence, so long as he was liberal with money and bangles of gold or silver; but they had no more respect for the Mahratta, than the sepoys at Delhi had for the Mogul Padishah.

Nana Sahib seems to have been more or less aware of this state of affairs. He had entertained a large number of Mahratta soldiers ostensibly to help the British to suppress the sepoys; just as the ex-Peishwa had raised a Mahratta army in 1817 ostensibly to help the British to suppress the Pindharis. Meanwhile Nana Sahib quietly sold out the half million sterling which had been invested in government paper. He had thus ample funds for carrying out his designs. But neither Nana Sahib nor the sepoys betrayed the thoughts that were agitating their brains. Secrecy and surprise, with the necessary element of duplicity, are the main strength of Orientals.

CHAP. VI.

Secrecy and duplicity

§ 8. On the 4th of June, the very day that Neill reached Benares, Sir Hugh Wheeler was warned that the sepoys were plotting mutiny and murder. Accordingly he ordered the British officers to leave off sleeping at the sepoy lines. That same night the sepoys broke out in mutiny. The cavalry galloped off to the treasury and helped the Mahrattas to plunder it. The British officers left the barracks and hastened to the lines, but were fired upon by the sepoys. The rebels loaded a number of country carts with plunder from the treasury and magazine, and then set off with all speed to the first stage on the road to Delhi.

Mutiny of 4th June.

Nana Sahib accompanied the rebels, but implored them not to go to Delhi. He swore that a large treasure was hidden away in the barracks, and urged the sepoys to return and capture it, and slaughter all the Feringhis. Asiatics will believe any stories of hidden treasure. The sepoys were also told that

Nana Sahib joins the sepoys.

CHAP. VI. enough guns and powder remained in the magazine to enable them to storm the barracks with ease. Accordingly, on the 6th of June, the sepoys returned to Cawnpore with Nana Sahib at their head.

Propitiates Mohammedans and Hindus. Nana Sahib now began to appear in his true colours. He pitched his camp in the centre of the station and hoisted two standards, to conciliate both Mohammedans and Hindus; namely, the green flag of Islam, and the Hindu god Hanuman, the friend of Rama, the avatar of Vishnu. He sent a body of horsemen into the town of Cawnpore to kill every European and Christian they could find. He mounted some heavy guns and prepared to assault the entrenched barracks.

Bombardment of European barracks. Next morning, the 7th of June, Nana Sahib sent a letter to General Wheeler threatening to attack the British garrison. Several guns began to open fire on the barracks, and volleys of musketry were discharged from all quarters. Meanwhile Nana Sahib was reinforced by mutineers from Allahabad, by irregulars from Lucknow, by rebels from Oudh, and by armed bands of brigands and blackguards from all the country round.

Cruelty and cowardice. At this period Nana Sahib was guilty of cowardly malice and revolting cruelty which appear incredible to Europeans. British refugees were flying from mutinous sepoys; floating down the river Ganges in boats in the hope of reaching Allahabad. They were arrested at Cawnpore, brought before the inhuman Mahratta, and brutally murdered. Men, women, and children were cut to pieces like cattle. The Europeans in the barracks heard nothing of these butcheries, or the story of Cawnpore would have had a different ending. But they knew enough to resist to the death every assault of the enemy. The rebels, on their part, kept up a hot fire, and made frequent rushes on the earthworks, but they never ventured on hand-to-hand encounters. Their one solitary exploit was to set fire to the hospital, and then, whilst the place was burning, and every effort was being made to save the inmates, a mass of rebels tried to storm the barracks. The assault, however, was a failure. The enemy was driven back by the British guns, but many of the sick and wounded Europeans perished in the flaming hospital.

Parleying and perfidy.

On the 24th and 25th of June there was some parleying. The British garrison could hold out no longer. Provisions and stores were exhausted. Nana Sahib was frightened and humiliated by the obstinate courage of the British. Moreover he was yearning for the pomp and pleasure of sovereignty. Under such circumstances he sent written messages to General Wheeler by the hands of a woman. He solemnly swore that he would provide boats for the passage of the whole of the beleaguered Europeans down the Ganges to Allahabad, provided the British would surrender their arms, and leave him in possession of the cannon, and of what remained in the treasury and magazine. Few men of Indian experience would have trusted in the good faith of Nana Sahib; but Sir Hugh Wheeler was bowed down by the weight of years, and by the terrible responsibility of the women and children, and in an evil hour he accepted the terms offered by the false-hearted Mahratta.

Massacre.

§ 9. On the morning of the 27th of June, 450 Europeans left the barracks and proceeded to the river side. The sick and wounded were carried in palanquins; the women and children were placed on elephants and bullock carts; the men went on foot. Forty boats were moored in the shallows of the river, and the men waded through the water whilst the others were carried to the boats. All were on board by nine o'clock, and the boats were loosened from their moorings. A crowd of sepoys and rebels was assembled on both banks of the river to witness the departure of the Europeans. Suddenly a bugle was sounded. Volleys of musketry were fired upon the boats, and shrieks of agony and terror rose from the hapless passengers. Presently the thatched roofs of some of the boats caught fire, and the flames rapidly spread as the boats were huddled together. Many of the doomed passengers jumped overboard. One boat escaped down the stream, but only four individuals survived to tell the story. Many were shot dead or were drowned in the river. The rest were all dragged ashore helpless and unarmed. The men were allowed a few moments to prepare for death, and one of their number who had preserved a Prayer Book, read a portion of the Liturgy. All the men were then shot dead by volleys of musketry. The women and children, who escaped alive, to the number of 125, were carried off and lodged in a building close to the head-quarters of Nana Sahib.

Triumph of Nana Sahib.

That night there were great rejoicings in the station at Cawnpore. The Mahratta Brahman was puffed up with his so-called victory over British captives. Money and bangles were freely distributed to the murderers, whilst salutes were fired from the cannon, and the whole station was ablaze with fireworks and illuminations. The infamous Nana Sahib, the last faint shadow of the Mahratta Brahmans who had once reigned at Poona, was proclaimed conqueror of the British, and Peishwa of Hindustan.

Terrors.

But the avenging furies were already at the heels of the Mahratta Brahman. Neither drugs nor dancing girls could quiet his terrors. The Mohammedan sepoys were already plotting his destruction; they wanted to restore the reign of Islam, not to set up the idolatry which was denounced in the Koran. The lavish distribution of treasures might please them for a while, but would not satisfy them in the end. Meanwhile, the Rajputs were ready enough to accept his rupees and bangles, but they were his masters, and compelled him to do their bidding. To crown his anxieties, a column of European soldiers was soon on its way from Allahabad to avenge the slaughter of their countrymen at Cawnpore, and to deliver British wives, mothers, and widows, together with their helpless children, from the hands of the perjured destroyer.

Massacre at Jhansi.

That same month of June saw a like massacre at Jhansi, about 150 miles to the south of Cawnpore, amidst the hills and jungles of Bundelkund. British rule had been introduced, together with a garrison of Bengal sepoys. The sepoys mutinied as they did elsewhere, and the Europeans, to the number of fifty-five men, women, and children, took refuge in an old fortress until the storm blew over. The sepoys could not capture the fortress. The widow of the deceased chief sent them elephants and guns, but they were of no avail. At last it was known that the provisions within the fortress were exhausted. The widow and the sepoys solemnly swore to conduct the besieged to another station, if they

CHAP. VI. would only lay down their arms. The terms were accepted; the besieged left the fortress two by two, and were all seized, bound, and butchered without further parley.

General Havelock. § 10. Early in July, General Havelock reached Allahabad with 1,000 Europeans and 200 Sikhs, and joined his forces with those of Colonel Neill, and took the command. The one object of the expedition was to relieve the British garrisons at Cawnpore and Lucknow, and to save the women and children.

Henry Havelock was short in stature, and spare in form. He was a pale man of ascetic habits, who might have served in Cromwell's Ironsides. He was a soldier to the backbone, but religious to the verge of fanaticism. His whole life was devoted to fighting and prayer. He thirsted for military glory and the conversion of Mohammedans and Hindus. He had seen much service. He had distinguished himself in the first Burma war and the first Afghan war, and had published clear and able narratives of both campaigns. He had also distinguished himself in the Gwalior war and the two Sikh wars; and he had just returned from the Persian expedition, in which he had commanded a division. But the straitness of his religious views had interfered with his promotion, and the greater part of his life had been spent in regimental duty. He was approaching the age when men usually retire from active service; but he was destined, during the last few months of his career, to become famous throughout the civilised world.

Advance on Cawnpore. On the 7th of July General Havelock left Allahabad for Cawnpore with less than 2,000 Europeans and

Sikhs. By this time the slaughter of the Europeans at Cawnpore was noised abroad, but there were still hopes of saving the women and children. There was a march of 120 miles between Allahabad and Cawnpore. An Indian sun glared down at intervals, but the heat was moderated by heavy rains, which were equally deadly. Fever, dysentery, and cholera, carried off more victims than the enemy's fire. But men and officers were one and all animated by the same determined spirit to be revenged on Nana Sahib and the rebels, and to save the women and children at Cawnpore.

Treachery of a deputy-collector.

At Futtehpore, about two-thirds of the way to Cawnpore, there had been a sepoy mutiny, and a civil rebellion, headed by a Mohammedan deputy collector. The European residents had already sent their wives and families to Allahabad, and when the outbreak took place they all escaped on horseback save one. The exception was Mr. Robert Tucker, of the Bengal civil service, the judge of the district, who refused to abandon his post. The Asiatics, headed by the Mohammedan deputy-collector, environed Mr. Tucker's house and overpowered him, but not until he had slain sixteen men with his own hands. He was then brought to a mock trial, at which the Mohammedan presided, and of course was condemned and executed, and his head, hands, and feet held up for the inspection of the rabble.

Defeat of the Nana.

When Nana Sahib was master of Cawnpore, he sent a large force of rebel cavalry to Futtehpore, to defeat the European column, and if possible to capture the fortress of Allahabad. But he was too late. Had the rebels advanced against Allahabad before the outbreak, they might have captured the

CHAP. VI. fortress, and blocked out all reinforcements from Bengal. As it was, they were utterly defeated and dispersed by Havelock's column.

Execution of a murderer. After the battle the Mohammedan deputy-collector appeared to offer his congratulations to General Havelock. To his intense surprise, he found that his crime was known to the British authorities. He was arrested on the spot, and within a brief interval he was tried, convicted, and hanged for the murder of the British judge.

Tragedy at Cawnpore. § 11. Next day another rebel force was routed, and then followed a crowning victory at Cawnpore. But now Havelock was too late. Maddened by defeat, Nana Sahib had ordered the slaughter of the women and children, and then had fled away in the hope of finding refuge at his castle at Bithoor.

The well. Never before had British soldiers beheld such a sight as met their eyes at Cawnpore. Other fugitive women and children had been captured by Nana Sahib, and 200 helpless beings had been imprisoned in the same building. A veil may be thrown over their sufferings. Some of the poor ladies were compelled to grind corn for the household of Nana Sahib, and they were glad to do so, as it enabled them to bring back some flour for their half-starved children. In this wretched plight, longing for relief but despairing of succour, they had been suddenly attacked by sepoys and rebels, and mercilessly hacked to pieces with swords and hatchets, and then thrust into a well. Never, so long as a Briton remains in India, will the ghastly well at Cawnpore be forgotten. Since then a Christian church has been built over the well, and a marble angel is seen with outspread wings, as if imploring forgiveness and mercy.

Destruction of Bithoor.

Havelock advanced to Bithoor, but Nana Sahib had fled into Oudh. At Bithoor Havelock demolished the castle, and brought away the guns. Within a few days he left General Neill at Cawnpore, and crossed the Ganges into Oudh with a force of 1,500 Europeans and Sikhs, for the relief of Lucknow.

Lucknow: May to July.

§ 12. It was now the middle of July, and it is necessary to glance at the progress of affairs at Lucknow since the 3rd of May. On that day an irregular corps of Oudh sepoys had threatened to murder its European adjutant; but that same night a force of European soldiers and Bengal sepoys marched against them. The mutineers surrendered their arms, and then rushed off in a panic of terror towards Delhi. The Bengal sepoys hotly pursued them, and arrested the ringleaders. But the scare at greased cartridges was rankling in the breasts of these very Bengal sepoys; and Sir Henry Lawrence had reason to fear that sooner or later they would break out in mutiny like the Oudh irregulars.

Bengal sepoys rewarded.

For the moment, however, the Bengal regulars had been overawed by the prompt action of the Europeans. Accordingly Sir Henry Lawrence determined on a public distribution of presents to the Asiatic officers and sepoys who had distinguished themselves on the 3rd of May; and thus to show that if the British government was prompt to punish mutiny, it was equally prompt in rewarding faithful service.

Durbar of 12th May.

A grand durbar was held on the evening of the 12th of May. The whole of the European civil and

CHAP. VI. military residents at Lucknow, all the officers and men of the Bengal regiments, and many Asiatic officials were assembled on the lawn in front of the Residency. Carpets had been laid down, and chairs arranged to form three sides of a square. Sir Henry Lawrence entered, followed by his staff, and a large body of officers, and took his seat at the head of the assemblage. Beside him were deposited the trays of presents. Before, however, distributing the rewards, he delivered a solemn and earnest speech in Hindustani.

Speech of Sir Henry Lawrence. Sir Henry Lawrence reminded the Hindu sepoys that Mohammedan rulers had never respected their religion, and had converted many Hindus to Islam by forcing beef down their throats. He reminded the Mohammedan sepoys that their religion had been cruelly persecuted by the Sikh rulers of the Punjab. He reminded one and all that for a whole century the British government had tolerated both Hinduism and Islam, and never interfered with either. He dwelt on the power and resources of Great Britain, her numerous ships and her exploits in the Russian war; and he declared that within a few months she could assemble an army as large as that in the Crimea in the vicinity of Lucknow. He urged all present to believe the assurances of the British government, and he solemnly warned the sepoys that if any of them became the dupes of fools or knaves, like the mutineers at Berhampore and Barrackpore, the British would inflict such a punishment as would be remembered for generations. The presents were then distributed, and Sir Henry Lawrence shook hands with the recipients.

The speech and the rewards made a deep impression on the sepoys, but it did not last. Four days later the news arrived of the revolt at Delhi, and mischief was again brewing. Another fortnight passed away without mutiny, and Sir Henry Lawrence gained time for making the necessary preparations. He entrenched the Residency and adjoining buildings, and collected large quantities of provisions and stores. Meanwhile the Europeans in Lucknow, who were not serving as regimental officers, were formed into a volunteer corps.

News of revolt at Delhi, 16th May.

General mutiny, 30th May.

On the 30th of May, in the middle of the night, about 2,000 sepoys of the regular Bengal army broke out in mutiny at the cantonment on the opposite side of the river. European officers were killed, and houses were pillaged and burnt. Sir Henry Lawrence hurried across the river with a company of Europeans and two guns, to protect the bridges and prevent the mutineers from communicating with the disaffected population of Lucknow. Presently the sepoys came rushing up to the bridges, but were driven back by a volley of grape. They dispersed, but made no attempt to reach Delhi. On the contrary, they halted at a place named Sitapore, within the province of Oudh, where they remained several weeks and did nothing.

Proposed retreat to Cawnpore.

Meanwhile the storm was gathering. Early in June news arrived of the treachery of Nana Sahib at Cawnpore. General Wheeler wrote to Sir Henry Lawrence imploring help and protection for the women and children in the barracks. But Sir Henry Lawrence was in sore straits and could not spare a European soldier. He had been authorised to withdraw from Oudh in case of emergency, and possibly had he beat a retreat from Lucknow to Cawnpore, he

CHAP. VI. might have prevented the massacres. But the step would have been more hazardous and desperate than the abandonment of Peshawar by his brother John. No one anticipated massacre, and reinforcements of Europeans from Bengal might reach Cawnpore at any moment, and stamp out the mutiny and crush the Nana. Retreat from Oudh would not only have involved the loss of a province, but imparted a fatal strength to mutiny and murder from Bengal to the Punjab. The flag of Mohammedan revolt was still floating over Delhi, and had it floated over Lucknow, the second Mohammedan city in Hindustan, British prestige would have vanished for a while from Northern India.

Mutineers in the districts. In June mutiny and murder were running riot at different stations in Oudh. At some places the atrocities committed on Europeans were heartrending. At one station there was an outbreak on a Sunday morning. The sepoys rushed into the church during divine service and killed the British magistrate and several officers. Some thirty Europeans, including ladies and children, fled for their lives, and escaped to a station named Mohamdi, where a detachment of Oudh irregulars were quartered under the command of Captain Orr. The very sight of European fugitives taking refuge at the station, drove the sepoys into rebellion. Captain Orr assembled the Asiatic officers and appealed to their common humanity. The men were moved to compassion. They crossed their arms on the head of one of their comrades, and solemnly swore to conduct all the Europeans in safety to another station.

The convoy started at five o'clock in the evening; the men on foot or on horseback, and the women and children in a carriage and baggage waggon. Suddenly they found that they were pursued by sepoys. They did their best to hasten on the carriage and waggon, but were soon overtaken and surrounded. A gun was fired, a British officer was shot down, and then followed a general massacre. Women and children were slaughtered with infernal cruelty. A few fugitives escaped the slaughter, but were doomed to privations and sufferings on which it is painful to dwell.

Massacre of Europeans.

Hostility at Lucknow.

§ 13. The Residency at Lucknow was still a place of refuge, although it might possibly be soon overwhelmed by numbers. No effort was spared by the disaffected to stir up the city population against the British authorities. Proclamations were posted from day to day on Hindu temples, and Mohammedan mosques and palaces, calling upon the people to wage a holy war against the Feringhi. Horrible effigies, dressed as British officers and children, but without heads, were carried through the streets by the rabble. Plots were discovered and individuals were arrested, but British prestige was dying out with alarming rapidity, and by the end of June British authority had little influence outside the limits of the Residency at Lucknow.

Disaster at Chinhut.

On the 29th of June reports came in that an army of 6,000 rebels was marching towards the British Residency, and that an advanced guard of 1,000 might be expected to arrive on the following morning. Sir Henry Lawrence marched out to attack the advance guard, with 300 Europeans, eleven guns, and about 300 Asiatics, including sepoy cavalry, and native artillery drivers. There was treachery

CHAP. VI. from the outset. Instead of an advanced guard of 1,000, the whole body of insurgents was hidden in the jungle behind the village of Chinhut, about six miles from the Residency. As Sir Henry Lawrence approached he was met by a heavy fire from a battery of guns posted in the village. The Europeans advanced; the British guns returned the enemy's fire with great effect, and victory was assured. At that moment the Asiatic artillery drivers turned traitors, cut the traces, tumbled the guns into a ditch, and deserted to the enemy. The 300 Europeans were thus left exposed to a terrible fire and forced to beat a retreat. They were compelled to abandon their killed and wounded, and only one hundred reached the Residency. Sir Henry Lawrence was severely wounded, and worn out with fatigue and despair, but was brought away on a gun-carriage.

Defence of the Residency

The rebel army followed the Europeans. They reached the bridge which led to the Residency, but were driven back by the fire of the British batteries. They forded the river at another spot, and began to plunder the wealthy quarter of Lucknow. This gave the British garrison breathing time. They abandoned the cantonment on the opposite bank, and many of the buildings near the Residency. Henceforth they contracted the area of defence to the British Residency and a few houses within the Residency enclosure.

Residency besieged, 30th June.

The siege of the British Residency soon began in right earnest. The besieged within the enclosure numbered 500 British soldiers, 150 British officers, 500 women and children, and some 300 or 400 sepoys who had remained loyal. The besiegers soon numbered from 25,000 to 50,000 rebels. They environed the Residency enclosure with a circle of guns. They kept up a heavy and continuous fire, and killed and wounded many of the British garrison, but they could not capture a single position. CHAP. VI.

Death of Sir Henry Lawrence, 4th July.

On the second day of the siege Sir Henry Lawrence was mortally wounded by the bursting of a shell. He died on the 4th of July, exhorting those around him to entrench night and day, and to shut their ears against all suggestions of surrender. Such was the terrible lesson which had been taught to every European in India by the treacherous massacres at Cawnpore.

Dissension amongst the rebels.

The besiegers increased in numbers with marvellous rapidity. They were joined by all the rebel sepoys in Oudh; by the vassals of the talukdars, who were mostly brigands; and by the scum of the population of Lucknow. They were, however, at constant strife with each other; torn by quarrels about religion, politics, or personal animosities. One prince was raised to the throne and another was placed in command of the army, but their authority was nominal. The rebels elected their own officers, and the officers chose their own generals; but cowardice and insubordination were rampant, and commanding officers often lost their lives in attempts to uphold their short-lived dignities.

Anarchy in the city.

Meanwhile there was a reign of terror in the city of Lucknow. The orderly and peaceful classes, which made up the bulk of the population, were overwhelmed by taxes and exactions of all kinds; and bankers, traders and other wealthy citizens, must have yearned for the restoration of a rule under which life and property were always respected.

At early morning, on the 21st of July, there was

CHAP. VI.

Repulse of rebels, 21st July: news of Havelock.

a general assault. The batteries opened on the Residency from all sides. The sepoys advanced in compact masses to the trenches, but were driven back by the fire of the Europeans. The next day the struggle was renewed, but with the same result. The British garrison, amidst all these toils and privations, exulted in the conviction that they could repulse the assaults of the rebel besiegers until help should arrive. That very night a faithful sepoy got inside the Residency with the news that General Havelock had compelled Nana Sahib to fly for his life, and had recaptured the city and cantonment of Cawnpore.

Havelock retreats.

§ 14. Havelock failed to reach Lucknow. His brave little column worked wonders. It scattered large armies of rebels by bayonet charges, but it was rapidly reduced by three fatal diseases—fever, dysentery and cholera. Havelock could not spare troops for keeping up his communications with Cawnpore; he was compelled to carry his sick and wounded with him, and he was losing fifty men a day. Before he had fought his way a third of the distance, he was compelled with a heavy heart to fall back on Cawnpore.

Mutiny in Behar: defence of Arrah.

Havelock reached Cawnpore just in time to save Neill from being overwhelmed by rebel armies. European reinforcements from Bengal had again been delayed by mutinies. At Patna there had been a Mohammedan plot which was quashed at the outset by Mr. William Tayler, a Bengal civilian. At Dinapore, ten miles west of Patna, three sepoy regiments had mutinied. At Arrah, twenty-five miles still further to the west, a large body of rebels had attacked and plundered the station; but sixteen Europeans and fifty Sikhs defended a single house against 3,000 rebels for an entire week, when they were relieved by a detachment of Europeans from Dinapore under the command of Major Vincent Eyre.

European garrison at Lucknow.

Meanwhile the suspense of the Europeans in the Residency at Lucknow was becoming intense. The provisions were coarse and beginning to fail. Most of the native servants and all the bakers had fled at the beginning of the siege. Balls, bullets, and fragments of shells fell into every dwelling-place; and ladies and children on beds of sickness were as much exposed to the fire of the enemy as the soldiers in the trenches. There was, however, no slackening on the part of the garrison. Every man in the Residency worked in the trenches. Officers, soldiers, and civilians were either returning the enemy's fire, or digging with spades and pickaxes. The rains allayed the burning heat; but fever, dysentery, and cholera carried off their victims. No one thought of capitulation. Cawnpore had steeled every British heart. Husbands and fathers would have slain their own wives and daughters, rather than they should have fallen into the hands of the merciless besiegers.

Delay of Havelock.

All this while General Havelock was impatient to attempt a second advance on Lucknow. His force was too small to fight a way through the streets of the city into the Residency enclosure. Could the garrison have cut their way out, he might possibly have convoyed the whole body in safety to Cawnpore. But Brigadier Inglis, who commanded the garrison, was hampered with 450 women and children. He had no carriage, and in any case he was unwilling to

CHAP. VI. abandon the guns and treasure. So Havelock and Inglis were both compelled to await the arrival of further reinforcements from Bengal.

Advance of Havelock and Outram, September. § 15. At last about the middle of September, a column of 3,000 troops was formed at Cawnpore, of whom 2,700 were Europeans. General Sir James Outram was sent from Calcutta to take the command, and Havelock must have smarted at the supersession; but Outram, who was known as the Bayard of India, chivalrously refused to supersede him. Accordingly the column left Cawnpore under Havelock's command.

Britons to the rescue. Never in British history had a more resolute or enthusiastic column of soldiers taken the field. It was something for the crusaders to wrest Jerusalem from the infidels. It was something to stand against overwhelming numbers at Agincourt and Cressy. But Havelock and his men had to rescue British women and children from the horrible fate that befell the victims at Cawnpore; and neither shot nor shell, bullet nor barricade, could have availed against British valour in such a cause.

City and Residency. There was a five days' toilsome march from the Ganges at Cawnpore to the city of Lucknow. Then a day's halt for rest. Then on the glorious 25th of September, Havelock and his men fought their way into the city, whilst Outram, with a sublime contempt for rebels, scorned to draw his sword, and hammered about with a walking-stick. But the work was no child's play. A rebel battery had to be carried with the bayonet. Then the high street was reached, which led from the suburbs to the Residency, but it was long and narrow. The British column might have suffered heavily from barricades, or from a raking fire which might have been opened from the houses on either side. Outram, however, was familiar with the whole labyrinth of roads and lanes. He led the main body through by-ways towards the Residency, whilst the high street was closed by Highlanders and Sikhs. Towards evening a junction was formed, and the united forces marched straight on to the Residency.

Anxieties of the garrison.

Throughout the whole day the beleaguered garrison in the Residency had been anxious and bewildered. In the morning they heard the roar of cannon in the distant suburbs. They beheld a mob of Asiatic fugitives from the city—men, women, and children, with terrified sepoys in full uniform—all rushing to the bridges, or wading and swimming through the river. The guns of the Residency opened fire, but the rebel batteries responded with a storm of shot and shell. In the afternoon discharges of musketry were heard; the fusillade drew nearer and nearer. Presently the Europeans and Sikhs appeared on the scene with mounted officers in front. Finally Havelock and Outram dismounted from their horses, and were carried on the shoulders of their men through an embrasure into the Residency.

Cheers and tears.

§ 16. Then arose ringing cheers which must have astonished the Hindu gods on Mount Meru. The pent-up hearts of the half-starved garrison could find no other way of giving vent to their emotions. From every pit, trench, and battery, from behind sand-bags piled on shattered houses, from the sick and wounded in the hospital, nothing was to be heard but shouts and cries of welcome. The British soldiers who poured into the Residency were equally moved

CHAP. VI. They had saved women and children from the destroyer. Rough and bearded warriors shook hands with the ladies all round. They took the children in their arms, kissed them and passed them from one to the other; and with tears running down their cheeks, they thanked God that all were rescued. But in the hour of gladness there was a dash of sorrow. The gallant Neill had met with a glorious death in the streets of Lucknow.

Havelock's dilemma. Havelock and Outram had cut their way into the Residency, but the question was how to get out again. It was comparatively easy to lead enthusiastic battalions into a beleaguered fortress, but it was a very different thing to convoy 400 women and children, 600 sick and wounded, and a quarter of a million sterling in silver, through the narrow streets of Lucknow exposed to the fire of swarms of rebels thirsting for blood and rupees.

Unexpected provisions. There was, however, no alternative. Provisions were exhausted. Suddenly the commissariat discovered a vast stock of grain which had been overlooked after the death of Sir Henry Lawrence. The problem was solved. The oxen which dragged the guns, ammunition, and baggage of Havelock's column would furnish the garrison with butcher's meat for months. Accordingly it was determined to remain behind the defences of the Residency enclosure until another European army advanced to the conquest of Oudh.

Sir James Outram in command. Sir James Outram was now chief commissioner of Oudh, and general in command of the garrison. Many positions were wrested from the rebels, and the area of defence was enlarged. The garrison was no longer in daily peril, and it was felt that an avenging army of Europeans and Sikhs would soon deliver them.

Advance of Sir Colin Campbell, November.

§ 17. Meanwhile, Sir Colin Campbell, one of the heroes in the Russian war, had been appointed commander-in-chief of the Bengal army, in succession to General Anson. He reached Calcutta in August, and prepared for a second expedition against Lucknow. In October an army of 4,700 Europeans and thirty-two guns was assembled at Cawnpore. In November the expedition set out for Lucknow, under the new commander-in-chief.[1] It included a detachment of sailors from the *Shannon* frigate, who had brought their guns to bear upon the rebels, under the command of Captain William Peel, a son of the illustrious Sir Robert. The sailors excited the wonder of Asiatics, especially as it was reported that they had fish-tails like tritons, and were harnessed to the guns.

Deliverance: death of Havelock.

Sir Colin Campbell did not attempt to drive the rebels out of the city of Lucknow. His one object was to bring away the besieged from the Residency. By Outram's advice he did not advance through streets or by-ways, but made a detour through the palaces and other royal buildings. After much hard fighting, he reached the Residency, and brought away all the besieged at twenty-four hours' notice. The besiegers were outwitted. They knew nothing ot what was going on, and continued to fire upon the Residency for hours after it had been abandoned.

[1] During the march, the 93d Highlanders suddenly stopped, broke their ranks, and rushed off right and left like madmen. It was thought that they were seized with a panic. It turned out that they were flying from bees, who were swarming at their bare legs and stinging like fury.

CHAP. VI. But again there was sadness. General Havelock lived long enough to receive the cross of Knight Commander of the Bath, and died amidst the tears of the women and children whom he had done his best to rescue.

Gwalior rebels at Cawnpore. § 18. Many a soldier grieved over the retirement from Lucknow, but the retreat was a painful necessity. The Gwalior contingent, maintained by Sindia under the treaty of 1843, had broken out in mutiny and joined the forces of Nana Sahib. An army of 20,000 rebels advanced on Cawnpore, defeated Brigadier Wyndham, who had been left in charge, and occupied the town. Sir Colin Campbell shipped the precious convoy from Lucknow on board a flotilla of steamers, and despatched them to Calcutta. He then took the field, and drove the Gwalior rebels out of Cawnpore.

Calcutta, 30th January, 1858. On the 30th of January, 1858, all the Europeans in Calcutta flocked to the banks of the Hughly, to welcome the return of the besieged from Lucknow; but when a procession of widows and orphans appeared in black raiment, with pallid faces and emaciated forms, the acclamations of the crowd died away in a deep and painful silence, and every eye was filled with tears for the sufferings of the survivors of the beleaguered garrison at Lucknow.

Conclusion. § 19. Here ends the story of the siege and reliet of Lucknow. In 1858 Oudh was conquered, the rebellion was crushed, peace and order were restored, and a compromise with the talukdars was effected on the battle-field. The reconciliation of the people of Oudh with British rule and supremacy will be noted in a future chapter.

CHAP. VI.

Causes of the revolt in Oudh.

Greased cartridges were the cause of the sepoy mutinies of 1857, but they were not the cause of the revolt in Oudh; and yet it was impossible for the British government to postpone the deposition of the king of Oudh or the annexation of the kingdom.

Unheeded warnings.

Oudh had been drifting into anarchy ever since it had been taken under British protection. Every Governor-General from Lord Wellesley to Lord Dalhousie had denounced the administration of Oudh as tyrannical, oppressive, and corrupt. Every ruler of Oudh had been threatened in turn; but as the Resident was warned not to interfere beyond tendering advice, repeated threats were as unheeded as the old cry of "wolf." Sir James Outram, the Bayard of India, and last British Resident at Lucknow, summed up his views in the following words:—"I have always been the upholder of native states as long as they retained a spark of vitality, and we could recognise them without infringing our treaties or our suzerain power. It is, therefore, most painful for me to have to acknowledge that if we persist in maintaining this feeble and corrupt dynasty, we shall be sacrificing the interests of ten millions of individuals whom we are bound by treaty to protect by ensuring them a good government, capable of defending the life and property of its subjects."

Feudatory states: mutinous contingents.

The feudatory states of India which owe allegiance to the British government displayed no sympathies with the Bengal sepoy, or with their mutinies against greased cartridges. Some may have trimmed and wavered, and were prepared to join the winning side. Contingent and subsidiary forces caught the infatuation against greased cartridges, and revolted against their British officers, and joined the mutineers.

CHAP. VI. The Gwalior contingent revolted, but Sindia remained loyal. Holkar's troops revolted at Indore, and murdered every European they could find; and this could scarcely have been a rebellion against greased cartridges.[1] But after the lapse of a generation any suspicions of disloyalty, that may linger in the minds of those who are familiar with the history of the time, may be dropped in oblivion.

[1] For an interesting account of the state of affairs in Central India during the mutinies of 1857, see *Life of Major-General Sir Henry M. Durand*, by his Son. 2 vols. 8vo. London, 1883. Sir Henry Durand was Agent to the Governor-General for Central India, and Resident at Indore, during the mutinies.

PART II.

THE BRITISH CROWN.

CHAPTER THE LAST.

CONSTITUTIONAL GOVERNMENT.

1858—1886.

§ 1. Awakening of the British Nation. § 2. Government Education in India: Toleration. § 3. British Rule after the Mutiny: Legislative Council of 1854 and Executive Council: Wrongs of Non-Official Europeans. § 4. Mr. James Wilson and his Income-Tax. § 5. New Legislative Council of 1861-62. § 6. New High Court: proposed District Courts. § 7. Lord Canning leaves India. § 8. Lord Elgin, 1862-63. § 9. Sir John Lawrence, 1864-69: Governments of Madras and Bombay: Migrations to Simla: Foreign Affairs. § 10. Lord Lawrence leaves India. § 11. Lord Mayo, 1869-72. § 12. Lord Northbrook, 1872-76: Royal visits to India. § 13. Lord Lytton, 1876-80: Empress Proclaimed. § 14. Second Afghan War. § 15. Political and Judicial Schools. § 16. Constitution of British India: proposed Reforms.

Extinction of the East India Company.

THE great and grand East India Company was brought to a close after a busy life of two centuries and a half, extending from the age of Elizabeth to that of Victoria. It was still in a green old age, but could not escape extinction. The story of mutiny and revolt raised a storm in the British Isles which demanded the sacrifice of a victim, and the Company was thrown overboard like another Jonah. In July, 1858, India was transferred to the Crown by Act of Parliament. In the following

CHAP. THE LAST. November proclamation was made throughout India that Her Majesty Queen Victoria had assumed the direct government of her Eastern empire. The Governor-General ceased to rule in the name of the East India Company, and became Viceroy of India. The old Court of Directors, which dated back to the Tudors, and the Board of Control, which dated back to William Pitt the younger, were alike consigned to oblivion. Henceforth India was managed by a Secretary of State in Council, and Great Britain was an Asiatic power.

Alarm and panic in Great Britain. § 1. The sepoy mutinies awakened the British nation from the lethargy of forty years. At one time it was aroused by the discovery that the East India Company had acquired an empire larger than that of Napoleon; but was soon immersed once more in its own insular concerns. The sepoy revolt of 1857 stirred it up to its innermost depths. The alarms swelled to a panic. Exeter Hall clamoured for the conversion of Hindus and Mohammedans to Christianity. Some called aloud for vengeance on Delhi. The inhabitants were to be slaughtered as David slaughtered the Ammonites; the city was to be razed to the ground and its site sown with salt. Others, more ignorant than either, denounced the East India Company and Lord Dalhousie; demanded the restoration of British territory to Asiatic rulers, and the abandonment of India to its ancient superstition and stagnation.

British ignorance. In the olden time India was only known to the bulk of the British nation as a land of idol-worshippers, who burnt living widows with their dead husbands, tortured themselves by swinging on hooks, thrust javelins through their tongues, prostrated themselves beneath the wheels of Juggernauth's car, and threw their dying and dead into the holy Ganges, under a child-like faith that the safest way of going to heaven was by water. Educated men knew that the greater part of India had been previously conquered by Mohammedans, just as Syria and Persia were conquered by Arabs and Turks. It was also known that Mohammedans hated idolatry, broke down idols and pagodas, built mosques in their room, and forced many Hindus to accept Islam. But few, excepting those who had lived in India, knew anything of its affairs, or cared to know anything about them, except when war was declared against Afghans, Sikhs, or Burmese, or when Parliament was about to renew the charter of the late East India Company.

Missionary and educational movements.

But the instincts of the British nation are generally healthy and sensible. It subscribed largely to missionary societies, and was led by flaming reports to expect the speedy conversion of Hindus and Mohammedans. Such aspirations, however, were not to be realised. The devout were obliged to wait and pray; the sensible urged the East India Company to provide for the secular education of the masses. For centuries the rising generation had learnt something of reading, writing, and arithmetic from village schoolmasters, mostly Brahmans. These hereditary schoolmasters taught the village boys from generation to generation, in the same old-world fashion, with palm-leaves for books, sanded boards and floors for writing lessons, and clay marbles for working out little sums. Christian missionaries had established schools from an early period, especially in Southern India; and to this day nearly every Asiatic servant

CHAP. THE LAST — in the city of Madras can speak English indifferently well. Meanwhile the East India Company had done little or nothing for the education of the masses, nor indeed had much been done by the British government for its own people in those illiterate days.

Government High Schools, 1841: Hindus and Mohammedans.

§ 2. In 1841, when a British army was still at Cabul, the British government established high schools at Calcutta, Madras, and Bombay. Hindu boys flocked to the new schools, but Mohammedans kept aloof. The followers of the Prophet would not accept an education which rejected the authority of Mohammed and the Koran. Meanwhile there was an agitation for teaching the Bible in the government schools. Had it succeeded, respectable Hindus would probably have followed the example of the Mohammedans.

State education, 1854.

At last, in 1854, a State system of education was introduced, beginning with primary schools and middle-class schools, and ending in British colleges with professors and lecture-rooms. The whole system in every presidency, and gradually in every province, was placed under the control of a Director of Public Instruction. Grants in aid were made to schools established by missionaries and others, according to the educational results of their teaching. A University was established at Calcutta, another at Madras, and a third at Bombay, for the conduct of examinations and the granting of degrees. In a word, secular education was proceeding on a liberal scale, and some Hindus, who took high degrees, got appointments in the revenue and judicial departments, whilst others entered the service of Asiatic rulers, and rose to the rank of ministers.

Then followed the terrible sepoy mutinies, and wild cries from the British Isles for teaching Christianity and the Bible in every government institution. Had British statesmen yielded to the demand, the general population would have felt that the rebel sepoys were in the right; that they had fought, not from childish terror, but for the defence of their religion and caste; that they were martyrs to their faith, who had been crushed by the European red-coats to clear the way for the conversion of helpless Hindus and Mohammedans who were without arms.

Bible teaching.

Fortunately, the Royal Proclamation of 1858 was drafted by a statesman who felt that the machinery of government had no more to do with religious movements than the machinery of workshops. It announced, in clear and unmistakable language, that the British government had neither the right nor the desire to interfere with the faith of its Asiatic subjects, and the question of religious toleration in India was settled for ever.

Toleration proclaimed, 1858.

§ 3. The sepoy mutinies had paralysed the executive government of India. To make matters worse, the non-official Europeans—the merchants, bankers, planters, and lawyers—had been hostile to the government of Lord Canning from the very beginning of the outbreak. The cause of this collision is important. It suggested the necessity for future reforms. It will be seen hereafter that something was done in this direction in 1861-62; but something else was undone, and further reforms are still needed.

Hostility of non-official Europeans.

The legislative assembly of 1854 has already been

CHAP. THE LAST.

Representation in the legislative council.

described as the earliest germ of representative government in India. This was due to the fact that in addition to the executive members of council, the legislative chamber included four representative members, each one chosen from the civil service of one or other of the four Presidencies; also two judges of the old Supreme Court, who were not in the service of the East India Company, but were appointed by the British Crown, and were consequently independent legislators.

Controlled by the executive.

In every other respect, however, the executive government, including Lord Canning and the members of his executive council, exercised supreme control over the Indian legislature. They introduced what measures they pleased. They excluded what measures they disliked. Being mostly Bengal civilians, they were accused of ignoring the representative members from Madras and Bombay, and Madras and Bombay had some ground of complaint. No member of the legislative council of India had the power to introduce a bill without the consent of the Indian executive; nor even had the power, common to every member of the British parliament, to ask any question as regards the acts of the executive.

Class legislation.

At this period there was a nondescript body in England known as the "Indian Law Commissioners." These gentlemen prepared an act cut and dried, and the Court of Directors sent it to India in 1857, and recommended that it should be passed into law by the legislative council of India. This act began with asserting the equality of Asiatics and Europeans in the eyes of the law; but laid down a still more invidious distinction between non-official and official Europeans. It proposed to subject all non-official Europeans to the jurisdiction of Asiatic magistrates, but to exempt from such jurisdiction all Europeans who were members of the Indian civil service, or officers of the army or navy.

Agitation and withdrawal.

The first reading was followed by alarm and indignation. The press thundered, outside orators raved in public meetings, and European petitions against the bill poured in like a rushing stream. For a long time not a single member of the legislative chamber raised a voice against such vicious legislation. The Penal Code had not become law, and judges and magistrates, whether European or Asiatic, administered the law very much at their own discretion, by the light of "equity and good conscience," and voluminous regulations. Then, again, the time was out of joint for such an innovation. Mutiny and revolt were at work in the upper provinces, and isolated European planters might soon be at the mercy of Asiatic magistrates who sympathised with the rebels. At last, however, Sir Arthur Buller, one of the ablest judges of the old Supreme Court, rose from his seat in the legislative chamber, and virtually tore the bill to shreds. From that day it was doomed. Bengali baboos vainly petitioned the British government to pass the bill in all its integrity. It perished in the maelstrom of the mutiny, and was then formally withdrawn by the Court of Directors.

Executive council remodelled.

When the mutiny was over, Lord Canning remodelled the executive council into the form of a cabinet. He divided the administration into six branches, namely:—foreign, home, legislative, military, financial, and public works. The Viceroy was

CHAP. THE LAST. the prime minister, who sat as president of the council. He took charge of "foreign affairs." The other members were ministers; each had charge of a separate department, and transacted the bulk of its business. All important business, however, was transacted by the whole cabinet of ministers, which held its regular sittings at Government House, as it had done in the days when the governor or president was only the head of a factory.

Ministers and Secretaries. The post of minister was not, and is not, doubled up with that of secretary, except during the earlier years of the public works department. In the present day there is a minister for every department. Every minister transacts the business of his branch at his own house; leaving the secretary and under-secretary to control the office of his particular department, conduct the correspondence, and carry out orders.

Mr. Wilson, Finance Minister, 1860. § 4. In 1860 an English financier, the late Mr. James Wilson, was sent out from England to put the Indian budget to rights. He was a famous man in his day; a noted leader of the anti-corn law league, and had a large reputation as a sound financier. He freely conferred with Calcutta merchants and bankers, and so far poured oil on the troubled waters; but in those days the merchants of Calcutta were as ignorant of India outside the city of palaces as Mr. Wilson himself, who was sent out to tax the people.

Income-tax. Mr. Wilson quoted the laws of Manu in the legislative chamber, and proposed an income-tax. It was not an ordinary tax on incomes above 400*l.* or 500*l.* per annum, with which India has since been burdened. It included a tax on Asiatic incomes rising from eight shillings a week to twenty shillings. It was as oppressive as the poll-tax which drove Wat Tyler and Jack Cade into rebellion. But India was prostrate. British red-coats were masters; and British financiers might do as they pleased.

Protest of Sir Charles Trevelyan.

Sir Charles Trevelyan was Governor of Madras and knew India well. He protested against the tax and sent his protest to the newspapers. The Viceroy and the Secretary of State were filled with wrath at an act of insubordination which amounted to an appeal to the public opinion of India against the ukase of the supreme government. Sir Charles Trevelyan was removed from the government of Madras, but within two years he was revenged. The obnoxious clause had filled 600,000 households with weeping and wailing, in order to collect 350,000*l.*, of which 100,000*l.* was spent on the work of collection. Accordingly the clause was repealed.[1]

Independent judges.

Later on, the two judges who sat in the legislative chamber were guilty of a still more flagrant act of insubordination. Whilst 350,000*l.* was exacted from 600,000 poor Asiatics in the shape of income-tax, the Secretary of State for India overruled a previous decision of Lord Dalhousie, and capitalised half a million sterling, in order to improve the pensions of the descendants of Tippu! The controversy is obsolete; the two judges ventured to question the justice of this measure, and the heinous offence was punished in due course.

[1] Mr. James Wilson died in 1860. He was succeeded by Mr. Samuel Laing as financial minister, who in his turn was succeeded in 1862 by Sir Charles Trevelyan.

CHAP. THE LAST.

Legislative council remodelled, 1861–62.

§ 5. In 1861-62 the legislative council of India was reconstituted by act of parliament. The two judges were excluded from the legislative chamber, and European merchants, and Asiatics of wealth and influence, were nominated in their room. The control of the executive was thus stronger than ever, but it is doubtful whether the legislature has profited by the change.

Legislative councils at Madras, Bombay, and Bengal.

Legislative councils, on a similar footing to that of India at Calcutta, were granted to the governments of Madras and Bombay, as well as to the Lieutenant-Governor of Bengal. They include both European and Asiatic members, who are nominated by the local government. They legislate on purely local measures, such as port dues, hackney carriages, canal tolls, and municipalities. They are, however, under the immediate control of the executive, and have no power to make laws, or to initiate legislation in the legislative council of India.

New High Courts.

§ 6. A still more important measure was carried out at this period. A new High Court of Justice was created at Calcutta, and also at Madras and Bombay, by the amalgamation of the Supreme Court and Sudder, which had been separate and rival courts ever since the days of Warren Hastings. In other words, the barrister judges appointed by the British Crown, and the civilian judges appointed by the Indian governments, sat together in the new High Court. Moreover, as a crowning innovation, an Asiatic judge was appointed to each High Court, to sit on the same bench as the European judges.

The amalgamation of the two courts is an epoch in British rule in India. The coalition of barrister and civilian judges, and the presence of an Asiatic judge on the same bench, enlarged and strengthened the High Court. It was, however, unfortunate that a European and an Asiatic judge did not also sit in the legislative chambers. Such an addition would have converted the chambers into schools of legislation. An Asiatic judge, who had graduated in the High Court, would have taught something to his Asiatic colleagues in the legislative council; whilst a European judge would have smoothed away many of the asperities which have sprung up of late years between the acts of the Indian executive and the rulings of the High Court. Judges in council.

The mixed constitution of the High Courts might be extended with advantage to the District Courts. If European and Asiatic judges sit on the same bench, why not European and Asiatic magistrates, deputy-magistrates, and subordinate judges? Such an amalgamation would prove a school for Asiatic magistrates and judges; whilst the evil spirit of race antagonism, which was raised by the unfortunate bill of 1857, and revived a few short years ago, would be allayed for ever. European and Asiatic magistrates.

§ 7. Lord Canning left India in March, 1862, and died in England the following June. His administration had been more eventful than that of any of his predecessors. At first he hesitated to crush the mutinies, and was named "Clemency Canning"; but he never lost his nerve. After the revolt at Delhi he rose to the occasion. Later on, non-official Europeans, as well as officials, learned to respect "Clemency Canning," and his sudden death was felt by all as a loss to the nation as well as to the empire. Lord Canning leaves India, 1862.

CHAP. THE LAST. — Lord Elgin, Viceroy, 1862–63. § 8. Lord Elgin succeeded Lord Canning. He was a statesman of experience and capacity, but cumbered with memories of China and Japan. Lord Elgin's reign did not last two years. He died in November, 1863.

Sir John Lawrence, 1864-69. § 9. In those days of imperfect telegraphs, there was an interregnum of two months. Meanwhile, Sir William Denison, Governor of Madras, acted as provisional Governor-General. With great presence of mind, he sanctioned all the measures which he had previously sent up from Madras for the confirmation of the government of India. In January, 1864, Sir John Lawrence landed at Calcutta as Viceroy and Governor-General.

Sir William Denison at Madras. Sir William Denison returned to Madras. He is said to have been hostile to competitive examinations, and anxious to govern Southern India without the help of an executive council. But his ideas of government were not in accord with those in power, and competitive examinations and civilian members of council have remained to this day.

Sir Bartle Frere at Bombay. At this period Sir Bartle Frere was Governor of Bombay. He was an Anglo-Indian statesman of the first order, with capacity and experience combined with diplomatic tact. He had done good service as commissioner of Sind. Since then he had graduated in the Indian executive as Home member of Lord Canning's cabinet. But, like many Indian civilians, he was too self-reliant, and fell upon evil times when Indian experiences could not help him.

American war: cotton famine. Sir Bartle Frere was transferred from the cabinet at Calcutta to the government of Bombay at the moment when war was raging between the North and the South in the United States of America. A cotton famine was starving Manchester, and Indian cotton rose from threepence a pound to twenty pence. Bombay cultivators loaded their women with jewels, and shod their cattle with silver shoes. The spirit of speculation was rampant. Europeans and Asiatics, shrewd Scotchmen and cautious Parsis, rushed blindly into the wildest gambling. Mushroom companies sprung up in a single night like the prophet's gourd, and flourished like the South Sea Bubble. Clerks and brokers woke up to find themselves millionaires, and straightway plunged into still madder speculations, dreaming, like Alnaschar, of estates as large as counties, of peerless brides, and of seats in the House of Lords.

Crash and panic.

Suddenly the American war collapsed, and cargoes of cotton were hurried from the States across the Atlantic. Prices fell to zero. There was joy at Manchester, but weeping and wailing at Bombay. The Bombay Bank had been drawn into the vortex of speculation, and loans had been advanced on worthless shares. How far Sir Bartle Frere was implicated is a disputed point; but the bank stopped payment, and Sir Bartle Frere lost his chance of becoming Viceroy of India.

Civilian experiences of John Lawrence.

The Viceroyalty of Sir John Lawrence was altogether exceptional.[1] Most Viceroys are noble peers, who land in India with parliamentary and diplomatic experiences, but with no special knowledge of Asiatic affairs, beyond what has been "crammed up" at the India Office during the interval between acceptance of office and embarkation for Calcutta. In 1864

[1] During the Viceroyalty he was plain Sir John Lawrence, but when it was over he was raised to the peerage.

CHAP. THE LAST. Lord Lawrence knew more about India than any previous Governor-General, Warren Hastings not excepted. He, and his foreign and home secretaries, the late Sir Henry Durand and the late Sir Edward Clive Bayley, were, perhaps, better versed in Indian history than any other men of the time. Lord Lawrence had gone through the ordeal of the mutiny with the salvation of the Empire in his hands. Since then he had sat on the council of the Secretary of State at Westminster, and learnt something of public opinion in the British Isles on Indian affairs.

Yearly migrations to Simla.

Lord Lawrence hated Bengal, and could not endure her depressing heats and vapour-baths.[1] He was the first Governor-General who went every year to Simla, and he was the first who took all his cabinet ministers and secretaries with him. Old Anglo-Indians disliked these migrations, and likened them to the progresses of the Great Mogul with a train of lords and ladies, in tented palaces, escorted by hosts of soldiers and camp-followers, from Agra to Lahore, or from Delhi to Cashmere. But the migrations of the British government of India required no army of escort, and entailed no expense or suffering on the masses. Railways shortened the journeys; telegraphs prevented delays; and civilian members of government, whose experiences had previously been cribbed and cabined in Bengal, began to learn something of the upper provinces.

Lord Lawrence, like his immediate predecessors, took the Foreign Office under his special and

[1] Calcutta is by no means an unpleasant residence for Europeans with tolerably sound constitutions. Sir John Lawrence was only in his fifty-fifth year, but he was sadly worn by hard work and unexampled anxieties.

immediate charge. At that time Colonel, afterwards Major-General Sir Henry Durand, was foreign secretary to the government of India. Both Lawrence and Durand were firm to the verge of obstinacy, but Sir John was sometimes hasty and impetuous, whilst Colonel Durand was solid and immovable.

CHAP. THE LAST.

Sir John Lawrence and Sir Henry Durand.

Foreign and political.

The main business of the Foreign Office is that of supervision. It directs all negotiations with the Asiatic states beyond the frontier, such as Afghanistan, Cashmere, and Nipal. It controls all political relations with the feudatory states of Rajputana and Central India, which are carried on by British officers known as political agents and assistants. In like manner it controls the political relations with other courts, which are carried on by "Residents." It also overlooks the administration in newly-acquired territories, which, like the Punjab, are known as "non-regulation" provinces.[1]

[1] British territory in India comprises 900,000 square miles, with a population of 200,000,000. Asiatic territory comprises nearly 600,000 square miles, with a population of 52,000,000.

NORTHERN INDIA is fringed on the west by Afghanistan, on the north by Cashmere, Nipal, and Bhotan; on the east by Munipore and Burma.

CENTRAL INDIA is traversed from west to east by a belt or zone of states and chiefships—Rajput, Mahratta, and Mohammedan —which extends from the western coast of Gujerat facing the Indian Ocean, and the western desert of Sind facing Rajputana, through the heart of the Indian continent eastward to the Bengal Presidency. This belt includes, amongst a host of minor principalities and chiefships, the three leading Rajput states— Jeypore, Jodhpore, and Oodeypore; the Jhat state of Bhurtpore; the Mahratta territories of the Gaekwar of Baroda in Western India, and those of Scindia and Holkar in Central India; and the Hindu states of Bundelkund, including Rewah, along the eastern hills and jungles to the south of the river Jumna.

The DECCAN includes the Mohammedan dominions of the

CHAP. THE LAST.

Afghanistan: death of Dost Mohammed Khan.

The main question of the day was Afghanistan affairs. Dost Mohammed Khan died in 1863, after a chequered life of war and intrigue, a labyrinth which no one can unravel. He had driven his enemy Shah Shuja out of Cabul; he had been robbed of the coveted valley of Peshawar by Runjeet Singh; he had coquetted with Persia, Russia, and the British government. He had abandoned his dominions on the advance of the British army in 1839-40; fled to Bokhara; then surrendered to Macnaghten; was sent to Calcutta as a state prisoner; played at chess with the ladies at Government House; and

Nizam of Hyderabad, to the eastward of the Bombay Presidency.

SOUTHERN INDIA includes the Hindu states of Mysore and Travancore to the westward of the Madras Presidency.

The term "foreign" as applied to the Indian Foreign Office is a misnomer, and has led to confusion. The term "political department" would be more correct, as it deals mainly with Asiatic feudatory states which are bound up with the body politic of the Anglo-Indian empire. The relations between the British government and its Asiatic feudatories are not "international" in the European sense of the word, and are not controlled by international law. They are "political" in the imperial sense of the word, and are governed by the treaties, and regulated by the sovereign authority which is exercised by the British government as the paramount power in India. A British officer is placed in charge of every state, or group of states, and is known as "political agent" or "Resident."

Lord Macaulay, versed in European history, but with no special knowledge of Asia, condemns the word "political," which had been used ever since the department was founded by Warren Hastings. He declared that Asiatic feudatories were "foreign states," and that the relations between those feudatories and the paramount power were diplomatic. Lord Macaulay in his time was as great a literary authority as Dr. Samuel Johnson. Lord Ellenborough took the hint when he was Governor-General, and changed the Political Department into the Foreign Office. It would be better to call it "Political and Foreign."

finally returned to Cabul. He seized the valley of Peshawar during the second Sikh war. Finally he had become friends with the British government, and made no attempt to take advantage of the sepoy mutinies to recover Peshawar.

Jacob *versus* Esau.

But old Dost Mohammed had a patriarchal weakness for youthful wives. He had been beguiled by a blooming favourite into nominating her son as his successor, to the exclusion of the first-born. It was nearly a case of Jacob *versus* Esau, and when the old man was gathered to his fathers, the younger son and the first-born, with their respective partisans, tried to settle the succession by force of arms. The British government did not interfere, but left the brothers to fight on, until the elder was carried off by death, and the younger, the late Shere Ali Khan, gained the throne.

Mysore.

Mysore was another vexed question. Lord Wellesley had acquired Mysore by the conquest of Tippu in 1799. He incorporated some provinces into the Madras Presidency, but formed the remaining territory into a little Hindu state, and placed a Hindu boy, a kinsman of the Raja who had been supplanted by Hyder, on the throne of Mysore. The boy grew to be a man, and turned out a worthless, extravagant, and oppressive ruler, deaf to all remonstrances and warnings. His subjects rebelled against his tyranny and exactions. Even Lord William Bentinck, a sentimental admirer of Asiatic principalities, was disgusted with his conduct and deposed him, and placed Mysore territory in charge of a British commissioner, and brought it under British rule.

Thirty years passed away. There was an outcry

CHAP. THE LAST.

Restoration of Hindu rule.

in the British Isles against annexation. It was proposed to restore the ex-Raja to his throne, but Mysore had become to all intents and purposes a British province. In the teeth of these facts, it was determined to restore this flourishing territory to the rule of the worthless Hindu who had been deposed by Lord William Bentinck a generation previously. Sir John Lawrence fought against the measure, but was overruled. At last there was a compromise. It was decided to place an adopted son of the ex-Raja on the throne, and to remove the British administration from Mysore, and place an Asiatic administration in its room. The ex-Raja was extremely annoyed at this arrangement. It put an end to all his aspirations. He did not want an adopted son, and would willingly have left his territories to the British government, had he been only allowed to handle the revenues during his own lifetime.

Opposition of Durand.

Sir John Lawrence, like every practical administrator in India, was most unwilling to replace Mysore under Asiatic rule. He submitted under pressure, but not without misgivings. Colonel Durand, however, opposed it tooth and nail. Had he been a Roman general, ordered to restore the island of Albion to an adopted son of Boadicea, or had he been an English lord of the marches ordered to restore the principality of Wales to a son of Llewellyn, he could not have felt more indignation. Durand was, of course, powerless to resist, and the restoration was carried out. The future alone can decide the merits of the question.

Oudh talukdars.

Next arose a controversy about the Oudh talukdars. Lord Canning had dealt liberally with the talukdars, restored most of their so-called estates, and converted them into landed proprietors. Sir John Lawrence discovered that the rights of joint village proprietors had been overlooked. Again there was a paper war, which ended in another compromise. The talukdars were eventually confirmed in the possession of their estates, but the rights of under proprietors and occupiers were defined and respected.

The cabinet and legislature.

Meanwhile Colonel Durand was transferred from the Foreign Office to the executive council, with charge of the military department. As a member of the council he had a seat in the legislative chamber, and on one occasion he voted against the other ministers. This raised a question as to the right of a member of the cabinet to vote against the majority of his colleagues in the legislative chamber. It was argued on one side that in England a cabinet minister must vote with his colleagues in parliament; in other words, he must either sacrifice his conscience for the sake of party or resign his post in the executive. On the other side it was urged that an Indian cabinet had nothing whatever to do with party, and that any cabinet minister might vote in the legislative chamber as he deemed best for the public service, without thereby losing his position as member of the executive council.

Sir John Lawrence leaves India, 1869.

§ 10. Sir John Lawrence retired from the post of Viceroy in 1869. With the exception of an expedition into Bhotan, a barbarous state in the Himalayas next door to Nipal, there was peace in India throughout the whole of his five years' administration. He returned to England and was raised to the peerage. He had strong attachments, but the

CHAP. THE LAST. — outer world only knew him as a strong, stern man, with a gnarled countenance and an iron will. He lived for ten years longer in his native country, doing good work as the chairman of the London School Board, and taking an active part in every movement that would contribute to the welfare of his generation, until, in 1879, the saviour of British India found a final resting-place in Westminster Abbey.

Lord Mayo Viceroy, 1869-72.

§ 11. Lord Mayo succeeded as Viceroy and Governor-General. To him is due the greatest reform in the constitutional government of India since the mutiny. He delivered the local governments from the financial fetters of the Viceroy in Council, and left them more responsibility as regards providing local funds for local wants, and devoting local savings to local expenditure. Hitherto every presidency and province got as much as it could out of the imperial treasury, and spent as much as it could during the current financial year, for any balance that remained was lost for ever by being credited to imperial funds. Henceforth every presidency and province was interested in improving its income and cutting down its expenditure, since it was entrusted with some discretion as regards the disposal of the surplus money.

Tragic death.

The assassination of Lord Mayo in 1872 by an Afghan desperado in the Andaman Islands, brought the career of a great and energetic Viceroy to a sad and sudden close. By force of character, noble address, and genial open-heartedness, Lord Mayo had charmed every Asiatic feudatory that came to do homage; and even brought Shere Ali Khan, the sour and suspicious ruler of Afghanistan, to put some trust in the good faith and good intentions of the British government. His death was a loss to every European and Asiatic in India, and a loss to the British empire. CHAP. THE LAST.

§ 12. The later administrations of Lord Northbrook in 1872-76, of Lord Lytton in 1876-80, of Lord Ripon in 1880-1884, and the advent of Lord Dufferin, the present Viceroy, are too recent for personal criticism. They have been characterised, however, by events and changes which have left their mark on British rule in India. Lord Northbrook, 1872–76.

The personal influence of Her Majesty, and the presence of princes of the royal blood, have imparted a new prestige to British sovereignty. The visit of the Duke of Edinburgh during the *régime* of Lord Mayo, and the extended tour of the Prince of Wales during the *régime* of Lord Northbrook, were welcomed in India with every demonstration of joy and loyalty. The old East India Company was a magnificent corporation, but had always been a mystery to Asiatics. The presence of British princes, the sons of Her Majesty, solved the problem for ever. Royalty in India.

§ 13. Finally the Imperial assemblage at Delhi on the 1st of January, 1877, when Her Majesty was proclaimed Empress of India by Lord Lytton, in the presence of all the members of the Indian governments, all the high officials of the empire, and of all the Asiatic feudatory rulers and their ministers, gave a reality to British sovereignty in India which had previously been wanting. When Queen Elizabeth Lord Lytton Viceroy, 1876–80: proclamation of the Empress.

CHAP. THE LAST. gave a charter to the East India Company, at the beginning of the seventeenth century, when Queen Anne received a present of "tay" from the Court of Directors, and even when George III. and Queen Charlotte graciously accepted an ivory bedstead from the polite Warren Hastings, not a soul in the British Isles could possibly have dreamed that the nineteenth century would see the Queen of Great Britain and Ireland reigning as Empress over the dominions of the Great Mogul. Neither could the Asiatic populations of that dim commercial period, who beheld the European gentlemen writing letters and keeping accounts in factories and fortresses, have imagined that a day would come when the descendants of the "European gentlemen" would be the rulers of India.

Second Afghan war.

§ 14. Under Lord Lytton's *régime* there was a second war in Afghanistan. Shere Ali Khan had become estranged from the British government. He imprisoned his eldest son, Yakub Khan, and refused British mediation. He was offended because the British government would not conclude an offensive and defensive alliance on equal terms. He received a mission from Russia at Cabul, and refused to receive a mission from the British government.

British designs.

Accordingly, it was resolved to establish British supremacy in Afghanistan; to advance the British frontier to the Hindu Kush; to convert the mountain range into a natural fortress, with Afghan-Turkistan for its *berme* and the river Oxus for its ditch. Russia already held the glacis, as represented by Usbeg-Turkistan.

Shere Ali Khan fled away northward as the British

army advanced, and died in exile. Yakub Khan succeeded to the throne, and submitted to the demands of the British Resident. Then followed the cruel and cowardly massacre of Sir Louis Cavagnari, the British Resident at Cabul, with all his officers and attendants; the abdication of Yakub Khan; and finally the accession of Abdul Rahman Khan, the present Amir, who was son of the first born of Dost Mohammed who was ousted in favour of Shere Ali.

Massacre and submission.

During the generation that followed the mutinies, the administration of British India has been undergoing an important change. The old patriarchal rule of non-regulation provinces has been fading away. The distinction between regulation and non-regulation is being effaced. The Punjab and Oudh, the Central Provinces and British Burma, which for years had been exclusively controlled by the Foreign Office, are being brought more and more under the Home Office; and the same laws and forms of administration will soon prevail throughout every presidency and province of the Anglo-Indian empire.

Regulation and non-regulation provinces.

§ 15. British India is a school for Asiatics in which Europeans are the masters. The teaching has hitherto been successful. Asiatic students are becoming monitors; some are under-masters; and some may in due course hope to be masters. The British government is appointing educated Asiatics to posts of responsibility and trust, which few European merchants and bankers have hitherto ventured to do. Accordingly, non-officials, as well as officials, are awaiting the results of an experiment that will serve to show how far the Asiatic has profited by his European education; and how far he may be entrusted with

Asiatic students: European masters.

CHAP. THE LAST. the higher duties of administration, or with the exercise of self-government and political power.

Hindu culture. Hindus have many virtues. They are obedient to parents, polite to equals, respectful to superiors, and reverential towards priests and preceptors. But for ages they have lived under the despotism of caste, custom, and religion, which is slowly melting away from European capitals of India, but is still rampant in Asiatic towns and villages. British education is elevating their intellects and enlarging their experiences, but cannot change their nature, nor hastily emancipate them from the usages of ages. The result is that to this day, both Hindus and Mohammedans lack those political ideas of constitutional government and public life, in which Englishmen have been trained since the days of Queen Elizabeth.

Child marriages. Hindus are married in their childhood, and are often husbands and fathers when British boys are still at school, or learning trades and professions, or competing at boating or cricket. All this while, and for years after they have attained manhood, the bulk of Hindus are living under the roof of their parents. Husbands are ruled by fathers as though they were still children, and wives are the victims of their mothers-in-law.

Temper and repression. Occasionally Hindus will exhibit a petulance and passion like that which drove the sepoys into mutiny; but as a general rule, they are kept within bounds by the despotism and discipline which reigns supreme in Hindu families, as well as by the severe self-control, which Asiatics esteem as one of the highest virtues. Moreover, during a long course of ages, they have become more or less enervated by that depressing heat, which often shakes the nerve and loosens the muscle of Europeans. Consequently, they have little relish for active life, and generally prefer sedentary duties which do not involve physical exertion.

Village communities.

Hindu village communities may have had some public life in the pre-British period. They governed themselves, and administered justice amongst themselves, but they in their turn were governed by caste, custom, and superstition. Sometimes they defended themselves against brigands or tigers, and they environed their domiciles with mud walls, wooden palisades, or hedges of prickly pear. If however there were any rumours of an enemy appearing in force, they all fled to the jungle until the danger was over. In Bengal, the villagers were helpless to resist dacoits, who occasionally committed the most horrible crimes; but since the organisation of police under European superintendence, such atrocities have disappeared from British India.

Despotic commonwealths.

Where the village community was strong, the little commonwealth was a despotism. The joint proprietary was an oligarchy, and tenants and cultivators were serfs or slaves. The officials and artisans were hereditary, and hereditary officials are almost invariably inefficient and untrustworthy. Village justice may have been administered by the elders, but generally at the dictation of some domineering Brahman or Guru.

Old civilian conservatism.

Indian civilians of the old school, like Thomas Munro and Mountstuart Elphinstone, were much inclined towards Hindu institutions. In those ancient times the whole village would turn out to welcome the arrival of a new British collector and magistrate. The Asiatic officials appeared with

CHAP. THE LAST. — music, flags, and garlands, whilst the village dancing girl performed before the "great man," and sung his praises. The "great man" in his turn was charmed with these manifestations of respect for British rule; but a later generation was aghast at the enormity, and the demonstration was stopped by the Court of Directors.

Failure. In the Madras Presidency Munro turned the head-men of villages into munsifs, and empowered them to settle all civil disputes up to the value of twenty shillings. The village munsifs might also summon a punchayet, or council of arbitrators, to settle disputes above that amount. In the Bombay Presidency, Mountstuart Elphinstone made similar attempts to utilise the Mahratta collectors and sub-collectors. But in both cases the experiment failed through hereditary incapacity or corruption.

Trained Asiatic officials. The creation of new classes of Asiatic officials has been more successful. Munsifs, trained and educated, are deciding civil cases in the districts, and have proved efficient and trustworthy. Deputy-collectors and magistrates, as well as subordinate judges, have also been found to do their work well. Pay and position have been improved, and the number has been increased; and possibly more might be done in this direction. But this question can be best worked out with that of placing European and Asiatic magistrates on the same bench.

Viceroy of India in Council. § 16. The Viceroy is sovereign over the whole of India. He is no longer drawn away from the cares of supreme control by the separate and direct government of Bengal and the North - West Provinces. Each of these presidencies has now a lieutenant-governor of its own. The Viceroy is thus the presiding deity of the whole of India. During the cold weather months he reigns at Calcutta on the banks of the Hughly, where he is president alike of an executive council and a legislative council. During the hot weather months, he is enthroned at Simla like another Indra, on the slopes of the Himalaya mountains, attended by his cabinet or executive council. He exercises sovereign authority over every presidency and every province; and every Asiatic ruler in India, Hindu or Mohammedan, Rajput or Mahratta, acknowledges the supremacy of the Viceroy and Governor-General as the representative of the Queen and Empress.

Secretary of State in Council.

But Indra himself is subject to some mysterious power, who is omnipotent and invisible. In like manner the Viceroy of India in Council is subject to a *deus ex machinâ,* in the shape of the Secretary of State for India in Council. The Secretary of State, or one of his under-secretaries, is sometimes asked questions in Parliament; but the Secretary of State for the time being generally manages to have his own way, or treads cautiously in the footsteps of his predecessors, or relies on the wisdom of the reigning Viceroy.

Strengthening of legislative council.

The executive council of the Secretary of State, as well as that of the Viceroy, are essential parts of the constitutional government of India. But the legislative council of India lacks strength and independence. It was a mistake to shut out the two judges from the chamber. One European and one Asiatic judge would be as useful in the council as on the bench. Again, in these days of railways and steamers, there seems no reason why

CHAP. THE LAST. governors of presidencies, and lieutenant-governors and chief commissioners of provinces, should not occasionally sit in the legislative council of India to exchange views and give the weight of their personal support to their respective representative members. The sittings are generally held in the cold season, when the British Parliament is not sitting. The occasional presence of high Indian officials and British members of Parliament would improve the debates, educate public opinion, and convert the chamber into a high school for Asiatic legislators.

British Residents in Asiatic states.

Meanwhile the idea of a school should be borne in mind in every branch of the administration, civil and judicial, and especially in the foreign or political department. A British officer at an Asiatic court is often the one solitary representative of civilisation and progress; and this feeble light ought to be fed, strengthened, and kept constantly burning like the fire of the Vestal virgins. By that light, Asiatic rulers may hope in time to rise to the level of Europeans; without it, they may sink back into the barbarism of the past century, when the Mogul empire had lost its hold, and was tottering to its fall.

INDEX.

A.

Adoption, question of, 175 ; present aspect, 177
Afghanistan, Elphinstone's mission, 103 ; Russian advances, 143 ; first Afghan war, 146 ; insurrection at Cabul, 149 ; British losses in the Khyber Pass, 150 ; end of war, 152 ; vulnerable frontier, 186 ; death of Dost Mohammed Khan, 290 ; fratricidal war, 291 ; Shere Ali Khan, *ib.* ; second Afghan war under Lord Lytton, 296
Agnew, Mr. Vans, murdered at Multan, 161
Agra, captured by General Lake, 95 ; presidency formed, 128 ; water way, 171 ; isolation during the sepoy mutinies, 215, 231
Ajmere, acquired by the British, 120
Akalis, Sikh fanatics, 156, 157
Akbar Khan, son of Dost Mohammed, heads revolt at Cabul, 149 ; murders Sir William Macnaghten, 150
Alam, Shah, Padishah, seeks British protection, 95
Alexander the Great, defeat of Porus, 163 ; his invasion of India, 225
Alighur, fortress of, captured by Lake, 94
Aliwal, battle of, 159
Allahabad, at the junction of the Jumna and Ganges, 171 ; position during the sepoy revolt, 215, 217, 220, 238 ; mutiny and massacre, 241 ; fortress besieged, *ib.* ; relieved by General Neill, 242
Amherst, Lord, Governor-General, 120 ; first Burmese war, 121 ; Bhurtpore war, 122
Amir Khan, an Afghan Pindhari, 105 ; founds principality of Tonk, 112, 113 ; surrenders to the British, 115
Amritsar, city of, 155
Andaman Islands, 294
Anderson, Lieut., murdered at Multan, 161
Anson, General, at Simla, 216 ; movements at the revolt of Delhi, 216-271 ; his death, *ib.*
Appa Sahib, defeated by the British, 117 ; flight from Nagpore, *ib.* ; succeeded by his grandson, *ib.*
Arakan, annexed by the British government, 122, 169
Arcot, captured by Clive, 34 ; suppresses mutiny at Vellore, 100
Arrah, besieged by rebels, 266 ; relieved by Major Eyre, 267
Asia, Central and Northern, the cradle of India, 142 ; rise of Nadir Shah, 143 ; rise of British power in, 145
Asiatics of India, better phrase than "native," 186 ; characteristic craft, 240 ; officials, 300
Asiatic rulers, acknowledge British supremacy, 301 ; British political officers in India, 302
Assam, overrun by Burmese, 121 ; acquired by the British, 122 ; tea cultivation, 123
Assaye, battle of, 94
Attock, fortress of, captured by Dost Mohammed Khan, 163
Auckland, Lord, Governor-General of India, 141 ; declares war against Dost Mohammed Khan, 145 ; sends expedition against Cabul, 146
Aurangzeb, the Great Mogul, 21 ; stops supply of saltpetre to the British at the bidding of Turkey, 25 ; his death, 31 ; persecutes the Sikhs, 155 ; detested by the Sikhs, 222
Ava, *see* Burma

B.

Baird, Sir David, commands storming party at Seringapatam, 86
Bala Hissar, fortress of, 148
Barlow, Sir George, provisional Governor-General, 98 ; political half measures, 99 ; sacrifices revenue in Bundelkund, 101 ; annuls protective treaties, 104
Barnard, Sir Henry, commander-in-chief in 1857, advances against Delhi, 218 ; his death, 230
Baroda, Gaekwar of, 112
Barrackpore, cantonment and park, near Calcutta, 192 ; story of the

Laskar and Brahman, 194; sepoy agitation, 196; incendiarism, 197; outbreak of Mungal Pandy, 201; disbandment of 19th Native Infantry, 202; of the 34th Native Infantry, 205
Barwell, Mr., member of the Council of Warren Hastings, 65
Bassein, efforts of the British at Bombay to acquire from the Mahrattas, 72; treaty of 1802 concluded with the Peishwa, 92, 119 *note*
Bayley, Sir Edward Clive, Home Secretary to Sir John Lawrence, his knowledge of Indian history, 288
Behar, a province of Bengal, 42—44, 127, 129; mutinies at Patna, Dinapore, and Arrah, 266
Benares, ceded to the British, 73; turbulent population, 235; triumph of Mr. Gubbins, 236; mutiny of sepoys, 237
Bengal, early English trade, 25; British supervisors, 55; terrible famine, *ib.*; British administration, 58; zemindari system of land revenue, *ib.*; no village communities, 128; people, 190
Bengal army, *see* Sepoys
Bentinck, Lord William, recalled from Madras, 101; Governor-General, 123; wise and just administration, *ib.*; civil and judical reforms, 126; appoints Asiatic officials, 127; settles land revenue in the North-West Provinces, 131, 167; popularity, 140; appoints Asiatic deputy collectors, 166
Berhampore, sepoys at, 192; mutiny against greased cartridges, 198
Berar, British relations with, 72; vacillations of the Raja, 95; *see* Nagpore
Bhotan, beyond Northern India, expedition to, 293
Bhurtpore, Jhat Raja of, pays a heavy fine to the British, 98; destruction of the fortress, 122
Bithoor, palace of Nana Sahib, 244; destroyed by Havelock, 259
Bombay, old fortress and town, 24; interference in Mahratta affairs, 73; bravery of sepoys, 118; acquires the territories of the Peishwa, 134; stagnation, 139; want of roads, 172; state education, 278; cotton speculations, 287; failure of Bank, *ib.*
Brahmans, hereditary schoolmasters, astrologers, and priests, 129; survival of, 131; position in the Bengal army, 188, 191
Britain, Great, an Asiatic power, 140, 180, 276
Buller, Sir Arthur, his opposition in legislative council, 281
Bundelkund, lawless condition of, 101; chiefs of, defy the British, *ib.*; peace restored, 102; condition, 255, 289 *note*
Burma, aggressive demands of the officials, 120; invade British territory, 121; end of first war, 122; second war, 168
Burnes, Sir Alexander, at Cabul, 148; environed by Afghan mob, 149; murdered, *ib.*
Buxar, battle of, 52

C.

Cabul, *see* Afghanistan
Cachar, under British rule, 122; tea cultivation, 123
Calcutta, founded, 28; captured by the Nawab of Bengal, 35; Black Hole tragedy, 38; recaptured, 42; auction sales of lands, 60; British garrison of, 186, 192
Campbell, Sir Archibald, at Rangoon, 121
Campbell, Sir Colin, commander-in-chief, Bengal army, 271; sets out for Lucknow, *ib.*; reaches Residency, *ib.*; brings away besieged, *ib.*
Canara, landholders and land revenue of, 133
Canning, Lord, Governor-General, 181; war with Persia, *ib.*; settlement with the Delhi family, 182; uneasy about Oudh, *ib.*; alarm of the sepoys at Barrackpore, 192; mutiny at Berhampore, 200; outbreak at Barrackpore, 201; disaffection in Oudh, 202; disbandments at Barrackpore, 202, 205; mutiny at Meerut, 206, 208; orders General Anson to Delhi, 217; refuses to abandon Peshawar, 229; offends non-official Europeans at Calcutta, 279; turns the executive council of India into a cabinet, 281; departure and death, 285
Carnatic in Southern India, conquered by Aurangzeb, 22; war between Great Britain and France, 32; interference of the Nawab, *ib.*; rival Nawabs, 33; invasions of Hyder, 74; acquired by Lord Wellesley and incorporated with the Madras Presidency, 87, 88
Cashmere, conquered by Runjeet Singh, 103; sold by Lord Hardinge to Golab Singh, 160; relations with the British government, 289
Caste in Bengal army, 191; its disadvantages, *ib.*
Cavagnari, Sir Louis, murdered at Cabul, 297

Cawnpore on the Ganges, British cantonment in Lord Lake's time, 94 ; position, 171, 175 ; outbreak of the sepoy mutinies, 233 ; story of Cawnpore, 243 ; peril of General Wheeler, 244 ; palace of Nana Sahib at Bithoor, 245 ; suspense, 248 ; mutiny, 251 ; treachery of Nana Sahib, 252 ; revolting cruelties, *ib.* ; massacre, 254 ; advance of Havelock, 256 ; story of the "well," 258 ; defeat of Wyndham, 272 ; victory of Sir Colin Campbell, *ib.*

Central India, feudatory Asiatic states and chiefships, 289 *note*

Central Provinces, under Home Office, 297

Chamberlain, Neville, his flying column in the Punjab, 224 ; services at the siege of Delhi, 227, 230

Charnock, Job, imprisoned and scourged by the Nawab of Bengal, 25 ; flies to Madras, 27 ; founds Calcutta, 28

Charters, *see* East India Company

Child, Sir Joseph, frames a municipal corporation for Madras, 16 ; makes war on the Great Mogul, 25 ; plans the protection of British trade in India by three great fortresses, 26 ; his humiliation, 27

Chillianwalla, battle of, 163, 164

China, East India Company's trade with, 138

Chout, paid by the Mogul to the Mahrattas, 28 ; plunder of Bengal and the Carnatic for non-payment, 32 ; Mahratta demands on the Nizam, 82 ; demanded by Holkar, 96

Clavering, General, appointed member of council, 66 ; insolence to Warren Hastings and Elijah Impey, 67, 68

Cleveland, Augustus, humanises the Sonthals, 78

Clive, Robert, saves British interests in India by the capture of Arcot, 34 ; expedition to Calcutta after the Black Hole disaster, 40 ; victory at Plassy, 42 ; instals a new Nawab, 43 ; relieves the Mogul Prince Imperial, 45 ; refuses the post of Dewan to the Great Mogul, *ib.* ; offers it to William Pitt, 46 ; Governor of British settlements in Bengal, 53 ; accepts the Dewani, 54 ; returns to England, 55 ; inferior authority to that of Warren Hastings, 56

Code, Penal, 281

Colvin, Mr. John, besieged in fortress of Agra, 220, 231 *note*

Combermere, Lord, captures fortress of Bhurtpore, 122

Company, *see* East India

Cornwallis, Lord, appointed Governor-General, 78 ; proclaims the perpetual settlement, 79 ; judicial reforms, *ib.* ; war against Tippu, 80 ; Governor-General a second time, 98 ; dies, *ib.*

Councils, executive and legislative, *see* Government

Courts, *see* Judicature

Currie, Sir Frederic, Resident at Lahore, 161

D.

Dalhousie, Lord, Governor-General, 161 ; enters on the second Sikh war, 163 ; annexes the Punjab, 164 ; introduces British administration, 166 ; second Burmese war, 168 ; annexation of Pegu, 169 ; progressive policy, 170 ; public works, *ib.* ; roads, 171 ; railways, 173 ; telegraphs, 174 ; Ganges canal, *ib.* ; annexation policy, 175 ; question of adoption, 176 ; annexation of Jhansi and Oudh, 177 ; opens the legislative council of India, 179 ; leaves India, 180

Deccan, definition of the term, 2 ; Mohammedan Sultans of Golconda, 22 ; bad roads, 172

Delhi, capital of the Mogul empire, 44 ; flight of the Prince Imperial to Calcutta, *ib.* ; proposed British expedition stopped by Clive, 53 ; defended by Ochterlony against Holkar, 95 ; occupied and plundered by Nadir Shah, 144 ; water-way to Calcutta, 173 ; family of the last of the Moguls, 182 ; occupied by the rebel sepoys from Meerut, 208 ; the city and its surroundings, 210 ; massacre of Europeans, 213 ; explosion of the magazine, 214 ; rebel successes, 216 ; avenged, 219 ; the siege, 221 ; the capture, 230 ; imperial assemblage at, 295

Denison, Sir William, Provisional Governor-General, 286 ; returns to Madras *ib.*

Dharna, sitting in, 81 ; abolished, *ib.*

Dhuleep Singh, nominal sovereign of the Punjab, 157

Dinapore, European regiment at, 186 ; mutiny at, 266

Dost Mohammed Khan, ruler of Afghanistan, 145 ; defeated by the British, 146 ; a prisoner at Calcutta, 147 ; returns to Cabul, 152 ; recovers Peshawar during second Sikh war, 162, 163 ; helped by the British in the Persian war, 181 ; death 290 ; wars between his sons, 291

Dravidian races, 142

Dumdum arsenal, near Calcutta, 186; musketry school at, 192
Dupleix, French Governor of Pondicherry, 32; his brilliant success, 33; appointed Nawab of the Carnatic, *ib.*; ruin of his schemes by Clive, 34; return to France, *ib.*; disgrace and death of, *ib.*
Durand, Sir H., Foreign Secretary, 288; relations with Sir John Lawrence, 289; proposed restoration of Mysore, 292
Dutch, settlements of, 9

E.

East India Company, charter and factories, 1; English house at Surat, 4; territory and fortress at Madras, 7; Fort St. George, 12; charter from James II. for municipal corporation, 16; settlement at Bombay, 24; at Hughly, 25; war against the Great Mogul, 26; submission, 27; war with France, 32; saved by Robert Clive, 34; Black Hole tragedy, 35; Plassy, 42; exasperated by their civil servants at Calcutta, 53; accepts the office of Dewan for Bengal, Behar, and Orissa, 54; orders Warren Hastings to assume the direct administration, 56; false position of the Company in Bengal, 69; first war against the Mahrattas, 71; Fox's hostile India bill, 75; Pitt's Board of Control, 76; trial of Warren Hastings, 77; wars of Lord Wellesley, 84; conquest of Mysore, 86; annexation of the Carnatic, 88; subsidiary alliances, 89; second Mahratta war, 94; recall of Lord Wellesley from Bengal, 98; recall of Lord William Bentinck from Madras, 101; war against Nipal, 108; Pindhari and Mahratta wars, 110; paramount power in India, 120; first Burmese war, *ib.*; administration of Lord William Bentinck, 123; stages in the relations between the Company and the Crown, 135; old East India House, 136; patronage under Pitt's bill, 137; charters of 1813 and 1833 granted by Parliament, 138; abolition of licences, *ib.*; constitutional changes, 139; appointment of Lord Macaulay, *ib.*; charter of 1833, its evil results, *ib.*; an Asiatic power, 141; first Sikh war, 154; second Sikh war, 161; acquisition of the Punjab, 165; second Burmese war, 168; splendid administration of Lord Dalhousie, 170; question of adoption, 175; annexation of Oudh, 177; end of charter of 1833, 178; competitive examinations for the Indian civil and new legislative council of India, 179; sepoy revolt, 185, 232; end of the East India Company, 275
Edinburgh, Duke of, visit to India, 295
Education in India, 277; state system, 278; Bible teaching, 279
Edwardes, Herbert, defeats rebels at Multan, 161, 162; opposes withdrawal from Peshawar, 229
Elgin, Lord, sends British regiments to Lord Canning, 233; Viceroy and Governor-General, 286
Ellenborough, Lord, Governor-General, 151; hears news of Khyber Pass disaster, *ib.*; interferes in Gwalior, 152; recalled, 154; proposes removal of the Delhi family, 182
Elphinstone, Mountstuart, his mission to Cabul, 103; Resident at Poona, 112; negotiations with the Mahratta Peishwa, 113; destruction of his library, 116; Governor of Bombay, 134; conservatism in India, 299; its failure, 300
Empress of India, proclamation of, 295

F.

Ferozshahar, battle of, 158, 159
Foreign Office, Indian, relations with Asiatic states, 289; misleading term, 290 *note*
Fort St. George, *see* Madras
Fort William, *see* Calcutta
Francis, Mr. Philip, member of Bengal Council, reputed author of the *Letters of Junius*, 66; jealous hatred of Warren Hastings, *ib.*; bitter charges against Hastings and Impey, 67, 68; denounces appointment of Impey to the Sudder, 70; fights a duel and returns to England, 75
Frere, Sir Bartle, Governor of Bombay, 286; his career, 287
Frontier tribes on the north-west, 225

G.

Gaekwar of Baroda, 112, 289 *note*
Ganges canal, 174
Ganges, river, 171, 175
George III., his hostility to Fox's India Bill, 137; accepts presents from Warren Hastings, 296
Ghorka, conquest of Nipal, 106; war against British government, 108—110
Gillespie, Colonel, commands garrison at Arcot, 100; suppresses mutiny at Vellore, 101
Goa, the capital of Portuguese India, 2

Goddard, Colonel, leads an expedition from Calcutta to Bombay against Mahratta country, 73

Godwin, General, commands expedition to Burma, 169

Golab Singh buys Cashmere from Lord Hardinge, 160

Goojerat, battle of, 164

Gough, Sir Hugh, commands army in Gwalior, 153; his victory at Maharajpore, 154; battles at Moodki and Ferozshahar, 158; at Sobraon, 159; Chillianwalla, 163; Goojerat, 164

Government, old merchant rule in Madras, 5, 8, 12; municipal experiments, 14, 16; Nawab rule in Bengal, 43; offer of the dewani, 45; Great Mogul installed in British factory at Patna, 48; collision between the British and the Nawab in Bengal, 49; Clive's double government, 54; Warren Hastings a sovereign ruler, 56; British zemindar at Calcutta, 59; appointment of British collectors, 61; members of council at Calcutta appointed by Parliament, 65; quarrels, 66; Governor-General in Council empowered by parliament to make laws, 69; changes under the charter of 1833, 135; executive council remodelled by Lord Canning, 280; legislative councils of 1854 and 1861-6, 179, 284; relations of legislative and executive, 293; British India a school for Asiatics, 297

Govind, Guru, 155; founder of the Sikh Khalsa, 156

Graves, Brigadier, commands station at Delhi, 209, 210; preparations to resist rebel sepoys from Meerut, 211; escapes to Flagstaff Tower, 213

Gubbins, Mr. Frederic, his municipal reforms at Benares, 235, 236

Gwalior, fortress of, captured, 73; interference and war by Lord Ellenborough, 152

Gwalior contingent formed, 154; mutiny of, 228, 229; victory of, at Cawnpore, 272

H.

Hands, Right and Left, Hindu antagonism in Southern India, 10, 11; *see* also 39 *note*

Hardinge, Lord, Governor-General, 154; commands the army at Moodki, 158; at Sobraon, 159; settles the government of the Punjab under a regency, 160; returns to England, 161

Harris, General, commands British army against Mysore, 86

Hastings, Warren, appointed Governor of Bengal, 56; virtually sovereign of Bengal, Behar, and Orissa, *ib.*; previous career, 57; introduces British administration, 58; dealings with the zemindars and land revenue 59, 61; judicial administration, 62 creates the Sudder Court, 64; surprised by the arrival of three new members of council, and the creation of the Supreme Court, 65; appointed Governor-General, *ib.*; quarrel with Philip Francis, 66; trial and execution of Nundcomar, 67; inaction, *ib.*; collision between the Supreme Court and the Sudder, 68; points in dispute, 69; settled by parliament, *ib.*; alleged corruption of Elijah Impey, 70; war with the Mahrattas, 71; plottings of three Asiatic powers, 73; Hyder invades the Carnatic, 74; interference of parliament, 75; India bills of Fox and Pitt, *ib.*; returns to England, 76; trial in Westminster Hall, *ib.*; case of the Oudh Begums, *ib.*; services of Hastings, 77, 78; presents to George III., 296

Hastings, Marquis of, Governor General of India, 107; war against Nipal, 108; converted from non-intervention to imperialism, 110; suppresses Pindhari raids and Mahratta disaffection, 111; humiliation of Sindia, 113; submission of Amir Khan of Tonk, 114; treachery, defeat, and flight of the Peishwa, 115; dealings with Nagpore, 116; defeat of Holkar, 117; capture and conquest of the Peishwa, 118, 119; renewal of protective treaties in Rajputana, 120

Havelock, General, his career in India, 256; advance on Cawnpore during the sepoy mutinies, *ib.*; hangs a deputy collector, 258; enters Cawnpore after the massacre, *ib.*; advances towards Lucknow, 259; retreats, 266; second advance with Outram, 268; relief of the garrison, 269; death, 272

Herat, besieged by Persia, 145; defended by Eldred Pottinger, 151; second siege by Persia, 181

Hindus, protected against European soldiers at Madras, 14; rebel against the house tax, 15; municipality in the 17th century, 16; abolition of Suttee, 123; overawed by Thugs, 125; village communities in the North-West Provinces, 128; in the Madras Presidency, 131; ancient colonisation, *ib.*; ancient migrations from Central and Northern Asia, 142; accept Sikh religion in the Punjab, 155; absence of roads in Hindu kingdoms, 172; belief in adoption but reluctant to adopt, 175; caste system, 188, 191; worship of the cow and horror of beef, 195; forced conversions to Islam, 196; hostility of the Brahmans at Benares, stamped out by Mr. Gubbins, 235; Hindu culture, 298; child marriages, *ib.*; temper, *ib.*; social despotism, 299; failure of hereditary officials, 300; successful training, *ib.*

Holkar, Jaswant Rao, the bandit, 92; drives the Peishwa from Poona, *ib.*; occupies Indore territory, 93; relations with the British, 95; defiance, 96; campaign of Lord Lake, *ib.*; Monson's disastrous retreat, 97; joined by Sindia, etc., *ib.*; flies to the Punjab, 99; confined as a madman, *ib.*; dies of cherry brandy, 111; *see* Indore

Holkar, *see* Indore

Holwell, Mr., elected Governor of Calcutta, during the siege, 38; sells Calcutta lands by auction, 60

Hughly, old Portuguese fortress at, 19; demolished in punishment for slave dealing, 20; British factory at, 25; Mogul oppressions, *ib.*; British retreat to Madras, 27

Hyder Ali, of Mysore, desolates the Carnatic, 74

Hyderabad, disbandment of French battalions, 85; subsidiary force at, 113

I.

Impey, Sir Elijah first Chief Justice of the Supreme Court at Calcutta, 65; charges against, 70

Indore, revolt of the army of Holkar, 115; defeated at Mehidpore, 117; subsidiary alliance, 118; outbreak during the mutinies, 272; political relations, 289 *note*

J.

Java, wrested from the Dutch, 104; restored to Holland, *ib.*

Jeypore, Raja of, fights for princess of Oodeypore, 105; asks British government to arbitrate, 106

Jhansi, massacre at, 176, 255

Jodhpore, Raja of, contends for princess of Oodeypore, 105; asks British to arbitrate, 106

Judicature, justices of the choultry at Madras, 13; mayor's court, 31; British zemindar at Calcutta, 59; magistrates and judges, 62; courts of circuit and appeal, 63; chief court or Sudder, 64; patriarchal system, *ib.*; supreme court of barrister judges, 65; collisions, 67, 68; judicial reforms of Lord Cornwallis, 79; of Lord William Bentinck, 126; Asiatic judges, 127; amalgamation of Supreme Court and Sudder in the existing High Courts, 284; Asiatic judges and magistrates, 285; proposed changes, 300

Julinder, mutiny at, 227

K.

Kali, goddess, worshipped by the Thugs, 124; Calcutta a corruption of Kali-Ghat, 125 *note*

Keane, Sir John, captures fortress of Ghazni, 146; created Baron of Ghazni, 147

Khalsas, the Sikh, 155; army of, 156; sent to plunder India, 158; defeated at Sobraon, 159; broken up, 164

Khyber Pass, British disaster in, 151; faces Peshawar, 225

Korigaum, glorious action of sepoys, 118

Kumaon, ceded to the British by Nipal, 109

L.

Lacouperie, Professor Terrien de, on the right and left hand castes, 39 *note*

Lahore, Council of Regency at, 161; sepoy mutinies at, 223, 224; European strength, 243

Lake, General, commander-in-chief of the Bengal army, 94; his campaign in Hindustan, 94, 95; attacks Holkar, 96; fails to reduce Bhurtpore, 97, 98

Lawrence, Sir Henry, Resident at Lahore after first Sikh war, 161, 164; chief commissioner of Oudh, 202; suppresses a mutiny at Lucknow, 216; holds a public durbar for rewarding sepoys, 259; preparations for the defence of Lucknow, 260; wounded at Chinhut, 261; dies, 265

Lawrence, John, chief commissioner of the Punjab, 165; patriarchal rule, 166; land settlement, 167; telegram to General Anson, 217; executions at Peshawar, 226; sends Punjab "Guides" to Delhi, *ib.*; proposes to withdraw from Peshawar, 228; overruled by Lord Canning, 229; disarms all Bengal sepoys in

the Punjab, *ib.*; created a baronet and afterwards a peer, 286 *note*; Viceroy and Governor-General, 286; yearly migrations to Simla, 288; relations with Sir Henry Durand, 289; leaves India, 293; burial in Westminster Abbey, 294
Legislation, no code of laws, 13; powers of, granted to the Governor-General in Council, 69; legislative council created in 1833 under the charter, 139; new legislative council of 1854 under Lord Dalhousie, 179; new Penal Code, 180; new legislative council of 1861-2, 284; relations of cabinet and council, 293; proposed changes, 301
Lucknow, capital of Oudh, description of, 203; the British Residency, *ib.*; first mutiny suppressed by Sir Henry Lawrence, *ib.*; further durbar for rewarding loyal sepoys, 259; general mutiny, 261; hostility of the city, 263; disaster at Chinhut, *ib.*; British Residency besieged by mutineers and rebels, 264; death of Sir Henry Lawrence, 265; anarchy in the city, *ib.*; retreat of Havelock, 266; desperate defence, 267; advance of Havelock and Outram, 268; triumphant entry, 269; final relief of Sir Colin Campbell, 271
Lumsden, Sir Peter, his mission to Candahar, 181
Lytton, Lord, Viceroy, 295; proclaims Her Majesty as Empress of India, 295; the second Afghan war, 296

M.

Macaulay (Mr., afterwards Lord) appointed legal member of the Council of India, 139; drafts the Penal Code, 180
Macnaghten, Sir William, British minister at Cabul, 146, 147; his difficulties, 148; murdered by Akbar Khan, 149, 150
Macrae, Mr., Governor of Madras, in the olden time, 31
Madras, foundation of fortress, 7; growth of Fort St. George and Black Town, 8; wars of the Right and Left Hands, 10; first Hindu town under British rule, 13; Asiatic revolt against European taxation, 14, 15; corporation founded, 16; trade in slaves, 18; abolished and revived, 21, 22; flourishing private trade, 23; Governors Pitt and Macrae, 31; Madras captured by the French, 32; restored, 33; village communities of Southern India, 131; creation of zemindars, 132; establishment of ryotwari, 134
Maharajpore, battle of, 154
Mahrattas, raids on the Mogul empire quieted by the payment of "chout," or blackmail, 28; origin of Mahratta power, 71; rise of the Peishwa and his feudatories—Sindia, Holkar, and the Gaekwar, 72; first British war against the Mahrattas, 73; refuse the British alliance, 89; rise of Sindia, 92; acceptance of British suzerainty by the Peishwa, *ib.*; campaigns of Wellesley and Lake, 94, 95; Holkar's defiance and successes, 97; non-intervention, 99; disaffection, 111; hostility, 115; final establishment of British supremacy, 116, 119; *see* also Sindia and Holkar
Malcolm, Sir John, sent on missions to Persia, 91, 103; negotiations with the Mahrattas, 112, 113; defeats Holkar, 117; captures the Peishwa, 119
Mayo, Lord, Viceroy and Governor-General, 294; his tragic death, *ib.*
Meerut, sepoy mutinies, 206—212
Mehidpore, battle of, 117
Metcalfe, Charles, his mission to Runjeet Singh at Lahore, 102; Governor-General, 140
Minto, Lord, Governor-General, 101
Mogul, empire in India, 2; his vengeance on the Portuguese at Hughly, 20; conquers the Deccan, 21; breaking up, 31; enthronement of a Great Mogul in the British factory at Patna, 48; settlement of Lord Clive, 54; flight to Delhi with the Mahrattas, 57; a pensioner of the British government, 95; makes common cause with the rebel sepoys, 209, 216; banishment to Rangoon, 231 *note*
Mohammedans, proportion of, in the Bengal sepoy army, 191; conversion of Hindus by force, 196, 210; revolt of Delhi, fanatics preaching rebellion, 220; capture of Delhi, 231
Moira, Lord, Governor-General, 110; *see* Hastings, Marquis of
Monro, Sir Hector, victory at Buxar, 52; takes possession of Oudh, 52
Monson, Colonel, disastrous retreat from Holkar, 97, 98
Moodki, battle of, 158
Mornington, Lord, *see* Wellesley, Marquis of
Mulraj, Sikh governor of Multan, his revolt, 161; murder of two British officers, *ib.*; surrenders, 164
Munro, Thomas, his career, 133, 134; his conservatism, 299

Munsifs, or civil judges, appointed, 80

Mutinies, *see* Sepoy

Mysore, Raja, restored to the throne of Mysore, 87

Mysore, conquest of, by the British army, 86; restoration of a Hindu Raja, 87; Mohammedan mutiny at Vellore, 100, 188; brought under British rule, 221; restored to Hindu rule, 292

N.

Nadir, Shah, checkmates Russia, 143; invades India, 144; an Asiatic Napoleon, *ib.*

Nagpore, 111; plottings against the British government, 116; annexed by Lord Dalhousie, 176

Nana Sahib, a *protégé* of the ex-Peishwa of the Mahrattas, 245; his preposterous claims against the British government, *ib.*; pertinacity and cunning, 246; pretended loyalty at Cawnpore, 249; deludes the British, 250; unpopularity with the Bengal sepoys, *ib.*; joins the sepoy mutineers, 251; parleying and perfidy, 253; massacre of Europeans, 254; his triumph, *ib.*; his terrors, 255; his army defeated by Havelock, 257; massacre of women and children, 258; flight into Oudh, *ib.*

Nanuk Guru, founder of the Sikh religion, 154; his teaching, 155

Napier, Sir Charles, defeats Amirs of Sind, 152; supersedes Lord Gough, 164

Natives, *see* Asiatic

Neill, Colonel, his advance towards Allahabad and Cawnpore, 234; delayed at Benares, 238; at Allahabad, *ib.*; restores order, 242; joined by Havelock, 256

Newars, Buddhist people of Nipal, 106

Nicholson, John, the sainted warrior, 227; worshipped by the Sikhs, *ib.*; crushes the rebel sepoy brigade from Sealkote, 229; mortally wounded at Delhi, 231

Nipal, Ghorka conquest of, 106; aggressions on British territory, 107; war, 108; peace, 110

Nizam of the Deccan, 33, 82; disbandment of his French battalions, 83; accepts subsidiary alliance with the British government, 89; political relations, 290 *note*

Non-intervention, policy of, 82; sad results, 99; bad effects in Rajputana, 106; in the Punjab, 158

Northbrook, Lord, Viceroy and Governor-General, 295

North-West Provinces, land settlement of, 167; revolt and suppression, 231

Nott, General, at Candahar, 146, 151; advances on Cabul, 152

Nundcomar, his charges against Warren Hastings, 67; arrested on charge of forgery, *ib.*; trial and execution, *ib.*

O.

Ochterlony, Colonel, defends Delhi from Holkar, 97; services in the war against Nipal, 109; operations against Bhurtpore, 216

Orissa, a province of Bengal, 44, 127; village communities, 129

Oudh, old aggressions on Bengal, 44, 47; settlement of Lord Clive with the Nawab Vizier, 53; case of the Begums, 76; acquisitions of Lord Wellesley, 91; annexation by Lord Dalhousie, 177, 178; land settlement, 182; disaffection of the talukdars, 183; discontent of sepoys, 184, 190, 202; Sir Henry Lawrence, chief commissioner, 203; disaffection, 220; mutiny and rebellion, 259, 262; peace restored, 272; causes of revolt, 273; settlement of Lord Lawrence with the talukdars, 292

Outram, Sir James, his mission to the Persian Gulf, 181; joins Havelock, 269; chief commissioner of Oudh, 270

P.

Parliament, interference in India, 75, 135; Charters of 1813 and 1833; opening out trade, etc., 138; creates the Legislative Council of India, and introduces competitive examinations, 178; transfers India from the Company to the Crown, 275; Council Act of 1861, 284

Patna, massacre at, 52; Mohammedan plots, 220, 266

Peacock, Sir Barnes, revises Penal Code, 180

Pegu annexed by Lord Dalhousie, 169, 170

Peishwa, Mahratta, his feudatories jealous of the British, 186; refuses the subsidiary alliance, 89; flight to British territory, 92; accepts subsidiary alliance at Bassein, *ib.*; disaffected, 99; intrigues, 111; hostility, 115; defeat and flight, 116; extinction, 119; at Bithoor, 245

Penal Code, drafted by Lord Macaulay, revised by Sir Barnes Peacock, 180

Persia, mission of John Malcolm, 103;

collision with British India, 140; menaced by Russia, 141; advance of Russia checkmated by Nadir Shah, 143; Persian invasion of India, 144; British expedition to the Persian Gulf, 181; its return to India, 217
Peshawar, valley of, wrested from the Afghans by Runjeet Singh, 103; re-occupied by Afghans in second Sikh war, 163; the key to India, 225; frontier tribes, *ib.*; peril during the sepoy mutinies, *ib.*; execution of rebels, 226; proposed withdrawal, 228; overruled by Lord Canning, 229
Peter the Great, covert advance to India, 143; checkmated by Nadir Shah, *ib.*
Pindharies, freebooters in the Mahratta armies, 104; horrible raids in British territory, 110; George Canning's denunciations, 111; campaign of Lord Hastings, 113; extinction of the gangs, 115
Pitt, Thomas, Governor of Madras, 29; his diamond, 30
Pitt, William, the younger, his India Bill, 75; creates a Board of Control, 76; marvellous statesmanship, 137
Plassy, battle of, 42
Pollock, General, avenges the British losses in the Khyber, 151; relieves Sale and restores British prestige, 152
Pondicherry, French settlement, 32; British carried prisoners to, *ib.*
Poona, head-quarters of the Sivaji family, 71; capital of the Mahratta Peishwas, *ib.*; interference of Bombay, 72, 73; negotiations of Lord Wellesley, 86; flight of the Peishwa to Bassein, 92; subsidiary alliance, *ib.*; intrigues, 112, 113; British residency burnt, 116; incorporated with the Bombay Presidency, 119
Portuguese in India, their fortresses, 3; thwart the British at Surat, 4; intermarriages with the British at Madras, 12; slave trade, 19; settlement at Hughly, 20; destroyed by the Great Mogul, 21
Pottinger, Eldred, Captain, 151
Provinces, regulation and non-regulation, 166, 289; distinction effaced, 297
Punjab, Sikh rule under Runjeet Singh, 102; relations with the British government, 103; attitude in the first Afghan war, 146; opened to British troops after the death of Runjeet Singh, 147; a Sikh army under French officers a menace to Hindustan, 153; review of Sikh history, 154; army of the Khalsa, 156; anarchy, 157; despotism of the army, *ib.*; Sikh invasion of British India, 158; Aliwal and Sobraon, 159; end of first Sikh war, 160; mixed government, *ib.*; revolt at Multan, 161; second Sikh war, 162; Chillianwalla, 163; Goojerat, 164; annexation, 165; patriarchal rule, 166; non-regulation system, *ib.*; land settlement, 167; frontier province of India on the north-west, facing Afghanistan and Cashmere, 186; musketry school at Sealkote, 193; John Lawrence, chief commissioner, sends the Punjab "Guides" to Delhi, 222; disaffection of Bengal sepoy regiments, 224; valley of Peshawar, 225; Sikh volunteers, 226; John Nicholson, the sainted warrior, 227; difficulties of John Lawrence, 228; fall of Delhi, 231

R.

Railways in India, 173, 174
Rajputana, princes and chiefs taken under British protection by Lord Wellesley, 95; annulment of treaties by Sir George Barlow, 99; plundered by the Mahrattas, *ib.*; ravaged by Sindia and Amir Khan, 105; renewal of protective treaties by Lord Hastings, 120; relations with the British government, 289
Rajputs, in Bengal sepoy army, 191
Rama, the ancient hero of Oudh, 104
Rana, of Oodeypore, his descent, 104; war for his daughter, 105; her death, 106
Rangoon, expedition to, 121; second Burmese war, 168
Rawlinson, Major, at Candahar, 146, 152
Revenue, Board of, 128
Rewah in Central India, 289 *note*
Roe, Sir Thomas, Ambassador to India, 135
Rohilcund, mutiny in, 228
Runjeet Singh, Sikh ruler of the Punjab, 102; relations with the British government, 103; attitude in the first Afghan war, 146; death, *ib.*; genius and depravity, 156; family pensioned, 165
Russia menaces Persia, 141, 143; driven back by Nadir Shah, 144; cat's-paw policy, 145; hold on Turkistan, 296
Ryotwari settlement, in Madras presidency, 133; introduced into Bombay presidency, 134

S.

Sale, Sir Robert, sent to Jellalabad, 149; besieged by Afghans, 151
Sealkote, mutiny at, 229
Secretary of State, Council of, 301
Sepoy army of India, 188; old mutinies, 189; separate armies of Bengal, Bombay, and Madras, 190; high caste in old Bengal army, 191; mutinies against greased cartridges, 193—274
Seringapatam taken by storm, 86
Shere Ali Khan, Amir of Afghanistan, 291; estranged from British government, 296; flight, *ib.*; death, 297
Shore, Mr. John, presses for an inquiry into rights of ryots, 79; Governor-General, 81
Sikh, kingdom founded by Runjeet Singh, 102; review of Sikh history, 154—157; first Sikh war, 158; second Sikh war, 161; annexed to British India, 165; help the British against Delhi, 222, 226, 237
Sind, Amirs of, defeat of, 152; their territories incorporated with the Bombay presidency, *ib.*
Sindia, Mahadaji, feudatory of the Peishwa, 71; established a dominion in Hindostan, 72; French battalions, 83; rule of Daulat Rao, 90; his vacillation, 93; flight at Assaye, 94; joins Holkar, 97; returns to the British alliance, 98; ravages Rajputana, 105; secret negotiation, 111; submission, 114
Sitabuldi Hill, battle on, 116, 117
Sivaji, hero of the Mahrattas, 71; his tomb repaired, *ib. note*
Slavery, Hindu and Mohammedan, 18; Mogul restrictions, 19; Portuguese trade, *ib.*; abolished at Madras, 22
Sobraon, battle of, 159
Sudder Courts, 127 *note*, 128, 284
Supreme and Sudder Courts amalgamated, 284
Surat, British traders at, 3; factory, 4; foreign guests, 5; decay, 24
Suttee, abolished, 123

T.

Talukdars, or zemindars, 130; discontent in Oudh, 220; healed, 293
Tayler, Mr. William, quashes plot at Patna, 266
Thomason, Mr., Lieut.-Governor, land settlement finished, 167, 168; constructs macadamised roads, 172
Thugs, atrocities of, 124; hereditary gangs, *ib.*; suppression, 125
Tippu of Mysore, first war against, 80; alliance with the French, 84; second war and death, 86; family, 100, 283
Trevelyan, Sir Charles, protests against income tax, 283
Tucker, Mr. Robert, at Futtehpore, murdered, 257
Turkey, menaced by Russia, 141

V.

Vellore, sepoy revolt at, 100, 188
Village communities in the North-West Provinces, 128; in the Madras Presidency, 131; changes, 299

W.

Wales, Prince of, his tour in India, 295
Water-ways in India, 171
Wellesley, Marquis of, Governor-General, 82; political system of subsidiary alliances, 89; fears of France, 90; mission to Persia, 91; acquisitions from Oudh, *ib.*; wars, 94; reversal of his policy, 98
Wellington, Duke of, opposes recall of Lord Ellenborough, 154
Wheeler, General Sir Hugh, commands at Cawnpore, 244—249; surrenders to Nana Sahib, 253
Willoughby, Lieut., blows up the magazine at Delhi, 214; murdered, 215
Wilson, Mr. James, Finance Minister, 282; proposes income tax, *ib.*; death, 283

Y.

Yakub Khan, imprisoned by his father Shere Ali, 296; succession and abdication, 297

Z.

Zemindars, status in Bengal, 59; created in the Madras Presidency, 132

THE END.

LONDON: RICHARD CLAY & SONS, PRINTERS.